RICHARD BEAN: PLAYS FIVE

Richard Bean

PLAYS FIVE

Introduction by Nicholas Hytner

Pub Quiz is Life

Pitcairn

Great Britain

The Nap

Kiss Me

OBERON BOOKS
LONDON

WWW.OBERONBOOKS.COM

This collection first published in 2017 by Oberon Books Ltd
521 Caledonian Road, London N7 9RH
Tel: +44 (0) 20 7607 3637 / Fax: +44 (0) 20 7607 3629
e-mail: info@oberonbooks.com
www.oberonbooks.com

A catalogue record for this book is available from the British Library.

PB ISBN: 9781786820990
E ISBN: 9781786821003

Cover image by Ansel Krut

Printed and bound by CPI Group (UK) Ltd, Croydon, CR0 4YY.

Contents

Introduction

The best time I had in a theatre in 2016 was at the Crucible Theatre, Sheffield, where I saw Richard Bean's play *The Nap*. As the audience walked into the theatre, home for two weeks every spring to the World Snooker Championships, it saw:

> *A British Legion snooker room in Manor Top in Sheffield S12.*

A young man comes in, a professional snooker player carrying nothing but a snooker cue case.

> *A snooker room, for him, is a church and so all his actions are reverential and ritualistic as if to do something wrong would be to upset the God of Snooker.*

For some minutes, he prepares to play, feels the nap on the table, chalks his cue, tests the balls, sets up a trick shot, and plays it. Then an older man, who turns out to be his father, arrives and offers him a prawn sandwich.

> DYLAN: I don't eat owt wi' a brain.
>
> BOBBY: They're prawns, they're not novelists.
>
> *BOBBY moans about their surroundings.*
>
> BOBBY: What a dump. What a dump! What a dump. What a dump. What a dump. I mean … what … what … what … I mean … what a fucking dump. What a dump?! What kind of … I mean, look at that … if yer gonna … I mean, stand to reason, knowhatimean. I mean … what the fuck is … what a fucking dump. What a dump. Do you like it?
>
> DYLAN: It's perfect.
>
> BOBBY: It's not the Crucible, is it?

Here are just some of the brilliant things about the first few minutes of *The Nap*, all of them typical of its author:

The play itself is a wonderful idea, in retrospect obvious, but it was Richard Bean who suggested to Daniel Evans, the Crucible's inspired artistic director, that he should stage a play about snooker at snooker's Mecca. Richard has a highly developed nose for the kind of material that people want to see on the stage.

The opening stage direction couldn't be more specific, even down to the postcode. Richard's stage worlds are never fake. He always knows what he's writing about, whether it's Sheffield, Hull *(Pub Quiz is Life)*, Bethnal Green *(England People Very Nice)*, a tabloid newsroom *(Great Britain)*, a bread factory *(Toast)* or a weekend cricket match *(The English Game)*. *The Nap* is utterly respectful about snooker and snooker players, too. It requires its actors to be rigorously truthful about the way they inhabit the people whose lives are snooker, in the way *Toast* and *Under the Whaleback* demand proper respect for bakers and trawler men.

Richard knows his audience. I wish I'd seen *Pub Quiz is Life*, and I particularly wish I'd seen it in Hull. It was thrilling to be part of a Sheffield audience watching Sheffield on its own stage. It felt like the theatre was fulfilling one of its ancient purposes: to reflect the community to itself.

And it fulfilled another of theatre's ancient purposes in making them laugh so often and so loud. They laughed from the moment Bobby came on, because Bobby was Mark Addy, who is one of Britain's funniest (and best) actors. You always know you're in for a good time when Mark comes onto a stage, and Richard's plays are like magnets for great actors because they give them room to do all the things they do best. Mark Addy got a laugh just by coming into the room: he didn't do anything, he made no signals, but the play allowed him to be disgruntled, and disgruntled is funny. Then the play gives him an excellent one-liner ('They're prawns, they're not novelists'); then a comic aria based on three words, repeated ad infinitum ('What a dump'); and finally, the big joke that everyone in the house had already told themselves, but another of Richard's virtues is that *he goes there*. And in *The Nap*, he went there within minutes of the play starting:

BOBBY: It's not the Crucible, is it?

Huge laugh. And the entire audience on side for the rest of a play, easily on side enough to take in its stride a one-armed transsexual called Waxy Chuff, who is the *capo di tutti capi* of world snooker, and who celebrates winning by crying:

This is beyond my wettest dreams.

It would be doing the play an injustice to insist only that it's funny. It included ten unbearably tense minutes when the plot required Dylan's opponent Danny Carr to make a break of one hundred and the audience slowly realised that John Astley – a proper snooker professional, but still – was actually intending to clear the table. The roar when he potted the final black was deafening, and testament to another of Richard Bean's gifts: an iron grip on what makes theatre theatrical. He'd realised that theatre and sport had a lot in common, and was the first playwright in my experience to exploit on stage the excitement of sport, played for real.

Asking a snooker pro to clear the table is all very well, but read the last page *The Nap* and you may wonder how any playwright would dare to build his climax around an actor potting a snooker ball to win the World Championship. Jack O'Connell, who played Dylan, nailed it and the audience left the theatre on cloud nine. I was still marvelling at it when I collected my coat. 'He doesn't always pot the ball,' said the cloakroom attendant. 'They have an alternative ending if he misses. It doesn't matter. He loses the championship but he gets the girl.' And there's another of Richard's unfashionable virtues: he's a romantic. There is, when he wants it, radiant warmth to his writing. 'She's my girlfriend. I love her,' says Dylan, as the stewards try to throw out Rosa just before his final shot. 'Unprecedented scenes here at the home of snooker,' says the commentator on live TV. Boy loves girl. Richard goes there.

In *Kiss Me*, Peter meets Stephanie under circumstances that seem to preclude romance, though over the course of a tightly written hour he slowly falls for her. Richard is voraciously curious, sniffing out stories in unlikely corners. The fictional meeting of a woman who lost her fiancé in the First World War and a man who has been sent by a psychiatrist to impregnate her is based on apparently true material that he encountered in the course of his reading. The play was performed at Hampstead Theatre's small downstairs studio. If you hadn't been told that the play was by Richard Bean, you wouldn't have guessed: his range makes him impossible to pin down and often hard to identify, though at least three of the plays in this volume *(Great Britain, Pub Quiz is Life* and *The Nap)* could hardly be by anyone else.

Pitcairn, a brutal and impeccably researched historical drama, feels a world away from *The Nap,* but both are written by a playwright who puts a gripping narrative high up his agenda. You want to know what happens next. And you care about what happens because Richard's peoples his plays so effectively – sometimes, necessarily, with deftly drawn caricatures; as often with fully complex, contradictory characters who are observed with forensic insight. *Pitcairn* has plenty of these, and it trades in big ideas and big ironies, too. But it works as much as anything as a good story.

The genesis of *Great Britain* was itself a story. After *One Man, Two Guvnors* opened at the National, Richard suggested 'a big, scabrous, state-of-the-nation satire. Working title: *Hacked*.' His friend and fellow dramatist Clive Coleman is also a journalist: he was covering the continuing legal proceedings around phone hacking at News International. We'd always known about the control the Murdoch press exercised over the political class. Now we knew about how close News International was to the Metropolitan Police: there was something increasingly ridiculous about the Met's red-faced outrage at anyone who dared question its refusal to act on the mountain of evidence against News International. The arrest in 2011 of Rebekah Brooks, its chief executive, at last promised to reveal how far the Murdoch press had sewn up politics, law enforcement and the country.

With help from Clive, Richard wrapped up the play long before the legal system wrapped up the case: the trial of Rebekah Brooks and her co-defendants had been postponed, and didn't start until 28 October 2013, more than a year after Richard first proposed the play. We knew we couldn't schedule it until the trial was over, as even a satirical caricature of the case would contravene the laws covering contempt of court. We suspected that it would take no more than a public announcement of our intention to produce the play to land us in hot water. So we postponed it for six months, left an unidentified gap in the programme, and within the National we referred to it only as the new Richard Bean. When it finally opens, we thought, maybe only a few months after the verdicts come in, it will at the very least amaze by its topicality.

As rehearsals approached, the trial dragged on. We consulted an expert in contempt of court. He confirmed that it would put us on the wrong side of the law to announce, let alone perform, the play while the trial continued. He reassured us that the contempt laws didn't extend to rehearsals: if we kept them secret we'd be OK. And that of course we wouldn't be able to perform the play Rebekah Brooks was acquitted. This stopped us in our tracks. We have to perform it, I told him, as there's a huge gap in the schedule for it. He said we'd lay ourselves open to a massive libel claim.

'But we're not seriously suggesting that Paige Britain is in fact Rebekah Brooks,' I said, 'or that Paschal O'Leary is Rupert Murdoch, or that any of the sleazy journos in the play are direct representations of the allegedly sleazy journos at the *News of the World*. Nobody is saying that anyone hacked the queen's phone or had sex with the prime minister! We have no opinion about the guilt of any of the defendants – we're happy to leave that to the jury. It's satire!'

The expert confirmed that satire can be a defence in law, but his advice was not to risk it. The problem was not that the play suggested there was industrial-scale phone hacking, or that there was an unhealthy relationship between sections of the press, sections of the Metropolitan Police, and sections of the political establishment. None of that was in dispute. The problem was who the play seemed to identify as guilty of breaking the law.

'So is Rebekah Brooks' defence,' we asked, 'that she was too stupid or too incompetent to know what was going on at her own paper?'

More or less, we all agreed.

'So what if instead of Paschal O'Leary promoting Paige Britain to editor, he promotes someone else who's too dim to know what's going on? If Paige Britain doesn't make it to editor, she can't be identified as Rebekah Brooks, can she? We'd have another editor, an innocent editor, and no suggestion that the editor has broken the law.'

Richard sketched out who the alternative editor could be: she'd love horses, she'd have long wavy hair, she'd be married to a soap star, she'd be stupid, she'd be innocent of any wrongdoing.

The trial, which had begun in October 2013, showed no sign of ending when rehearsals started on 28 April 2014. I told the cast that there were two versions of the play. In the one they had, Paige Britain, guilty as sin, becomes editor of the *Free Press.* In the second version, horse-loving Virginia White becomes editor, Paige Britain stays news editor, hacks and lies her way through the play, and poor, innocent Virginia is too dim to notice.

'You'd better learn both versions,' I said to the actors. 'If the jury convicts the defendants, we'll do the first version. If it acquits them, we'll do the second. Meanwhile, not a word.'

But nobody outside the National knew the play was happening, so we hadn't sold a single ticket, and the trial looked like it would run longer than *The Mousetrap.* We had a mole, of sorts: somebody an Old Bailey judge, and called him to ask what the word was on when the trial might end? Maybe the middle of June was the good news. The bad news was that the jury could take anything up to six weeks to consider its verdict.

'And by the way,' said the Old Bailey judge, 'don't even think of letting anyone know what you're up to.'

On the day of what should have been the first performance, Mr Justice Saunders was summing up in the trial of Rebekah Brooks. We performed the play, now finally called *Great Britain,* to about fifty friends and family. I made a speech to them before it started: 'If you tell ANYONE about this, you'll be arrested and Mr Justice Saunders WILL SEND YOU TO PRISON FOR CONTEMPT OF COURT.' They sat in total silence throughout the play.

'Thanks for the speech,' said Richard.

The next day, the jury retired to consider its verdict. That night, another fifty friends and family pitched up. I toned down my speech, and they started to laugh. We stuck with the Paige Britain Guilty version because I thought it would be too confusing for the actors to keep two versions in their heads simultaneously.

We played it eight times in secret to tiny invited audiences, and then it stopped to allow Sean O'Casey's *The Silver Tassie* back into the repertoire.

On 24 June, two weeks after it was supposed to have opened, my assistant ran into my office and yelled that the jury was about to give its verdict. Two of the defendants were guilty but Rebekah Brooks and five other defendants were acquitted on all charges.

'That's a much better ending!' I cried, 'Rehearsals start this afternoon for the Not Guilty Version! Start selling tickets!'

We decided to wait until the next morning to announce the play and put it on sale, so it wouldn't have to compete with news of the verdicts. At 9.00 a.m. on 25 June, we convened a press conference and told the assembled journalists that Richard Bean had written a play called *Great Britain*, that it would open on Monday night, that its first public performance would be its press night, and that I hoped they'd be there.

The entire run sold out within a few days, and when it finally opened, stupid, horse-loving Virginia White got one of the biggest laughs of the night when the cops arrived to arrest her and the rest of the staff of the *Free Press*, and she cried in panic, 'What have we done?!'

After her trial, Rebekah Brooks went to the US to lie low. A year later she came back as CEO of News International, a development that was beyond even Richard's satirical imagination.

I've directed three of Richard's plays so far: *Great Britain, One Man, Two Guvnors* and *England People Very Nice.* As I write this, I'm looking forward to a fourth: when I needed a play to open the new Bridge Theatre in London, he was the obvious first port of call. This volume is a perfect introduction to the many reasons why.

Nicholas Hytner, 2016

PUB QUIZ IS LIFE

Acknowledgements

This play is dedicated to Mabel, the ex-landlady of the Rose and Crown N16, and the finest Pub quiz MC there will ever be. I would like to thank the following for their help in the research.

Mick Beecroft
Denise Anderton
Marcus Hails
Petta Godney
Norma Howarth
Nicola Baker

and to 'Brown Trout', 'Tom's Sebaceous Cyst', 'Scottish Pound Notes Are Welcome at the Bar' and all the regulars and staff at the Rose and Crown in Stoke Newington. (Pub quiz every Tuesday, first question 8.30pm)

Characters

LEE
Male, mid thirties

MELISSA
Female, late thirties

MABEL
Female, fifties

WOODY
Male, late forties

BUNNY
Male, 70

BAZ
Female, thirties

ANGIE
Female, thirties

CATH
Female, twenty

MOURNER

MAM

Set

The set needs to be multi-location: the Pub, the Range Rover, the Street, and Bunny's Flat.

The Pub is big, functional, and more modern than traditional. Upstage left is the bar area with the usual wines, optics, pumps etc. On the downstage side of the bar, stage left, is a bar stool, microphone and file of papers. This is the normal location for Mabel when on the microphone asking the pub quiz questions.

Upstage in the back wall are three doors. The main entrance/exit to the street; a door to the LOUNGE, so labelled, and the toilets.

The set should suggest that the pub extends into the audience. Actors, particularly Mabel, will be trying to communicate to the audience as if they were the other teams in the pub quiz.

A blackboard announces the weekly calendar. Monday is 'LADY'S DART'S' (*sic*); Tuesday is 'QUIZZ!!!' (*sic*); Wednesday is 'KARIOKE' (*sic*); Thursday is 'DART'S' (*sic*); Friday is blank; Saturday is 'HAPPY HOUR'. Another blackboard has a pub food menu.

Bunny's council flat is on the fifteenth floor of a block overlooking the River Humber. It is accessible by the lift. Although it may be set above the pub it is important to define it as not being a flat above the pub.

It's a typical old man's flat; there is evidence of his dead wife's influence, but no photos of her. A newish TV, books such as *Reader's Digest* selections. Paintings or photographs of submarines and trawlers. An Airfix model of a submarine.

Pub Quiz is Life was first performed by Hull Truck Theatre Company at Hull Truck Theatre on 10 September 2009. The cast was as follows:

LEE	Marc Bolton
MELISSA /ANGIE	Esther Hall
MABEL	Sarah Parks
BUNNY	David Hargreaves
WOODY	Adrian Hood
BAZ /CATH	Rachel Dale
MAM / MOURNER	Sarah Follon
Director	Gareth Tudor Price
Design	Foxton

Week One

SCENE ONE (SEPTEMBER 2009)

The audience take their seats. The set is visible to them, though unpopulated, an audible but not ostentatious pub atmosphere is produced by sound effects. Then lights down. Then a spot on MABEL. She is an impressive woman, busty, brash, rather over-painted, like a ship's figurehead.

MABEL: It's Tuesday, at the White Horse. That can only mean one thing. Yesterday was Monday. Welcome to my pub quiz night adventure, an orgy, I wish, of trivia. A magical mystery tour without seatbelts down the highways and byways of the known universe. I'll be stopping the bus every two hours for a pee. My name's Mabel, and my quiz is much better than Master Mindyourownbusiness, cos Magnus Magnusson an't got much of a cleavage, and I mek up all me own questions using only me general knowledge, and the internet's wikipaedophilia. Any road, Magnus Magnusson's dead, so that's the end of that argument with a door. Anyone caught using a mobile phone will have their nuts crushed, they'll be stripped naked, and nailed to a sun bed and left outside Hammonds. If you need me to repeat a question, I have been known to repeat, then put your hand up, and I'll sort you out one at a time, as the actress said to the gathered synod. Round one, who played keyboards with the Hitler Youth Orchestra and the 1970s jazz fusion band Weather Report?

Snap to black, then lights up on the pub. It's after the quiz. BUNNY, in his wheelchair, alone at a table. LEE, wearing an outdoor coat, is looking at a sheet of paper. MELISSA is playing the General Knowledge machine. LEE, standing, has in his hand BUNNY's notebook.

LEE: What's this question Dad? I can't read your writing.

BUNNY: Where, on earth, does the wind always blow from the south?

LEE: You should've got that one.

BUNNY: Aye.

LEE: What did you put?

BUNNY: Bridlington.

LEE: That's ridiculous.

BUNNY: I was under terrible pressure.

LEE: How terrible can the pressure be, it's a pub quiz?

BUNNY: I was dying for a piss.

LEE: The mad thing is you've actually been to the North Pole.

BUNNY: Aye.

LEE: When you were there, where was the wind coming from?

BUNNY: I dunno. I was in a bloody submarine. I rang your Janet, she said you went up to caravans. Any luck?

LEE: Yeah. One of the jiggers is leaving. Don's put my name on his job. Pint of mild?

BUNNY: Half.

LEE goes up to the bar, nearly bumping into a MOURNER who has come in dressed in black.

MABEL: *(To MOURNER.)* You're in the lounge bar love. That one there.

The MOURNER goes into the lounge.

LEE: Pint of Kronenbourg and half a mild please Mabel. Who's died?

MABEL: Jimmy Parks's lad, the one who worked at Flamingoland. One of their Bengal Tigers got him. Now he's dead and gone.

(*Singing.*) 'Don't want nobody to mourn beside my grave.'

LEE: When I'm dead and gone, McGuinness Flint.

MABEL: Bonus point for the year.

LEE: Seventies. Nineteen seventy-one?

MABEL: Nineteen seventy, highest chart position, two. They had the funeral this afti, and this is the party. Kaw! It's like a bloody wake in there. You'd think somebody had died.

LEE: You shouldn't keep a Bengal Tiger in a cage.

MABEL: What else can you do with a Bengal Tiger? You can't have it selling the ice creams. Three pounds fifty-seven varieties.

The drinks are poured.

LEE: Ta.

MELISSA wins on the General Knowledge machine. LEE pays.

LEE: Who's that on the General Knowledge machine?

MABEL: You're married Lee Bunting.

LEE returns to the table, clocking MELISSA as he goes. At his dad's table LEE picks up an A4 sheet with about 10 celebrity pictures on it.

LEE: Did you get any of this picture round?

BUNNY: No. They're all celebrities I've never heard of.

LEE: What have you written down there for number seven?

BUNNY: I thought it was the Berlin Wall before they knocked it down.

LEE: That's Ann Widdecombe Dad.

BUNNY: I didn't have me glasses.

LEE: Has Woody been in?

BUNNY: He's at the KC. Hull City. He's gonna call in later.

LEE: Did he drop your gear off?

BUNNY: *(Taps a package on the table.)* Aye.

LEE picks up the package, looks at the contents.

LEE: Don't leave it on the table dad. Cannabis has been reclassified from Class C to Class B.

BUNNY: Woody never told us owt about that.

LEE: He's not gonna is he. Just cos it's for your MS, he's not gonna do you an information leaflet. He's Woody the dealer, not Boots the chemist. Is this the right stuff this time?

BUNNY: It's cannabis resin yeah.

LEE: Good. That skunk he sold you was too strong.

BUNNY: It got me out the house.

LEE: Out the house?! You went to Mars and back in an afternoon. You were the first retired docker in space.

BUNNY: I walked that day. I walked unaided across East Park.

LEE: That wan't walking Dad. That was a cross between Fred Astaire, and Hurricane Katrina. Drugs are wrong, you used to say to me, 'just say no'. Twenty years later, look at you, busy puffing your way through two ounces of Lebanese every week… It's only a matter of time before you discover Rastafarianism. In ten years' time you'll be the only eighty-year-old Hull bloke with dreadlocks. You can come off this when you get your Beta Interferon.

BUNNY: It lessens the pain, but I saw yer mam again last night.

LEE: What was she doing this time?

BUNNY: Sawing a leg off.

LEE: Sawing a leg off what?

BUNNY: Her own leg.

LEE: Where?

BUNNY: Below the knee.

LEE: I mean, where in the flat?

BUNNY: Living room.

LEE: Cannabis is a psychoactive narcotic Dad.

BUNNY: She hated me.

LEE: She didn't *hate* you. She found you annoying.

BUNNY: She hung hersen, and it was my fault son.

LEE: Hanged. How many questions did you get right?

BUNNY: Four.

LEE: Four!? Out of sixty?

BUNNY: I woulda got five but Mabel wouldn't let me have 'palletising' as an anagram. She said 'palletising' in't in her dictionary.

LEE: Summat you've spent your whole life doing and it in't even in the dictionary?

BUNNY: Dockers don't write dictionaries, good job an'all. There'd be a lot more Fs.

Enter BAZ from the street. She is a woman of about thirty, rough, white dreadlocks, tattoos, track suit, midriff showing, bum tattoo, a broken arm in plaster. She is a disaster area. She has a carrier full of booze and fags. She gets a subtle nod from MABEL and enters the pub assertively.

BAZ: Alright Bunny!? Touch bruv!

She punches fists with BUNNY. BUNNY does this in a surprisingly skilled manner.

Alright Peace! In the wheelchair again eh?

BUNNY: Aye.

BAZ: Did you enjoy the para olympics last year?

BUNNY: No.

BAZ: What! I'm disappointed in you bruv! An't you never heard of empathy!

BUNNY: I think it's really boring, and a bit embarrassing.

BAZ: Alright bruv, don't rub it in! They can't help it you know. Lee?! Bredren! Back from Afghanistan eh? Peace! Or in your case, war!

LEE: Hi Baz.

BAZ: You're home safe cos Jesus loves you, you know that don't you?

LEE: Yeah, thank him from me will you.

BAZ: *(Producing it from her bag.)* Big bag o' Drum.

LEE: You got any vodka, Grey Goose?

BAZ: I don't buy nothing on spec. This is orders. I work in that chippy top of Barnsley Street, the one run by Kosovans. Come in, I'll take your order.

LEE: Is Mabel alright about you selling bootleg in her pub?

BAZ: None of your fucking business is it Lee?

LEE: Yeah, you're right. Carry on.

BAZ: Respect. Alright. Do you want a blue badge? Park anywhere, disabled bays, you know.

LEE: I've got a blue badge.

BAZ: No!? Who d'yer buy that off?

LEE: It's a real one. I was given it.

BAZ: You're not a disabled.

LEE: He is.

BAZ: So?!

LEE: I'm his carer.

BAZ: I'm trying to make a living, and you're telling me there's people just giving them away.

BUNNY: It's off the council.

BAZ: Oh, riiight! MOT?

LEE: What would I want with a Belgian MOT?

BAZ: What makes you think it's Belgian?!

LEE: Everything else you're flogging's from Belgium.

BAZ shows him an MOT with emissions statement.

BAZ: I need an old MOT, and your emissions statement. Forty quid.

LEE: That's not much of a saving.

BAZ: Oh yeah! And that jalopy of yours is gonna pass first time is it?

LEE: How much money is my dad saving buying his Drum off you?

BUNNY: I'm not saving owt, you're paying for it.

LEE: What am I saving then?

BAZ: Saving your tax innit. Eight quid please. What was Helmand Province like?

LEE: It was like a quiet night down Preston Road.

BAZ: Was you scared?

LEE: Yeah, but I like being scared. You should go. Everyone should go. If you go, take your own towel.

LEE pays BAZ.

BAZ: You gone weird Lee. You got that post-traumatic stress disorder.

LEE: No. I'm not mad, no.

BAZ: Don't matter if you are, cos Jesus loves you. You see the great thing about Jesus right, is he –

LEE: – it's alright Baz. I know about Jesus.

BAZ: And he knows about you.

BAZ exits.

LEE: Is she off the skag?

BUNNY: She's stopped offering me sex.

LEE: Must be then. Which team won tonight?

BUNNY: Your teacher friends. I think they cheat. One of them's gorra Bramble.

LEE: *(Beat.)* Blackberry. They're not friends Dad. They know me because they humiliated me, patronised me, beat me. They prepared me for a life of hourly-paid wage labour, unemployment, or the army.

BUNNY: Aye, it was a good school, David Lister.

LEE: Mr Ellerington. 'Hard-on' we used to call him. Look at him, he hasn't changed. Goatee beard, chalk marks on his flies, permanent erection. He's got a hard-on now, looks like a giraffe fighting its way out of the wrong end of a one-man tent.

MABEL comes over, spying an empty glass.

LEE: Any good questions tonight Mabel?

BUNNY: HMS Belfast.

MABEL: What do HMS Belfast moored at Tower Bridge on the Thames and the London Gateway Services on the M1 have in common?

LEE: Both opened, launched by the Queen? Dunno.

MABEL: If HMS Belfast fired its guns it would hit London Gateway Services.

BUNNY: I'd do better if you asked questions on summat I knew summat about.

MABEL: What's your specialist subject Bunny?

LEE: The containerisation of East Hull docks.

BUNNY: Alexandra Dock. Don't know owt about George Dock.

LEE: How much did the teachers win tonight Mabe?

MABEL: Forty-two pound sterling.

MABEL moves on.

LEE: How does this quiz work?

BUNNY: It's a five-week league, works like superleague. At the end of the month the top two teams have a play-off final. But every week there's about forty quid up for grabs. I love it, but the teachers always win.

LEE: That forty quid could pay for your drugs. Remember, I'm not working. How many can you have in a team?

BUNNY: Four maximum. But it's just me and Woody usually.

LEE: You, Woody, me, so we need one more.

MELISSA wins again. And immediately starts another game.

MABEL: Sh! Love! That's a funeral party in there, and they're all still a bit melancholyflowercheese, about the whole thing.

MELISSA: Sorry. I've won twice now. I'm beginning to feel a little ostentatious.

MABEL: If you're not feeling well love, I'd go and have a lie down.

LEE stands, approaches MELISSA.

LEE: Hi. My name's Lee.

MELISSA: Melissa.

LEE: Melissaphobia. A fear of bees.

MELISSA: One point. What do you call the side of a hill sheltered from the wind?

LEE: The lee side.

MELISSA: That's another point. You're doing well.

LEE: Do you like pub quiz?

MELISSA: I love Mabel. Is it every Tuesday?

LEE: Yeah. You're not from round here are you?

MELISSA: I work in Hull. We were looking at a site today, just over the bridge.

LEE: What's your specialist subject Melissa?

MELISSA: Men.

LEE: OK.

MELISSA: Men and unrequited love.

LEE: Cool. Would you like to join my pub quiz team? I wanna beat the teachers. They used to teach me, called me thick, I'm not thick.

MELISSA: It's about revenge is it?

LEE: Yeah.

MELISSA: I'm with people from work.

LEE: OK. I apologise.

MELISSA: You don't have to apologise.

LEE: Who do you work for?

MELISSA: Hull Advance. We're the regeneration company.

LEE: Oh, you're one of them are you?

MELISSA: On second thoughts, maybe you can apologise.

LEE: No, no, I didn't mean anything by it. OK, nice to meet you, get back to work. Someone's got to save Hull haven't they, and the clock's ticking, know what I mean.

MELISSA: Maybe I've had enough work for one day.

LEE: Course you have. Do you want to meet my dad?

MELISSA: I've been in Hull six months, that's the best offer so far.

LEE: Dad. This is Melissa.

MELISSA: Hi. I thought Mabel was wrong not to allow your palletising answer.

BUNNY: Oh, you know what the word means do you love?

MELISSA: It's a noun drawn from the past participle of the verb to palletise, describing the action of using pallets in logistics.

BUNNY: Fucking hell. What's logistics?

LEE: It's the new word for warehousing and storage.

BUNNY: Oh aye, they're trying make it sound clever are they?

WOODY: *(Off / singing.)* 'Mauled by the Tigers!
You're getting mauled by the Tigers'

LEE: And this is the fourth member of the team, Woody.

WOODY enters, singing. He's in full head-to-toe Tiger costume.

WOODY: 'Mauled by the Tigers!
You're getting mauled by the Tigers'/

MABEL: Shhhh!!!

WOODY kisses MABEL, and moves on, ignoring her.

WOODY: 'Mauled by the Tigers!
You're getting mauled by the Tigers'

WOODY opens the lounge bar door and stands in the doorway.

'Mauled by the Tigers!'

WOODY walks into the lounge bar. MABEL shuts the door on him.

(*Off.*) 'You're getting mauled by the Tigers.
Mauled by the –'

There is a crash of breaking glass, and the collapsing of a table. The singing stops.

End of scene.

Scene change. MABEL isolated in a spot.

MABEL: What was the last British Rail steam service? Shoulda been easy enough for any geriatric Hull gits in tonight. *And* I gave you a bloody clue. 'PS'. PS stands for Paddle Steamer, yes! The PS Farringford, Humber Ferry, was the last British Rail steam service, and the very ship on which I met my fourth husband, Eddie. Eddie had got the draw string of his cagoule caught in one of the paddles and he was going round and round with the paddle wheel. He was in the Humber for thirty seconds, and then he'd pop up on the wheel and chat me up for thirty seconds before going under again. By the time we'd got to New Holland he'd asked me to marry him, and not expecting him to survive, I'd stupidly said yes.

SCENE TWO (HALF AN HOUR LATER)

In BUNNY's flat. A coffee table set with a mug and a cup and saucer set. LEE and BUNNY (in wheelchair) just inside the door.

BUNNY: Who's she then?

LEE: Melissa works for Hull Advance. One of them regeneration companies.

BUNNY: Is it them what's gonna knock down the old fruit market?

LEE: It's not an old fruit market dad, it's a strategic development area. It's gonna be a thousand-acre open-air piazza. Bob Carver's gonna open a sushi restaurant. Get out your wheelchair. I want you to walk to the settee.

BUNNY: It hurts.

LEE: I know it hurts. You don't get Beta Interferon unless you're walking.

BUNNY: You're hard on me.

LEE: You were hard on me. As a kid.

BUNNY starts to walk. It's painful. He sits on the settee and starts to smoke a pre-prepared joint from a tin on the coffee table.

BUNNY: I never hit you son.

LEE: You knocked one of me teeth out.

BUNNY: It was loose. It was a milk tooth.

LEE: A grown man punching a ten year-old is child abuse.

BUNNY: Everybody used to hit their kids.

LEE: You could've been different.

BUNNY: People back then, didn't think so much, about anything. You was who you was, and you were how you were, and that was that.

LEE: Did you ever hit me mam?

Silence.

What'd she done?

Silence.

BUNNY: I don't want to talk about your mother. She might make an appearance.

BUNNY takes a long and skilled toke on the joint. Holds in the smoke. And releases it slowly.

LEE: Where was she the last time you saw her?

BUNNY: She jumped up from behind this settee. She had a chainsaw.

LEE: She never went near power tools in her whole life.

BUNNY: Mebbe she's been on a course.

LEE takes the joint from BUNNY and takes a toke.

BUNNY: See that there, her cup and saucer.

LEE: It's a cup and saucer, yeah.

BUNNY: I use a mug. She's been in, while we've been at the quiz.

LEE: Has your occupational therapist seen her?

BUNNY: No.

LEE: Has she attacked meals on wheels with an axe as they come in the door?

BUNNY: No.

LEE: Has your physio seen her?

BUNNY: No. But he's blind.

LEE: Has he felt her?

BUNNY: No.

LEE: Have you ever seen her when you're not out of your head on psychoactive drugs?

BUNNY: What are you suggesting Lee?

LEE: That you're smoking enough puff every week to bring Bob Marley back from the dead.

BUNNY: Can I come and live with you?

LEE: No, you can't.

BUNNY: Your Janet dun't like me does she?

LEE: She dun't like *me* half the time.

BUNNY: That's cos you had a vasectomy. Women always wanna have at least one girl. She not talking to you?

LEE: I'm not gonna discuss my sex life with me own father.

BUNNY: I think you should give that flower shop idea of hers a go.

LEE: I don't want to run a flower shop.

BUNNY: You could run it together.

LEE: That's her dream. I'm off.

BUNNY: Don't get mixed up with Woody. You'll find work soon enough.

LEE: I didn't pay him for your gear. Is it working?

BUNNY: Aye, but it's her I'm worried about.

LEE: It's the drugs Dad, it's not real. Tarra.

He leaves. The cup and saucer begin to rattle. BUNNY watches. The cup and saucer then moves slowly along the coffee table and then flies off the end. BUNNY is terrified.

End of scene.

SCENE THREE

In the pub. WOODY is sat there with an elastoplast on both eyes and a packet of frozen peas against one of them. LEE is already sat there beside him, he's counting out notes.

LEE: Here's your money.

WOODY: I only take cheques. Make it out to South Cave Cakes.

LEE: Your wife's cake shop?

WOODY: Yeah. It's doing well.

LEE: I an't got a cheque book on me.

WOODY: Friday lunch then. At your 'team talk'.

LEE: I think a meeting will help. Clarify roles.

WOODY: You not found work?

LEE: I've only been back two weeks.

WOODY: Got two kids an't you?

LEE: Yeah. Jamie, he's eight, Paul's ten.

LEE shows a leaf in his wallet with photos.

WOODY: What are the schools like round here?

LEE: Alright.

WOODY: Kids is all there is Lee. Mine are off my hands now. It was expensive but it was worth it. I put both of them through Pocklington, gap year, university. Tilda's in publishing now, London, and Millie's singing with Opera North.

LEE: Wow. My Jamie's supposed to have a talent for piano.

WOODY: You got to get him a piano then, lessons.

LEE: How much is a piano?

WOODY: Two grand, three grand. I pay well. I need someone with army training. I got a problem. It's called North Hull Estate.

LEE: The Wild West.

WOODY: I like a good western, but this is more like *Apocalypse Now.* As a soldier I reckon you must know how to keep cool under pressure.

LEE: No thanks Woody.

WOODY: I'm looking to take early retirement. I miss performing you see.

LEE: You gonna start playing bass again?

WOODY: Rock and Roll's a young man's game. Comedy. Stand-up.

LEE: Yeah, you always like your stand-ups.

WOODY: Writing my own material. Gonna do the talent night, end of the month.

LEE: How many jokes have you written?

WOODY: One.

LEE: Good luck. Did you see where Melissa went?

WOODY: She rang for a taxi. You worked for me before you know. On Longhill. You wouldn't have known you were working for me.

LEE: The foreman at Coachman's is a mate of mine. He says one of the jiggers is going to give his notice in Thursday.

WOODY: Caravans? How much an hour?

LEE: Eight quid.

WOODY: Tut! I got part-time too you know. You got an attic?

LEE: I'm not gonna store stock for you Woody, alright.

WOODY: Hydroponics.

LEE: Skunk?

WOODY: It's farming Jim, but not as we know it. No pig shit, no sheep shagging, and you can stay in bed 'til lunchtime.

LEE: What are the risks?

WOODY: If it snows you're fucked.

LEE: Why is snow a problem?

WOODY: Hydroponics heats up the attic, melts the snow on the roof. Soon as it snows the cops are up in the air in the helicopter.

LEE: No thanks Woody.

WOODY: What's the problem Lee? I mean, how often does it snow?

LEE: I've got a flat roof.

LEE stands.

End of scene.

SCENE FOUR

MELISSA and LEE on the street outside. LEE has just clicked off his mobile phone.

LEE: You're getting a taxi from East Hull to Cherry Burton?!

MELISSA: I'll put it on expenses. That *Heart of Darkness* question –

LEE: – Joseph Conrad. Mister Kurtz.

MELISSA: Yes, you got it right.

LEE: And you were very impressed.

MELISSA: I'm sorry, Lee, if I sounded patronising, I can only –

LEE: – do you expect soldiers to be thick?

MELISSA: What I said was that it was 'brilliant' that you'd read *Heart of Darkness.* If you're paranoid about –

LEE: – I'm paranoid now am I?

MELISSA: One wouldn't normally expect a squaddie to be able to quote from a classic novel.

LEE: What do you think we do in our downtime? Play computer games and watch porn?

MELISSA: Yes. *(Beat.)* Sorry.

LEE: It's the only proper book, novel, I've ever read.

MELISSA: Why did you read it?

LEE: I saw *Apocalypse Now*, the film. I loved it. Dad said it was based on a book. He had a copy. I read it and then I went out and bought my own.

MELISSA: You went out and bought a book? Sorry! And pub quiz reduces your favourite novel to trivia, one quotation, 'the horror, the horror'.

LEE: I don't care.

MELISSA: OK. I'm impressed. You're unique and special, a soldier who reads Conrad.

LEE: I was a soldier. I like it when you get angry.

MELISSA: Are you making a move Lee?

LEE: What's Hull Advance doing in East Hull. Are we gonna get regenerated?

MELISSA: A dry ski slope, down that street there.

LEE: A dry ski slope, down Clough Road?

MELISSA: Are you suggesting that the people of Hull don't deserve a dry ski slope?

LEE: Skiing is summat you do after work, with your disposable income.

MELISSA: You're bitter aren't you?

LEE: Two pints of bitter. Na. We haven't had full employment here since the fishing finished.

MELISSA: Fishing was a very dangerous way to make a living.

LEE: It's better for men to die with dignity fishing, knowing who they are, than to die on welfare, on drugs, on a dry ski slope.

MELISSA: Nobody dies on dry ski slopes.

LEE: You don't know much about Hull do you, just you fucking wait.

MELISSA: Would you respect me more if I told you that I went to the roughest comprehensive in North East Surrey?

LEE: I'm all for regeneration me. I like bistros.

MELISSA: Hull could be a top ten town. We have two hundred thousand ABC1s living in the Wolds villages who shop in Sheffield or Leeds.

LEE: So the future of Hull is in the hands of people who don't live here?

MELISSA: Regeneration has given Hull a music venue, St Stephens shopping, a brand new theatre.

LEE: I'd go to the theatre if I thought that I might see someone like meself up on stage.

MELISSA: And what are you like Lee?

LEE: I'm not a king.

MELISSA: Plays aren't always about kings.

LEE: They're all about unemployed soldiers now are they?

MELISSA: Yes, actually. What did the army train you to do?

LEE: Some Personnel Officer asked me that this morning. I told her I'd been trained to kill a man with my bare hands.

MELISSA: What did she say to that?

LEE: She said there's not a lot of call for that at Jacksons.

MELISSA: Did you kill any Taliban?

LEE: Three that I know of.

MELISSA: I've never been alone with a killer. But you're a killer with a heart, I mean, I think what you're doing with your dad is brilliant.

LEE: I don't even like him.

MELISSA: I don't talk to my parents at all. They wanted grandchildren.

Taxi pips.

My taxi.

LEE: You know town end of Bev Road?

MELISSA: Sorry?

LEE: Beverley Road. Three years ago this bloke opened a sex shop and at Christmas he put decorations up on the outside, Santa with a sleigh, Rudolph. But running a sex shop put a strain on his heart and so he closed the place down, but he left Santa and Rudolph outside, up on the shop front. Three years they've been up there now, rain, sleet, sun. Santa's smile has got wiped from his face, Rudolph is frozen, sodden, lying dead next to a pink vibrator.

Taxi pips.

That's not the kind of thing you see in a top ten town. Forget your Wolds villages and their ABC1s and get that fucking Santa sorted.

MELISSA kisses him. It's a proper kiss. During which BAZ enters and notices what's happening. BAZ exits, saying nothing.

MELISSA: *(As she's leaving.)* I'll see you here, Friday lunch time.

MELISSA sees BAZ.

LEE: Yeah, team talk.

LEE watches as the taxi drives off. A moment's thought.

(*Quietly, to himself.*) Just say no.

End of scene

Week Two

SCENE ONE (LATER THAT WEEK, FRIDAY LUNCHTIME)

A food menu on the blackboard. LEE, BUNNY, WOODY (with plaster over the eye) and MELISSA at a table. On the table are empty plates from lunch, maybe the odd chip. BUNNY and LEE can still be eating if needed. On WOODY's plate is an uneaten battered fish skin and the odd chip.

WOODY: *(To MELISSA.)* Are you vegetarian?

MELISSA: No, but I only eat happy chickens.

WOODY: I think organic farming's cruel. If the animals are happy, yeah, killing 'em must be wrong. Factory farming's much better, cos at least when you kill 'em you're putting them out their misery.

LEE: *(Beat.)* Is that the joke you've written?

WOODY: Yeah.

MELISSA: It's funny, but it's rubbish. *(She spots MABEL.)* Mabel! Could you possibly do me a receipt for lunch please?

MABEL: You want all four of them on one ticket?

MELISSA: That'd be perfect.

LEE has clocked this example of exploitative expenses. MABEL moves off.

Why do you want to do stand-up?

WOODY: I want a change of career.

MELISSA: But you seem to me to be very successful. That Lexus in the car park, that's yours isn't it?

WOODY: No, I borrowed it off the enemy.

LEE: His wife.

WOODY: It's a good car that Lexus. Goes like taramasalata off a shovel.

MELISSA: What's your line of business?

WOODY: Buying, selling, distribution.

MELISSA: Because it's useful for me to know which sectors of the economy are flourishing in Hull. Are you involved in manufacturing?

WOODY: No. That's all overseas.

MELISSA: What kind of products?

WOODY: Alternative lifestyle solutions, pyramid selling, yeah.

MELISSA: That's my card. Next week I'm running an 'investors in youth forum' at Bridlington Spa. Do you know Bridlington Spa?

WOODY: Brid Spa, yeah, that's where I started.

LEE: He was in a band. Bass.

MELISSA: Cool.

WOODY: Cool? No we weren't cool, no. We were shit.

MELISSA: Hull Advance want to see successful entrepreneurs going into the schools, talking to the kids.

WOODY: I already have people doing that.

MELISSA: The danger is that for the kids on the big estates the only person they see driving a Lexus is the local drug dealer.

WOODY: Normally I drive a Range Rover. And I live in South Cave.

MELISSA: Where is South Cave?

WOODY: It's south of North Cave.

MABEL comes over to take the dishes.

MABEL: There's your receipt, love.

MELISSA: Thank you.

WOODY: Lovely haddock that Mabe.

MABEL: I wouldn't know. I haven't eaten fish since I signed on to that Estonian cruise ship fully intending to present my own particular brand of tasteless erotica. But they forced me to do a cabaret act as a female impersonator.

MELISSA: But you are a woman.

MABEL: And in fact, unlike some people I could name, I always have been. The ship turned out to be a floating brothel for the Russian fishing fleet. That's where I met me first husband, Leff. He was a winch operator from Murmansk who had webbed feet that he could tuck behind the back of his head. I hope that image hasn't ruined your lunch. I nursed him for ten months as he slowly died from passive smoking, like Roy Castle.

MABEL is genuinely moved, hanky, sniffs.

WOODY: Count your blessings Mabel, at least he never played the bugle.

MABEL moves off.

So why am I here on a Friday lunch, Lee Bunting?

LEE: I want to win the league. It's an injustice that the teachers always win.

WOODY: Pub quiz and injustice, you can't have one without the other. I was in Spain, at the villa last year, and the local had a quiz, one of the questions was 'where in England would you find the Land of Green Ginger'.

BUNNY: 'ull!

WOODY: Of course. But they wouldn't give me a point.

LEE: What had you put?

WOODY: Bottom o' Whitefri'gate.

LEE: There is a lesson there. OK. First off guys, thanks for coming in –

WOODY: – you sound like an officer.

LEE: We can win this quiz. But it does need focus.

WOODY: Prince Harry in Afghanistan! The Taliban are here, here, here and here!

MELISSA: We've all agreed to this meeting.

WOODY: You can't do homework for pub quiz!

LEE: Setting the questions for pub quiz is a form of self-expression. What are Mabel's obsessions? What is the wallpaper of Mabel's life?

WOODY: Wood chip.

MELISSA: She's going to Crete for her holidays.

LEE: Brilliant. Melissa, can you swat up on Minoan Culture.

WOODY: Fucking hell!

LEE: Woody, you're our music man. What is the soundtrack to Mabel's life?

WOODY: Glen Campbell, Neil Diamond, Glen Campbell, Gary Glitter and Glen Campbell.

LEE: Get all their lyrics, all their stories, go on the internet –

WOODY: I'm not looking up Gary Glitter on the internet.

BUNNY: Mabel likes her flags from when she was on cruise ships.

LEE: You were in the navy so can you swat up on flags please.

MELISSA: She always has questions about Hull and it's part of my job to learn about Hull and Hull people so I'll take that one.

LEE: Brilliant. Now, the other thing is how we work as a team. As a training exercise –

WOODY: – fucking hell.

LEE: – I'm gonna set you a question.

WOODY: You'll be giving us an half-time bollocking sat on the grass next.

LEE: What are the rooms in *Cluedo*?

WOODY: *(Loud.)* Conservatory.

LEE: Very good Woody, but keep your voice down.

WOODY: It's Friday lunchtime. It's not quiz night.

LEE: This is a role-play, we're training.

WOODY: Fucking hell.

MELISSA: Library, Dining Room –

LEE: Good. Dad?

BUNNY: What's *Cluedo*?

LEE: It's a board game Dad. Just say some names of rooms in a house.

BUNNY: Toilet.

LEE: No. There's no toilet.

BUNNY: What kind of house an't gorr a toilet?

LEE: Alright, dad. I take your point.

MELISSA: Kitchen.

LEE: Brilliant.

WOODY: Study. Snooker Room.

MELISSA: No, Billiard Room.

LEE: Yeah, Billiard Room, not Snooker Room, well done Melissa.

WOODY: Fucking hell.

BUNNY: Pantry?

LEE: No Dad.

MELISSA: Hall.

BUNNY: Front room.

LEE: No. Lounge.

LEE: Good. That's eight, there's only one left.

WOODY: Bedroom.

MELISSA: I don't think there is a bedroom actually.

WOODY: There must be a bedroom.

LEE: OK. We have a dispute. We have to use some conflict resolution procedures.

WOODY: Fucking hell.

MELISSA: I always think there should be a bedroom, because Miss Scarlett is so obviously a bit of a, you know, –

WOODY: – nymphomaniac.

MELISSA: And I remember always feeling surprised that there isn't a bedroom.

LEE: Woody?

WOODY: It's a house. There must be a bedroom.

LEE: There is no bedroom.

BUNNY: Scullery.

LEE: In this team if anyone's going to guess, the team captain, that's me, is going to ask you to support your guess with information. This is our team tin. Pens, pencils, scrap paper, a rubber.

WOODY: What's all this about Lee?

BUNNY: I like it. It's about getting organised. It's about collective action. The same things that brought the working class of this country some modicum of justice can be mobilised to –

WOODY: – win at pub quiz?

BUNNY: Yeah, course!

LEE: Thanks Dad.

MELISSA: I think this has been useful. Well done Lee.

MELISSA stands.

I'm sorry, I have to go. I'll see you all on Tuesday.

WOODY: Important meeting?

MELISSA: Yes.

WOODY: What? Toyota are gonna open a car factory? Mebbe East Yorkshire's gonna be one big wind farm, and we're gonna get to build the turbines?

MELISSA: We're unveiling plans for an iconic footbridge over the River Hull to connect the Old Town with The Boom.

WOODY: What's The Boom?

MELISSA: It's a new development. Shops, offices, restaurants.

WOODY: How does building a footbridge over the River Hull cause a boom?

MELISSA: Sometimes I think the Luftwaffe had the right idea.

MELISSA turns and leaves.

LEE: They got us The Deep.

BUNNY: I went round that Deep in ten minutes, can't see what all the fuss is about.

LEE: You've never got over Luton becoming 'Number one crap town'.

BUNNY: We was robbed there! I've been to Luton, there's some quite nice bits.

WOODY: That title's Hull's! Ours by rights!

BUNNY is trying to get up out of his chair.

WOODY: What you doing Bunny?

BUNNY: Need to spend a penny. He makes me walk everywhere.

WOODY stand to help him.

LEE: Sit down Woody. He has to do this for hissen.

BUNNY, using sticks, staggers off to the loos.

WOODY: It's hurting him.

LEE: He has to be walking, on his own, or they won't give him Beta Interferon.

WOODY: I see. You've got a plan. A plan for everything eh? Did you get that job at Coachman's then?

LEE: The bloke who was going to leave, changed his mind.

WOODY: Bad luck. The piano's on hold then?

LEE: I guess.

WOODY: In my business you meet a lot of scum. I don't like working with them.

WOODY puts an envelope on the table.

There's five hundred quid there. I'm talking about two days' work.

Silence

I laid on some stock, on tick, for this muppet, said she wanted to work for me. She's late paying. I think she hasn't got the money, because she's getting high on her own supply.

LEE: You want me to give her a yellow card?

WOODY: What would you do if the Taliban broke their word and needed scaring?

LEE: We'd go round and kill a few of them.

WOODY: This is Hull not Nottingham. I just want the stock back, or the money. Two thousand quid.

LEE: I don't know how to scare people without a gun.

WOODY: Tell her you want two thousand quid by Monday. Then go in her bathroom, piss all over the carpet, piss up the walls.

LEE: Why don't you go round and piss on the carpet?

WOODY: I've been serving it up for twenty years now and the longer I go without getting nicked the more nervous I get. You're army trained. I've seen the ads on telly. Road block, hundreds of Africans, women screaming, and the soldier, keeps cool, does the right thing.

LEE: How's your business work?

WOODY: The gear comes into Hull through the docks, goes to Liverpool, gets bashed, comes back to Hull, gets bashed again, not by me obviously, and then it goes out to the street dealers. Two problems in this business, stock and cash. I never go near the stock, and I get the cash clean as soon as I can. Cakes, casino, property, whatever. Just do this one job will you. Put the money in the piano fund.

A couple of beats, and then LEE takes the envelope.

Good. Here.

WOODY gives him a business card.

LEE: Brough Pianos?

WOODY: He won't rip you off. He's a Rotarian, like me.

End of scene.

SCENE TWO

North Hull Estate. A kitchen. ANGIE is sitting with her back to the audience, hoodie up.

ANGIE: Look bro, do I look like I've got two thousand quid?

LEE: I'll take the stock then.

ANGIE: *(Laughs.)* Why has Woody got excited about two K?

LEE: I think his main concern is that you've broken an agreement.

ANGIE: Woody's a joke man. The rumour is he wants out. I'm not paying him. What are you gonna do now? How you gonna scare me?

LEE: I'm army trained.

ANGIE: Have you been to Iraq?

LEE: Afghanistan.

ANGIE: What right have we got to invade other people's countries?

LEE: What right have they got to fly aeroplanes into our iconic buildings?

ANGIE: So, they killed three thousand fat American capitalists, you know what I mean bro, who gives a fuck?

LEE: Saddam Hussein killed a million of his own people. Don't you care about them?

ANGIE: No. When them soldiers marched in Luton right, and all those anti-war Muslims demonstrated, I thought that was dead good that.

LEE: They're not anti-war, they're pro the other side.

ANGIE: I'm pro the other side an'all bro. There in't no money to be had. You can't squeeze me. What you gonna do now?

LEE: I need a pee. Can I use your loo?

ANGIE: There.

LEE goes into her loo, closing the door behind him.

End of scene.

SCENE THREE

Lights up on WOODY, LEE, and BUNNY at their alcove table. BAZ is sat upstage of our team facing into the alcove behind. The impression is that she has her pub quiz team in that alcove, unseen.

MABEL: *(On the mic.)* And that is the last question in round one. Team positions after last week's debacle – 'The Staff of Life' on three points are top; second on two points is 'This is What Happens When Cousins Marry'; third on one point is 'I left my heart on Sutton Bridge, and I don't want it back', bit of a mouthful that, as the actress …no, I won't go there. They're on one point, and no other teams have any points. Swap your 'round one' answer sheets now please with your neighbouring team. Come on!

BAZ stands, sheet in her hand.

Swap these answer sheets. Hurry up!

She sings the start of Sham 69's 'Hurry up Harry'.

(*Speaking.*) I can feel a bonus point coming on. All together now.

ALL join in with the chorus.

MABEL: *(Speaking.)* The name of the band?

CONFEDERATE: Sham 69!

MABEL: Yes! Sham sixty-nines, I've had a few of them in me time, an enjoyable recreational activity once you've got used to the view. Bonus point, the teachers.

BAZ approaches our team's alcove.

BAZ: I should see the other bloke yeah?

WOODY: There were twenty-three of them. All of them professional boxers.

LEE: Gis your answer sheet Baz.

WOODY hands BAZ his team's answer sheet.

BAZ: You're funny!

BUNNY: Woody's gonna do Talent Night at the end of the month.

BAZ: Yeah?

Enter MELISSA, she's been in the loos.

(*To MELISSA.*) Alright?

MELISSA: Yes, thank you. Melissa.

BAZ: *(To MELISSA.)* Baz. Peace!

BAZ moves away and sits down.

LEE: I think the only one we didn't get in that round is the quotation.

MELISSA: I've seen it somewhere in Hull. On a statue. 'Had I now had the sense to have gone back to Hull, and have gone home, I had been happy'.

WOODY: Dean Windass.

LEE: It's not Deano.

BUNNY: Might be. He won't settle in Darlington.

MELISSA: No, it's not contemporary, the language suggests a different century.

WOODY: Dean Windass is from a different century.

MELISSA: Who is Dean Windass?

LEE: He was Hull City's oldest player last season.

MELISSA: How old is he?

WOODY: Eighty-four.

BUNNY: We should have had a guess even if we didn't know.

LEE: Didn't you put a guess down Woody?!

WOODY: Oh it's my fault is it?

LEE: We should never leave an answer box blank!

WOODY: I an't come here for a bollocking, I can get that at home.

MABEL: Exchange answer sheets now! Just answer sheets, keep your bodily fluids to yourself. I'm gonna begin the beguine now. Fuck that, I'm not dancing an'all. Question one, which screen star wore the same coat in every film?

BUNNY: Lassie.

MABEL: Thank you Bunny, Lassie the wonder dog. Two. Who was the first couple to be shown in bed together on prime time British TV? The answer is not Morecambe and Wise –

She sings start of 'I can't help falling in love with you'.

All together:

ALL join in with the chorus of the song.

The answer is Fred and Wilma Flintstone. TV companies didn't like to show people in bed together cos they thought it was rude. Ruud Gullit, a good-looking Dutchman, had an argument once with my sister over a bread roll. It was the last one they had in the shop. Question three, what is the longest river in Saudi Arabia? Well there in't one is there.

LEE: Yes!

BAZ: NO!

MABEL: Question four, who said 'Had I now had the sense to have gone back to Hull, and have gone home, I had been happy'? Robinson Crusoe.

MELISSA: It's on that statue in Queens Gardens!

MABEL: Robinson Crusoe sailed from Hull in 1651, and was shipwrecked for twenty eight years. That's fucking P&O for you. Question five. Who said these famous last words, 'I wish I'd had more sex?'

BAZ: Mother Theresa of Calcutta.

LEE: That's our answer to question six.

BAZ: It's written in the number five answer box.

MABEL: Quiet gentlemen please! 'I wish I'd had more sex' were reputed to be the last words of the poet John Betjeman. *(Reciting:)*

She recites the first four lines of John Betjeman's poem 'Slough'.

What a miserable git, no wonder he never got his leg over.

LEE: Baz? We put John Betjeman.

BAZ: Yeah, you did, in box four.

LEE: If all this round is out of sync Woody –

WOODY: Oh, it's Woody's fault is it?

MABEL: Which Roman Catholic nun ran an orphanage in India?

BAZ: Don Revie!

LEE: – we've got them in the wrong order Baz.

MABEL: Mother Theresa, of course. Question seven. Who was England manager when we failed to qualify for Euro '76?

BAZ: Linda Lovelace!

MABEL: Don Revie. Eight. Who starred in the pornographic film *Deep Throat*?

LEE: *(To BAZ.)* Go on.

BAZ: Baden-Powell.

MABEL: It's not Baden-Powell actually, though I would pay good money to watch that, it was Linda Lovelace. *(Reading.)* '*Deep Throat* was the most financially successful pornographic film of all time, however the three follow-up movies she made were less successful.' Which just goes to show that one swallow doesn't make a summer. Question nine. Baden-Powell was the British general at Mafeking. Question ten for a maximum of four points, name four English towns with a part of the body in the name, to make an example of you, as a lesson to others, Manchester – 'chest', and no more chests allowed please, I've got enough going on with these two here. Answers I can allow are liver, Liverpool; foot, Footscray; arm yes, Armley; head, Maidenhead and that's about it, I'm not allowing Scunthorpe.

WOODY: *(To LEE.)* Fag break!

LEE and WOODY head for outside.

BAZ: Two out of ten. Bad luck.

MELISSA: Three out of ten. Well done.

BAZ: Are you patronising me?

MELISSA: I beg your pardon.

BAZ: You said 'well done', when I only got three.

MELISSA: I didn't mean, anything, by it.

BAZ: Lee Bunting is married to Janet, a good friend of mine. See that scar?

She shows a cut, scar on her wrist.

That's from me and his Janet sharing blood. We're blood brothers.

MELISSA: I'm not having an affair with him if that's what you mean.

BAZ: That's alright then innit. Do you want a Blue badge? Park anywhere.

MELISSA: No thank you.

BAZ: MOT. Designer underpants, Colin Klein.

MELISSA: No thanks.

BAZ: Anything from Belgium? Spirits, sleeves of fags.

MELISSA: I don't smoke actually.

Outside. LEE and WOODY having a cigarette.

WOODY: Did you piss on the mat?

LEE: I pissed in her toothbrush mug.

WOODY: What makes you think she cleans her teeth?

LEE: Do you want me to go back?

WOODY: Yeah. She won't have the money but see if there's any of the stock left. I think she keeps it in the cistern.

LEE: I don't suppose she'll let me use the loo again.

WOODY: The brown she got from me was already bashed. If you find any in little bricks, that's not mine, we don't want it, but we want to know about it.

LEE: We?

WOODY: Yeah. Could be we if you wanted it to be. I'm impressed with you. Even the pub quiz team, the planning, the whatdoyoucallits –

LEE: – objectives.

WOODY: I could train you, couple of years, then I'll sell the whole business to you. Two hundred thousand.

LEE: I need a piano, then I'm out.

WOODY: Is your lad Paul gonna go to school round here?

LEE: I guess.

WOODY: Pocklington is about four thousand pound a term. Good school. Good values. You don't want your kids growing up round here, they might get into drugs. I'm serious.

Enter BAZ.

BAZ: What do you want from Belgium Woody?

WOODY: Box of chocolates please.

BAZ: Comedy! That's why God put you on this earth Woody.

WOODY: Yeah. What's his excuse for you?

BAZ: To love my fellow man.

WOODY: By selling bootleg from Belgium?

WOODY exits.

LEE: Do you make money?

BAZ: I do East Hull, alright, if you're gonna start go West Hull or North Hull.

LEE: Don't Customs ever stop you?

BAZ: Personal use, innit.

LEE: You'd have to be an alcoholic with a nicotine addiction.

BAZ: Yeah.

LEE: I need a favour.

BAZ: I don't turn tricks no more Lee. Since Jesus saved me, my body is not a means to an end, it's a chapel.

LEE: Temple.

BAZ: Whatever.

LEE: I need something from Belgium.

He gives her the money.

BAZ: What?

LEE: A Cuno Melcher replica.

BAZ: *(Beat.)* A lizard?

LEE: A Cuno Melcher ME 38 Magnum. It's a facsimile of a gun. It's legal, you can declare it. Are you working in the chippy tomorrow?

BAZ: Six til late yeah.

LEE: I'll call in. And, I'll pick you up Monday morning when you come off the ship, give you a lift.

BAZ: Cool. Do unto others as they would have you do unto you. Summat like that. And a bottle of Grey Goose, yeah?

LEE: Yeah.

BAZ moves off happy.

MABEL: *(On the mic.)* Final round. Question one. Fingers on buttons, I wish. Where would you find a Shogun?

BUNNY: I know this one…oh what is it…it's er…

WOODY: In a car park. A Shogun is a big four-by-four.

MELISSA: That can't be what she means. It's Japanese.

WOODY: Yeah, it's a Mitsubishi.

MELISSA: I think it's a soldier. So where would you find a Japanese soldier?

WOODY: In a shop, in bed, on the bog! What a stupid question?

BUNNY: No, their shoguns was like our Hitlers, or Mussolinis.

MELISSA: Yes! So where would you find a military dictator?

WOODY: In a shop, in bed, on the bog!

MELISSA: No. 'Running ancient Japan'.

Enter LEE. He sits.

MABEL: Question two. Name four examples of jobs done by a woman that end in 'tress', T R E double S.

MELISSA: Seamstress.

BUNNY: Waitress.

LEE: Head Mistress.

WOODY: *(Loud.)* Mattress.

BAZ pops up.

BAZ: Sexist! What do we want!? Equali'y! When do we want it! Now!

WOODY: Fuck off Baz, you shouldn't be listening.

BAZ: Oh yeah, sorry, respect!

LEE: Actress.

MABEL: Question three. The word 'alarming' has only one anagram. What is it? Talking of alarming, my second husband Tony, –

WOODY: – which one was he?

MABEL: He was the one I murdered. I say 'murdered', actually the jury's verdict was manslaughter despite the fact that I'd planned it meticulously with Tony's brother, Les, who was to become my third husband, and who only this week was discovered by the Child Support Agency living in an upturned coracle in the Forest of Dean.

LEE: I bet you're good at anagrams.

MELISSA: Not bad.

WOODY: Anagram of Alarming. Grim Anal.

MABEL: Question four.

LEE: Melissa, ignore this next question, carry on with the anagram.

MABEL: The letters L S D stand for what? And I don't mean Lucy in the Sky with Diamonds. *(Singing:)*

She sings the first two lines of 'Diamonds are forever'.

They don't need batteries either. Bonus point. Who –

CONFEDERATE: – Shirley Bassey.

MABEL: Ooh, a little premature there from the teachers, probably not the first time either. I wanted the name of the lyricist, who also wrote *Born Free.*

WOODY: Don Black.

MABEL: Correct. One point to 'My Dad's a Drug Addict'.

LEE: Woody – What does LSD stand for?

WOODY: Lysergic Acid Diethylamide.

MABEL: Question five. For two points. Name the singer and the song. I'm going to play you the first bar only.

MABEL plays the first bar of 'Rhinestone Cowboy' then turns the system off.

That's all you're getting of that one.

BAZ pops up.

BAZ: NO!

MABEL: Too difficult? Alright, I'll play it again.

She plays it again.

WOODY: 'Rhinestone Cowboy'.

LEE: Glen Campbell! Alright come on, the teachers won't have got that.

MELISSA stands suddenly, holding her piece of paper.

MELISSA: Got it! Marginal. The anagram of Alarming.

LEE: We are flying!

MABEL: Question six, the Panama Canal links the Caribbean Sea with the Pacific Ocean, but how long is it? And I'll give you a clue, it's not as long as you might expect, as the Chief Rabbi said to the Pope.

BUNNY: Oh I know this one…ah…it's er…

LEE: Have you been through the Panama Canal?

BUNNY: Aye, o' course I have.

WOODY: Underwater?

BUNNY: Don't be daft. It's onny fifty mile.

LEE: No.

MELISSA: It's a lot shorter than you might expect.

LEE: The teachers won't get that. We're gonna win.

LEE writes it in.

MABEL: Question seven. Which is the only national flag –

LEE: – Flags! I don't believe it.

MABEL: – which is neither oblong nor square.

WOODY: Flags Bunny, come on!

BUNNY: Oh bugger, I know this…it's… er…

LEE: *(To BUNNY.)* Did you do your flags homework?

BUNNY: No.

WOODY: Ooh, you're a selfish bugger you.

MELISSA: I went to Nepal in my gap year. Their flag is like two pennants, one on top of the other.

LEE: Brilliant.

He writes it in.

WOODY: What did you do in your gap year Bunny?

BUNNY: Went round the world underwater in a tin can.

MABEL: Question eight, final round. Who closed the gates of Hull on the King, and thereby started the English Civil War –

She sings the first two lines of Edwin Starr's song 'War'.

And a bonus point for the year the Civil War started.

MELISSA: He must have at least a street named after him.

LEE: Ferensway, Anlaby, Bricknell, fuck, Dad, Woody, gimme some roads in Hull that could be people's names.

WOODY: A63? Sorry. Spring Bank West?

BUNNY: Sutton Road, Clough Road, Fairfax Avenue. Hotham Road.

MELISSA: Hotham. Sir John Hotham.

BUNNY: And it's 1642, for the start of your English civil war.

WOODY: How come I don't know that then?

BUNNY: Cos folk don't want you to know stuff like that.

LEE: What you on about Dad?

BUNNY: If Hull kids was taught that this town has a tradition of violent revolution how many caravans would get made, eh? We'd all be on the streets, rioting. Instead we're shopping in Tescos. Breaks my fucking heart.

LEE: He's an old commie.

MABEL: Question nine, what do Barack Obama, Bill Clinton, and George W Bush have in common. All Presidents of the USA is not the answer.

BUNNY: Oh I know this…er…what is it…it's er…

WOODY: They're all Irish, way back.

MELISSA: Barack Obama – Irish?

WOODY: Yeah. O'Bama. O, apostrophe, Bama. Like O'Connor, O'Leary. O'Bama.

LEE: I bet this is Mabel's trick question for the night.

BUNNY: They've all got white mothers.

LEE: Brilliant!

MABEL: Last question in tonight's quiz. With a pot of forty-five pounds at stake. On a standard qwerty keyboard, what is the letter above the K.

LEE: I dunno, I have to look at the keyboard.

MELISSA: I touch type, hang on –

MELISSA starts to touch type. WOODY turns his phone on, looks at it under the table.

MELISSA: K? It's the right hand, middle of the right hand. I'd say O.

LEE: O? Are you sure? This could be crucial.

MELISSA: I'm not a hundred percent sure. It's a guess.

WOODY: That's wrong. The answer is I. I. I got a full qwerty keyboard on me phone.

LEE: That's cheating. I'm putting O.

BUNNY: Hang on, hang on!

LEE: I'm putting O.

MELISSA: But that's wrong. We know it's wrong.

LEE: It might be wrong but it's our answer.

LEE writes it in.

MABEL: That's the last question tonight. Swap your answer sheets.

LEE stands and takes the answer sheet over to BAZ.

WOODY: Oi Lee! Fucking hell.

To black.

SCENE FOUR

Lights up on the street outside. MELISSA, with LEE waiting for a taxi.

MELISSA: Everybody cheats Lee. MPs, Lords, the electorate.

LEE: You got Mabel to give you a receipt for four meals the other day.

MELISSA: That's what anyone with an expense account would do. It's normal.

LEE: This taxi, I bet he gives you two blank receipts, for you to fill in.

MELISSA: He did last time.

LEE: What did you do with them?

MELISSA: Twenty pound. Thirty pound. Different coloured biros.

LEE: Why is the whole of the UK on the fiddle?

MELISSA: You're gonna cheat on your wife.

LEE: Am I?

MELISSA: Yeah.

MELISSA initiates a kiss. Makes him stand up and kisses him properly. It's a long snog.

Should I be worried about Baz? Telling your wife.

LEE: No. She hasn't spoken to Janet for fifteen years, not since she caught impetigo off her.

MELISSA: How did she catch impetigo from your wife?

LEE: Some teenage sharing blood, blood sisters thing.

MELISSA: How does anyone get like Baz?

LEE: She left school, with no qualifications, started work at Reckitts sixteen, she got into nicking tamalgesics off the line, got sacked, started bombing amphetamines and turning tricks.

MELISSA: She was a prostitute at sixteen?

LEE: I've never seen her on the street, but she'd do the men in her life a favour. One day someone offered her heroin, which she injected. Hull's pretty hard core, we inject. You ever done heroin?

MELISSA: Are you kidding? Have you?

LEE: Yes. I chased the dragon, smoked it.

MELISSA: What's it like?

LEE: I've never injected but from what I've heard, you shouldn't feel sorry for Baz, she'll have known more happiness in one trip than you'll know in the whole of your life.

MELISSA: Don't exaggerate.

LEE: Heroin is addictive because it's fucking brilliant.

MELISSA: She's not on heroin now though is she?

LEE: She went down for persistent shoplifting, Newhall prison, did her rattle, got clean. You had university, she had Newhall. In prison she discovered Creationism, Mao Tse Tung, and Radical Feminism. So now she's clean but full of shit.

MELISSA: She's not an addict then?

LEE: Bit of trauma comes along, who knows. She might reach for it again.

They kiss again.

MELISSA: We need a room.

LEE: I've got to take my dad home.

MELISSA: We get a discount at the Holiday Inn on the Marina.

LEE: You're gonna put me on expenses?

MELISSA: Yup! I'll see you in the bar.

End of scene.

SCENE FIVE

In BUNNY's flat. BUNNY is wheeled in by LEE. The door is fully ajar.

BUNNY: It's hardly cheating. He only looked at his phone.

LEE: *(Off.)* He had to turn it on. Walk. You can do it.

BUNNY walks to the sofa. During the next he lights a spliff and smokes heavily.

BUNNY: Are you gonna cheat on your Janet with that posh lass?

LEE: I haven't touched her Dad.

BUNNY: You're married with two kids.

LEE: Did you cheat on me mam? Mebbe she's got to heaven, found out about that and that's why she's come back to torture you.

BUNNY: What would you do if I said 'Yes I did cheat on her'?

LEE: I'd think badly of you.

BUNNY: You already think badly of me. Aye. I cheated on her. For a couple of years after you was born.

LEE: Who with?

BUNNY: Her sister.

LEE: Auntie Pam from Sproatley?

BUNNY: Aye.

LEE: I always fancied Auntie Pam.

BUNNY: You'll understand why it was difficult to say no then.

LEE: We used to go and visit a lot didn't we.

BUNNY: Aye, any excuse for half a day at Sproatley.

LEE takes the spliff and has a major toke.

LEE: You said that talking about mam meks her put in an appearance.

BUNNY: Aye it does.

LEE: She's bound to show herself after these revelations.

BUNNY: Oh don't please. I can't handle it.

LEE: We're gonna get the bus to the hospital, and you're gonna walk, alright?

BUNNY: We have to talk. I've got some savings. Premium bonds.

LEE: Dad, that's your money. Jamie, the piano, that's my responsibility.

BUNNY: I wan't talking about his piano. I want to cash them bonds in so you and me can go to Switzerland.

LEE: What we doing? Skiing, snowboarding, what?

BUNNY: There's a clinic there, Zürich. The one on the telly. It's illegal in this country, but it in't over there.

LEE: That's stupid talk Dad. They're gonna put you on Beta Interferon, it's all gonna be alright. I gotta go.

BUNNY: I'm serious.

LEE: That's stupid talk Dad. Good night.

LEE closes the door. Behind the door hanging from a rope is his mam, dressed in a fifties rock and roll dress, but with the hair and rot of a corpse. BUNNY does not see it as he is looking forward.

End of scene.

INTERVAL

Week Three

SCENE ONE

One week later. BUNNY's flat. BUNNY on the sofa. A holdall upstage. LEE enters having just made a mug of tea for his dad.

BUNNY: Never mind Multiple Sclerosis, it's pub quiz what's ruined my life. I'll be sitting here on me tod and for no reason I'll say summat out loud like, I dunno – 'Kemal Atatürk' or 'Burkina Faso' or 'an extra leg'– and they're all answers to pub quiz questions what are spinning around inside me head, driving me mad. Yesterday I was watching the test match and I started to feel a bit peckish so I went in the kitchen to mek a sandwich, and I start mekking the sandwich and I says to mesen, why is a sandwich called a sandwich, and I stop mekking the sandwich and come in here, and look up sandwich in the dictionary, and discover that it's named after the Earl of Sandwich who didn't wanna leave the card table for proper meals so he invented the fucking sandwich.

LEE: Did you get a sandwich in the end?

BUNNY: No! That's the bloody point I'm trying to make. I completely forgot to mek mesen a sandwich! On the other hand if it weren't for pub quiz I coulda gone through the whole of me life not knowing that all the Village People are not gay.

LEE: Who was straight then? The Indian?

BUNNY: He's not a real Indian you know. That's just a get up he's got on.

LEE: Yes! But is he gay?

BUNNY: The Indian's gay, according to Mabel, although how she knows –

LEE: – who is straight!?

BUNNY: Two of them are.

LEE: Which ones?!

BUNNY: I've forgotten.

LEE: I've got the whole day to get through not knowing!? Is it the cowboy?

BUNNY: No. The cowboy's a gay.

LEE: The construction worker?

BUNNY: Gay.

LEE: The sailor.

BUNNY: Definitely a gay. I think he started it.

LEE: What? Homosexuality?

BUNNY: The Village People.

LEE: The cop?

BUNNY: Yes, the cop, he's not a gay, he's just acting.

LEE: The other one must be the biker?

BUNNY: Don't matter what he is anymore, cos he's dead. *(Beat.)* I let you down.

LEE: They let you down. I got summat to tell you Dad.

BUNNY: Janet's kicked you out.

LEE: How did you know?

BUNNY: There was lasagne on your windscreen.

LEE: Yeah, she threw me dinner at me.

BUNNY: What is it? Not having no work? You got an interview tomorrow. What is it again? I've never heard of them.

LEE: HobbyCraft.

BUNNY: What's that? A shop? What do they sell?

LEE: You know, stuff for hobbyists. Glue.

BUNNY: I blame your vasectomy.

LEE: Baz saw me give Melissa a goodnight kiss.

BUNNY: We could go to Switzerland together and they could put us both down.

LEE: *(Laughing.)* – buy one get one free!

BUNNY: *(Laughing.)* – yeah!

LEE: That's not gonna happen dad, Zürich, Dignitas, Switzerland – it's not on the menu. I'm not discussing it.

BUNNY: You'll get fed up of living here then, cos that's all I talk about. What am I gonna do?

LEE: Plan A was that they see you walking, and they put you on Beta Interferon.

BUNNY: What's plan B?

LEE: I don't have one.

LEE stands, goes upstage. Unseen by BUNNY he takes the Melcher replica from the holdall and puts it in his pocket. He picks a sheaf of papers from the table – flags of the world.

BUNNY: Where are you going?

LEE: Out. I've got to go see woman about a dog.

BUNNY: Kaw! You're busier than a man with a job, you.

LEE: Here.

BUNNY: What is it?

LEE: Two hundred and seventy five flags of the world. Memorise them. I'll test you when I get back.

LEE exits.

End of scene.

SCENE TWO

ANGIE's flat.

ANGIE: You're not getting tea. No liquids bro. Not after last time. I had to get a new toothbrush.

LEE: What's the idea Angie? Not paying.

ANGIE: Look bro, are you pressurising me? What you gonna do next? Shit in me dinner? You wouldn't hurt a woman?

LEE: I shot a woman in Afghanistan.

ANGIE: Did you kill her?

LEE: Course I killed her.

ANGIE: What had she done?

LEE: She owed me money and was pissing me off.

ANGIE: You shouldn't have been in her country.

LEE gets the Cuno Melcher replica gun out.

Is that a replica?

LEE: Dunno. Shall we find out?

ANGIE: Yeah, shoot me go on, I'm on heroin mate I won't feel a fucking thing, it's a painkiller didn't you know that.

LEE: Tell me where you keep your stash.

ANGIE: No, shoot me. You can't can you bro? Cos that's a toy innit. Fuck off. You're pathetic.

LEE: You stay here.

LEE goes into the loo. FX cistern lid lifted off, and then replaced.

ANGIE: I've cleaned in there. I bet you think all smackheads live like pigs.

Enter LEE.

LEE: What happened to the money?

ANGIE: I spent it on cleaning products.

LEE: There's a lot of bricks of heroin in your cistern. You didn't get them from Woody did you?

ANGIE: No, I didn't.

LEE: Are you gonna bash them yourself, and start trading? You got plans to work your way up the food chain haven't you?

ANGIE: You're smarter than you look you.

LEE: Where did those bricks come from? What's his name?

ANGIE: Fuck off.

LEE: Tell him to stay away from Hull. Hull's ours. Woody's. Mine.

ANGIE: You're a joke mate. Do you know that? It is innit, that's a replica, you're taking the piss.

LEE: Maybe it started life as a replica. Maybe I hired a 50 mill precision bench drill from HSS hire shops down Stoneferry and drilled the barrel out.

ANGIE: You wouldn't know what you were doing.

LEE: I was in the army twelve years.

ANGIE: I bet you was a cook or summat. You spent twelve years frying chips. You're thick, I mean if you're thick what else are you gonna do eh?

LEE: I'm not thick, alright?

ANGIE: You're threatening me with a toy gun, you must be thick.

LEE: It's loaded.

ANGIE: Oh you knocked up some bullets an'all did you?

LEE: Maybe I came back from Afghanistan with a few souvenirs.

ANGIE throws the salt pot at him, it hits him. He does nothing.

ANGIE: I just threw a salt pot at you! Fire it go on! See, it dunt work!

LEE: I'll be back for the money, on Monday.

ANGIE: Yeah, yeah, bring a replica tank mate.

LEE is gone. The door closed.

I'm gonna tell my man you threatened me with a toy. Wanker!

End of scene.

SCENE THREE

Spot on MABEL.

MABEL: Round three ladies and gentlemen. Hands out your pockets, ears syringed. Question one. Music. Today is the anniversary of my divorce from my seventh husband, Reg, the one with eczema. I didn't mind the scratching, or his affair with the lad from Rentokil, but I put me foot down when he started keeping iguanas in the airing cupboard. I don't miss him, but I do miss the love-making, cos although I had to get one, you can't keep your bed warm with a court order.

Karaoke backing starts.

This is for you Reg. Wherever you are, you tight bastard.

She sings 'Help me make it through the night', with her own additions.

Take the ribbon from your hair
[*why are you wearing a ribbon Reg?*]
Shake it loose and let it fall
[*itchy flaky scalp*]
Layin' soft upon my skin
[*soft again Reg! That's no use to me!*]
Like the shadows on the wall
[*turn the fucking light out will you*]
Come and lay down by my side
[*I'll be glad when you're back on nights*]

Till the early mornin' light
[*stop! that's as much quilt as you're getting*]
All I'm takin' is your time
[*but my solicitor's got a much better idea*]
Help me make it through the night

I don't care who's right or wrong
[*with morals like that I could be an MP*]
I don't try to understand
[*I'll Google it later*]
Let the devil take tomorrow
[*yup! everything's on tick*]
Lord tonight I need a friend
[*I think I'll give that Facebook a go*]
Yesterday is dead and gone
[*wahey! the decree nisi's come through*]
And tomorrow's out of sight
[*I celebrated by getting pissed*]
And it's sad to be alone
[*in the back of an ambulance, getting your stomach pumped*]
Help me make it through the night

Applause.

Thank you.

In the pub. LEE is drinking heavily. MABEL at the mic. WOODY, LEE, BUNNY, MELISSA at the table. WOODY has in his hand an A4 piece of paper with the league table on it.

WOODY: We're third in the league. That in't good enough. Three points.

MELISSA: 'Staff of Life' first.

BUNNY: How many points have they got?

MELISSA: The teachers.

WOODY: They got six points.

BUNNY: Who's second?

WOODY: 'This is What Happens When Cousins Marry'. Four points.

MABEL: For one point, who wrote 'Help me make it through the night', and for a bonus point which famous married couple did a cover version?

MELISSA: Who wrote it?

WOODY: Kris Kristofferson.

MELISSA: Cover version?

BUNNY: I know this! Oh bugger what's their names? Double act, he was tragically blind, wore sunglasses –

WOODY: – Stevie Wonder?

BUNNY: No. This fellah died of bone cancer in his fifties. He lost an eye in a car crash when he was onny five year old –

WOODY: He shouldn't have been driving.

BUNNY: – then, later on, someone chucked a brick at him and he lost the other eye.

WOODY: – later on the same day, what? after the car crash?

BUNNY: Later on in life! Oh whatshisname!? He had a hit with 'Why Me?'.

WOODY: He lost an eye when he was five in a car crash; another eye later on when someone threw a brick at him; died in his fifties of bone cancer; and had a hit song called 'Why Me?'.

BUNNY: Yeah.

LEE: Peters and Lee.

BUNNY: That's them!

WOODY: They wan't married! Dianne Lee married the bassist out of Wizzard, Rick, shit –

MELISSA: – Rick shit? Were Wizzard a punk band?

WOODY: Oh, …Rick er…

LEE: – for God's sake! We don't need the name of the bassist from Wizzard!

BAZ: Don't take the Lord's name in vain!

LEE: Don't you start!

WOODY: Rick Price. He was in Electric Light Orchestra an'all.

LEE: The answer's Johnny Cash and June Carter Cash.

WOODY: You knew all along didn't you?

WOODY writes the answer down. MELISSA takes the sheet and has a scan.

MELISSA: Do you want to look at the league table, Lee? We're in third place.

LEE ignores her and the sheet.

What's going on?

BUNNY: Leave him be love.

MABEL: Question two. A quote from a film. 'You're gonna need a bigger boat.' Name the film.

MELISSA: In what film does anyone need a bigger boat?

WOODY: *Titanic.*

BUNNY: *In Which We Serve.*

LEE: Trivia.

MELISSA: What's the matter with you tonight Lee?

WOODY: He's pissed.

LEE: You got a problem with that?

MABEL: Question three.

MELISSA: We need a guess for question two!

LEE: It's *Jaws.*

MELISSA: You want to beat the teachers, not me, I don't have a chip on my shoulder.

BUNNY: Leave him alone love.

MABEL: What was the name of the British Regiment in *Carry On Up the Khyber*?

LEE: Who fucking cares?

WOODY: I know this. The 3rd Foot and Mouth.

MELISSA: Brilliant.

WOODY: I love Carry On films. It's my life up there. I watch 'em in tears. They call that catharsis.

MABEL: Question four. Cricket. What is the maximum number of active players you can have on the field at any one time?

MELISSA: Eleven fielders, and two batsmen. Thirteen.

WOODY: Na, it'll be one of her trick questions.

LEE: Fifteen. Write it down.

MELISSA: No. Not until you've had the grace to explain why.

LEE: Eleven fielders, two batsmen, each with a runner.

LEE stands.

White wine spritzer?

MELISSA: I'm alright thank you Lee.

LEE: Shutup. You're getting one. Diet coke. Half a mild.

LEE goes to the bar.

MELISSA: What's the matter with him tonight?

BUNNY: He's upset cos Infirmary aren't gonna give me Beta Interferon.

MELISSA: Oh God. I'm sorry.

MABEL: Question five. Who was the only Prime Minister of Great Britain to marry a divorcee.

BUNNY: Oh I know this…whatshisname, …wore a coat…

WOODY: He wore a coat. That narrows it down.

BUNNY: Smoked a pipe, had an affair with his secretary…

WOODY: Harold Wilson? He never married her.

MELISSA: Denis Thatcher was divorced wasn't he?

BUNNY: That's it! Denis Thatcher.

MELISSA: Margaret Thatcher.

MABEL: Question six.

LEE grabs the microphone.

Oi Lee!

LEE: Question six. Why can't my father, you all know Bunny, who left school at fifteen to serve his nation in the Royal Navy in submarines, and every year of his life since has paid a stamp every week into the NHS, never been unemployed, never signed on, now he's got Multiple Sclerosis, and now when he needs the Health Service, and this is pretty much the first time he's ever been to hospital, the question is,

BAZ: – Oi Lee!? Is this question four?

LEE: This is question five.

WOODY: Six.

LEE: Six. Why can't he have the painkilling drugs he needs? Write your answer down. Question seven. Why does Sir Fred Goodwin get seven hundred thousand pounds a year pension after spending three years at the Royal Bank of Scotland, time he obviously spent eating crisps and wanking in the stationery cupboard. At least the *forty* years my dad worked on the docks was spent doing something useful.

MABEL: That's enough now love, go and get a bit of fresh air.

WOODY: Don't get involved Mabel!

LEE: Question eight. Why are our lads dying in Afghanistan in the name of democracy when this country has no democracy, itself, and I'm not talking about MPs expenses, you're all on the fiddle. We're run by unelected committees in Brussels, Gordon Brown's cabinet has seven unelected ministers, seven Lords, they're not elected, they're cabinet ministers! They're running the country and they an't been elected!

BAZ: – how many points do you get if you get this right?

WOODY: Shutup Baz!

LEE: – I lost two friends in Afghanistan, one of them, Jed, nice lad, eighteen, he had his leg blown off, an IED, and I sat with him, and I lied to him, I told him he was gonna be alright – and he died on me.

BAZ: You're mental you Lee Bunting!

LEE: Religion. There are nine established world religions, they all believe different things yeah –

BAZ: – yeah, and?

LEE: They can't all be right, but they can all be wrong. And another question for you Baz, as a Christian, where does it say thou shalt grass up your neighbour to his wife? Eh?

BAZ: Are you accusing me of not forgiving my fellow man?

LEE: Yeah.

LEE smashes a bottle or glass and advances on BAZ. WOODY steps between them. WOODY goes over and puts himself between the two of them, physically restraining LEE.

WOODY: I'm going outside for a fag, are you coming Lee?

LEE: Sorry Mabe.

MABEL: That's alright love.

Silence. LEE puts the broken bottle on the bar. LEE follows WOODY off.

MABEL: Question five. What was the name of Popeye's father?

Outside.

WOODY: What's occurring? Your dad?

LEE: Yeah. And Janet's kicked me out.

WOODY: Baz grassed you up?

LEE: Yeah.

WOODY: Grass her back then. Ring up Customs and Excise.

LEE: Yeah, I might. We need to talk business.

WOODY: In the office.

Back in the pub.

MABEL: *(On the mic.)* The last question in round one – Who was murdered by four knights in 1170, stabbed during vespers, very painful that, don't try it at home. Or as the actress said to the bishop, once a king always a king, but once a night's enough.

BUNNY: I know this one, it's er…oh bugger whatshisname, it's on the tip of me tongue, er…he was a big nob in the er… whatsitcalled –

MELISSA: – the church?

BUNNY: Yeah!

MELISSA: The Archbishop of Canterbury, Thomas Becket.

BUNNY: That's him!

MABEL: End of round one. Get your drinks in, and go and test the plumbing, back in five, I'm having a fag, if I can find him.

MELISSA: I think we got most of those.

BUNNY: Aye, we don't need them two nutters.

MELISSA: I was on the docks today.

BUNNY: Quiet?

MELISSA: Yes, actually. How many dockers used to work on the docks?

BUNNY: About half of them.

MELISSA: Is your MS caused by working on the docks?

BUNNY: Not that I know of. It could be dangerous though. One day I turned up there was a pair of lions on the wharf.

MELISSA: Where had they been imported from?

BUNNY: They was export.

MELISSA: Export? Where to?

BUNNY: Africa. I liked ships, outdoors, and I liked working with men.

MELISSA: What's so good about working with men?

BUNNY: The swearing. Don't know how you young lasses can work in an office. Them regeneration companies are just make-work schemes for women like you.

MELISSA: I used to like you Mister Bunting.

BUNNY: You should be gerrin work in for the men.

MELISSA: I'm trying to make Hull a shopping destination for the Wolds villages.

BUNNY: I been round St Stephens shopping, and there's no proper men's jobs there. A man's gorra be summat, he can't have babies can he? A man's gorra be proud of what he does. 'I'm a docker, and proud of it', 'I'm a trawlerman', 'I'm an engineer'. What kind of a man is gonna stand up in the pub and say – 'I work for Build-a-Bear Workshop'?

MELISSA: OK. If you had my job what would you do?

BUNNY: I'd build a massive bloody concrete island offshore at With and stick a thousand windmills on it. And I'd mek sure we got the contract to build 'em. Wun't upset no-one, you don't go to With for the view.

MELISSA: With?

BUNNY: Withernsea. And then there's fishing.

MELISSA: Fishing's gone, and thank God too.

BUNNY: Fishing an't gone! Iceland's bankrupt and running to the European Union cap in hand, and what have they got to offer? Nowt but them rich cod grounds of theirs the ones we used to fight ovver.

MELISSA: It was a disgusting, smelly, industry.

BUNNY: That's what men like! You just don't understand that do you! Aagh!

A spasm of pain.

MELISSA: Oh God, are you alright?

BUNNY: The more muck, stink and danger there is the more men bloody love it! That's what the Irish call the craic.

MELISSA: It was dangerous. I know that a lot of Hull men died.

BUNNY: It's better to die with dignity knowing who you are, than to die on the dole.

MELISSA: That's what Lee said. Almost word for word.

BUNNY: Where do you think he got it from?

Enter WOODY and LEE bringing on the car.

LEE: You got your Range Rover back then.

WOODY: Yeah. What do you think of this?

WOODY picks up the squeegee / ice scraper as if it were a microphone.

I was in the phone shop –

LEE: – What's that?

WOODY: That's the microphone. This is one of the jokes I've written.

LEE: How many jokes have you written now?

WOODY: Two. I was in the Vodafone shop the other day –

LEE: – I don't believe it. 'The other day'. That's what all comedians say. Be specific.

WOODY: I was in the phone shop, at half past ten Tuesday morning –

LEE: – I believe it.

WOODY: – and they've got this slogan 'Talk to anyone, anywhere in the world'. So I said, I'd like to talk to Cameron Diaz in a hot tub in Barbados please. Is it funny?

LEE: Am I laughing? I see what you're getting at, but it doesn't quite work.

WOODY: You've upset me now. I'm sensitive.

LEE: You live in South Cave, you're always complaining about the mobile reception. Why don't you say – 'Vodafone have got a new slogan, – ring anyone from anywhere in the world, except South Cave'.

WOODY: *(Laughs.)* That's funny.

LEE: Because it's true. You should write about what it's like being tall.

WOODY: You think?

LEE: I'm sure. You've got a serious problem with Angie. She had a boyfriend in the house. He's got a gun. He put a gun to my head.

WOODY: No? You serious?

LEE: The truth. Why would I lie to you? It's an Uzi automatic. He's got a Manchester accent.

WOODY: Oh shit. I knew this was gonna happen.

LEE: Technically an Uzi's a sub-machine gun, but it's small, so it's the perfect street gun. He held it to my head, like this –

LEE holds his fingers to WOODY's head. WOODY starts shaking. LEE mimes a gun against WOODY's head. WOODY is panicked even by the mime, and puts his hands up automatically.

LEE: He said tell Woody –

WOODY: – he used my name?

LEE: Oh yeah. He knows you.

WOODY: Do I know him?

LEE: No.

WOODY: Oh shit.

LEE: He said tell Woody if Angie gets any more stress, I'm coming to South Cave to blow him away.

WOODY: He actually said South Cave?

LEE: Yeah.

WOODY: Oh no, no, no, no, no. My daughter, Millie –

LEE: – she's the singer?

WOODY: Yeah, she's got her Opera North debut at the Music Centre tomorrow and I've never seen her sing professionally. I might be dead by then.

LEE: Possibly. What are we gonna do?

WOODY: Let me think. Can you put that gun down please, I can't concentrate.

LEE stops miming a gun, smiles. WOODY head in hands.

WOODY: There's nothing we can do. I'm getting out though, for definite.

LEE: I could go round –

WOODY: Forget it. It's only two grand. I'll sell the business to you. A hundred thousand. Do you want it?

LEE: It was two hundred thousand two weeks ago.

WOODY: It's worth less now, there's a threat. A threat I can't deal with.

LEE: I don't have a hundred thousand.

WOODY: I'll lend you it. You pay me five thousand a month, you'll be clear in a couple of years.

LEE: Let me think about it.

WOODY: I haven't got time. I need an answer.

LEE: Give me a week.

LEE stands and leaves the car, and goes back in to the pub. WOODY looks at his notebook.

WOODY: *(With squeegee mic in hand.)* I went for a haircut, half past eleven Wednesday morning. The barber said 'You got the day off son?', I said 'Why, how long's this gonna take?'

WOODY thinks, looks at his notebook. Puts his head in his hands. In the pub.

BUNNY: Hull folks think the dockers was all strike-happy. They'd say stuff like 'The daffodils are out, and the dockers have come out in sympathy'. Conditions, it was all piece-work you know, oh aye. You'd go along to the pen and, and you raise your book up and if you weren't well in with the foreman you'd have to spend all week dinting.

MELISSA: Dinting? Where does that word come from?

BUNNY: Dint gerr any work. Dint. I dunno. If you dint get owt you'd go in the black hut and wait.

MELISSA: What was the black hut, a café?

BUNNY: No, it were a black hut. One time, Ellermans had this ship come in from India with a cargo of human bones from the river Ganges and they was all crawling with maggots, and flies.

Enter LEE.

I picked a sack of bones up and I went into the building where Ellermans offices was and I chucked the sack on the boardroom table and I said 'How much would *you* want paying for handling that?'

MELISSA: What did they say?

LEE: 'Ellermans is next door, we're a solicitors' office.'

BUNNY: I'd got the wrong offices! Ha!

MELISSA: I didn't know your dad was a working class hero.

LEE: Yeah, he was a proper real life Robin Hood.

MELISSA: Did anybody ever steal anything?

LEE: Does Dolly Parton sleep on her back?

BUNNY: One day I filled a wheelbarrow full of straw. Dock police stopped us and searched in the straw, there's nowt in there, he lets me through. Second day, wheelbarrow, straw, he searches us, nothing, lets me through. Third day, wheelbarrow, straw, he searches us, let's me through. I managed to nick six wheelbarrows that week! Ha, ha! Aghh!

BUNNY is crippled with pain. MELISSA stands fussing. LEE is cool. WOODY returns.

MELISSA: Are you OK? Can I get you anything?

LEE: He punched me once, has he told you? I was eleven.

WOODY: Leave him alone Lee.

LEE: Knocked a tooth out.

WOODY: Lee!

LEE, in a sulk, scoops up his stool and takes it downstage right.

MABEL: Round two. Sit down, shutup, and keep your hands to yourself. Question one. Which famous actor had his top lip paralysed during the first world war?

WOODY writes the answer down.

BUNNY: Oh I know this one…oh…talked funny, er…agh… you know…er…

MELISSA: I don't know this sorry.

BUNNY: – couldn't act, won one Oscar, played that private eye, oh you know whatshisname –

WOODY: 's alright, take your time.

MELISSA scoops up her stool and joins LEE.

BUNNY: *African Queen*!

WOODY: He was a gay black man?

BUNNY: No! Big ugly square face.

WOODY: Meryl Streep.

BUNNY: Meryl Streep din't have her top lip paralysed in the First World War?

WOODY: Oh yes she did. Not a lot of people know that.

BUNNY: *Casablanca*! The big star.

WOODY: Ingrid Bergman?

MELISSA: Talk to me.

BUNNY: Humphrey Bogart.

WOODY: Yeah, you're right.

BUNNY: You knew all along. You'd written it down.

WOODY: I like listening to you Bunny. It's better than television.

LEE: In Afghanistan there's no homeless, no old people starving. Islam, tribe, family. Family is everything. I admire them.

MELISSA: Why can't he get the medication?

LEE: It costs ten thousand pounds a year. The consultant said to me if everyone paid their taxes, paid their VAT, stopped buying knock-off, or bootleg, stopped fiddling the social, then the NHS would have the money.

MELISSA: People have to find ways to survive.

MABEL: Question two. I've never seen a bigger one than this, as Sherpa Tenzing said to Edmund Hillary. For eleven points! What have the Romans ever done for us?

BUNNY: Oh what's that film called, er…oh, oh I know this…

WOODY: *Life of Brian.* Aqueduct!

WOODY writes.

LEE: He wants me to take him to Switzerland, that clinic in Zürich, Dignitas.

MELISSA: You're not serious are you?

LEE: For one point, what's the right thing to do?

BUNNY: What's it called? You know, sewers.

WOODY: Sanitation.

MELISSA: You didn't ring me. All week.

LEE: You didn't ring me.

MELISSA: You're married. I can't ring you.

LEE: She's kicked me out. I miss the kids. Sorry, I'm not supposed to mention kids around you am I?

BUNNY: The Romans built roads everywhere they went.

WOODY: Brilliant! Roads.

MELISSA: What I said last week, I was serious. Really.

BUNNY: Drinking water?

WOODY: The fresh water system!

BUNNY: O' course.

LEE: If you got pregnant you'd have to leave work.

MELISSA: I've been working twenty years non-stop.

LEE: Is this what you really want?

MELISSA: No! Christ! I want to fall in love, buy a cottage with roses round the door, and make love in a sand dune and conceive that way. But in twenty years it hasn't happened and it's not so much that my clock is ticking, it's more like the alarm's gone off, and the snooze button's wearing the batteries down! I'm serious Lee.

BUNNY: It's everything a civilised society needs.

WOODY: Wine.

BUNNY: Medicine!

WOODY: Education!

MELISSA: I'd get a legal contract drawn up.

LEE: Yeah, I don't want the Child Support on my back.

MELISSA: I wouldn't do that to you.

LEE: They might though. My country has a habit of shafting me.

WOODY: Public order.

BUNNY: Yeah.

MABEL: Question three.

WOODY / BAZ / BUNNY: No!

MABEL defers.

BUNNY: How many we got?

WOODY: Eight.

BUNNY: Three more. Hot water?

WOODY: No, but public baths, yes.

LEE: You might not want my genes. I didn't leave the army you know. I was discharged.

MELISSA: You got sacked from the army? What for?

LEE: Fighting.

MELISSA laughs.

I punched one of the Ruperts.

MELISSA: That's understandable. Every other day a young kid gets killed. The war's going badly –

LEE: Twenty thousand were killed on the first day of the Somme. I fucking loved Afghanistan. It was rock 'n' roll.

WOODY: Got it. Irrigation.

BUNNY: One more.

MELISSA: Why did you punch the officer?

LEE: I knew that this warlord, not a Talib, had killed this aid worker.

MELISSA: So you killed him?

LEE: I ran him over. You ever seen a cat in the road?

MELISSA: Oh, God.

LEE: His guts popped out. It was my village really, never saw a Rupert from one day to the next. Didn't always wear uniform, that's very naughty.

MELISSA: Are you telling me you went native? You were the Kurtz of Afghanistan.

LEE: I respect their culture. An eye for an eye. They don't fuck about with lawyers.

BUNNY: Peace!

WOODY: Peace? Of course, peace.

WOODY writes.

LEE: Thought you should know that if you're thinking of getting pregnant.

MELISSA: I'm glad you told me, but I want to do it.

LEE: I'll still be cheating you though.

MELISSA: How? If I get pregnant I'll be happy. If I don't, I'll have had fun trying.

LEE: I'll try me best. Where are we staying tonight?

MELISSA: Ramada, Willerby.

LEE: Bloody hell, that's almost the Wolds. Do I need oxygen?

MABEL: You've had long enough on that one, as Mother Superior said to the novice nun. Question three: 'Call me Ishmael' was the first line of what novel? And for a bonus point, what was the name of the author. I'll give you a clue, I've not slept with him.

LEE: I'm going outside. I've got a call to make.

LEE exits. MELISSA enters and passes the team table on her way to the loos.

BUNNY: It's that book about the whale…you know…er with the…er…oh fuck…

MELISSA: *Moby Dick.* Herman Melville.

WOODY: Are you going?

MELISSA: Of course not, just going to the loo.

WOODY: We're in the middle of a round.

Outside.

LEE: *(On the phone.)* Hello, could you put me through to the Customs Office please at the P&O Ferry Port, Hull, Kingston Upon Hull. Thank you… – Hello, can I give you some information about a professional smuggler travelling this weekend?… It's a woman, Barbara Calvert…travelling alone… Zeebrugge…she'll be coming in Monday morning… Who am I?

LEE flips the phone off.

End of scene.

Week Four

SCENE ONE

North Hull Estate. Night. The kitchen. Music loud on a CD – 'Yoshima Battles the Pink Robots', The Flaming Lips. ANGIE is gauched out on the floor. The bell rings. ANGIE rolls over, declines to get up. ANGIE has got to her knees. Enter LEE. LEE puts the lights on. ANGIE recoils, she's really out of it. He sees her. There is evidence of heroin paraphernalia – the blackened spoon, needle, water. There is a carry cot with a baby in it. The baby is asleep.

ANGIE: What is it bro? Is that you Danny? You're late innit. Stop pissing about will you. Oh fuck it's you. The Enforcer, not.

LEE turns the music down, but not off.

LEE: You've got a baby. I didn't know you had a baby.

ANGIE: I can have a fucking baby if I want can't I?

LEE: You been working your way through the stock haven't you Angie? You've confused the system. You're supposed to be the retailer not the consumer. It's like a newsagent eating all the Mars bars.

ANGIE: Don't patronise me bro.

LEE: It's not professional.

ANGIE: Nobody talks to me like that.

The baby cries.

That's you that is. You turned the music off.

LEE: Sit up. I need to talk to you.

ANGIE: Bro? What is it you don't understand?

LEE: I want your stock, what's left of it.

ANGIE: Leave me alone.

LEE gets the gun out.

Oh no, it's the Terminator again!

LEE: And I want the new stock. The stock you haven't bashed yet. The Manchester stock.

ANGIE: I'm fucked, can't you see that, I can't handle a discussion.

LEE goes into the loo, lifts the cistern, comes out with a single brick of heroin. Then he turns the music up loud. It is now playing 'Funky Cold Medina', Tone Loc. LEE casually shoots ANGIE. There is no deliberation, or consideration in this act, it is sudden, unexpected, and functional. She collapses. Dead. LEE kicks her body over so she's scrunched into the wall. He turns the music off, goes back into the loo and returns with the rest of the stock. The baby has started crying again. Enter CATH. A girl of about twenty, she has shopping.

CATH: Hi. Are you Danny?

LEE: Danny? Yeah. I'm Danny.

CATH: Mam. Mam! You left the door unlocked again! She's been fucked all day. Lazy cow. Gauched out like that on her favourite bit of floor. How long you been here Danny?

LEE: Not long.

CATH: Have you managed to get a word out of her?

LEE: No. She was nodding when I arrived.

CATH: Best ignore her, she's happy. Mate of mine lives in Stretford. Louise. Do you know her?

LEE: No.

CATH: Bet you do. What's that smell? Burning. Have you had a pipe going?

LEE: Yeah.

CATH: I like a bit of pipe. I don't like heroin. I tried it, once, chucked me guts up. Bit of a toke on a crack pipe, that's all I need. Wouldn't work any road would it, if we was both of us fucked all the time. She says it's good brown you're bringing in Danny. Thank God for the Taliban eh? You must be disappointed in my mum, yeah well, I know how you feel, she's disappointed me every day of me fucking life. But she's happy you know, she an't gorr a care in the world, long as she can get enough gear.

LEE: Are you gonna look after the baby?

CATH: Me? No way. I'm not a safety net while she's out of it. I made that very clear. Anyhow, you got a cheek. You're the father.

LEE: Am I?

CATH: That's what she told me. Sorry! *(Laughs.)* I thought you knew.

LEE: I've got to go. I'm going back to Manchester.

CATH: Do what you like, I'm gonna bed.

CATH exits. The baby starts crying.

LEE: I'll put some music on.

LEE goes over and puts on some music. 'Do you Realise?', The Flaming Lips. The music plays and the baby stops crying. LEE takes out his gun considers shooting the baby, decides against and leaves.

End of scene.

SCENE TWO

Lights up in WOODY's Range Rover. WOODY and LEE. WOODY is in a state.

WOODY: I've been banged up in Queens Gardens all morning! The police have been to South Cave to search the cake shop!

LEE: Did they find anything?

WOODY: A dead mouse. They said they could close me down.

LEE: Did you know you had mice?

WOODY: I couldn't give a fuck about the mouse! It's the accounts I'm worried about. I'm shaking, look.

LEE: Why are the accounts a problem?

WOODY: It's the only cake shop in East Yorkshire turns over two million quid a year.

LEE: They're nice cakes but they're not that nice. What are you panicking about?

WOODY: Prison.

LEE: You like snooker, cards, anal sex.

WOODY: They said I could go down for murder!? Angie's dead. Someone shot her! Lee, tell me, you will tell me won't you? Was it you?

LEE: Do you really want to know?

WOODY: No, actually no, I don't want to know. I'm gonna have to go to Spain, shit, I can't stand Spain, I wish I'd never bought that fucking villa. I'm allergic to everything over there.

LEE: You can't go to Spain, we're in the pub quiz final.

WOODY: I'm gonna have to get rid of the stock.

LEE: Give me the business. I'm not paying a hundred thousand.

WOODY: *(Beat.)* It's a deal.

They shake.

LEE: Does this include a certain cake shop with a rodent infestation?

WOODY: No. That's the enemy's.

LEE: Alright, I'll open my own cake shop.

WOODY: Are you mad? South Cave could never sustain two cake shops. Flower shop's good.

LEE: A flower shop? Alright. Janet'll like that. How's it feel? Retirement.

WOODY: I feel good about it. I might get a greenhouse.

LEE: What should I do with this? This is what's left of Angie's stock.

LEE shows WOODY a holdall full of heroin.

WOODY: Christ Lee, you've taken some stock from a murder scene! I can't have stock in this car! The police have got dogs. All their spaniels, they're all smack heads. Them dogs could find heroin in the Queen's knickers! NEVER TOUCH THE STOCK! This car's fucked now! Take it. It's yours. It's got nothing to do with me.

WOODY gets out of the car. He gives the keys to LEE. Exit WOODY. LEE looks at the car keys and adjusts the driver's seat, adjusts it, not being as tall as WOODY. Enter BAZ. She is wrecked, looking desperate, dressed like a prostitute.

BAZ: Lee?! Is that you?

She taps on the window.

LEE: I'm not talking to you Baz. You grassed me up.

BAZ: No Lee, lover, you don't understand –

LEE: Lover?! What's got into you?

BAZ: Come on Lee. What do you say?

LEE: I say no. No way.

BAZ: Just a tenner. Go on mate, be reasonable. I'm good.

LEE: What happened? Turning tricks in not very Christian or did you discover Darwin this morning?

BAZ: It was Customs. They busted me. Took everything. They've searched the flat. I got sacked from the chippy. I missed work, one day, one fucking day. Bastard Kossos. I don't know what I'm gonna do.

LEE: What do you need?

BAZ: I need ten quid. I can get a wrap then. I've always fancied you Lee. Ten quid that's all. I did you a favour didn't I? I went to Belgium for you.

LEE: Get in.

BAZ: I'll get in the back, yeah?

LEE: No! Get in here. The front.

BAZ gets in.

You back on the smack then?

BAZ: I just need a little holiday, you know how it is. It's the stress.

LEE: Ten quid holiday. That'll solve all your problems.

BAZ: I'll let you do what you like Lee.

LEE: I'm gonna give you this big bag.

BAZ: Where did you get this? Is this Woody's car?

LEE: No. First I want some information. Who are you getting your wraps from?

BAZ: Preston Road.

LEE: I didn't ask where. Who? It's good stuff, this. Name, phone number.

BAZ: Terry.

LEE: I want his number.

She gets her phone out, boots up Terry's number. LEE takes the phone and enters the number into his phone.

LEE: OK. It's yours. In future come to me. But that's the only freebie.

BAZ: I haven't got any money.

LEE: I'm sorry. I can't take favours as payment. You'll have to start earning.

BAZ: I can't go shoplifting down Holderness Road no more, they've all got photos of me.

LEE: Hull's been regenerated. We got a retail triangle now.

BAZ: I can't shoplift in town. If I get caught, with my record, I'll go down. I'll have to go on the streets, I've never worked on the street, it's dangerous.

LEE: You've got God, he'll look after you.

BAZ: What's got into you Lee? You've changed.

LEE: I learned something from the Afghans. It's a brilliant culture. Family. Look after your own. Now get out of my car.

BAZ gets out. Wanders off, sits on the wall. LEE gets out the car, walks a pace or two, turns and flicks the wireless locking device. A light flashes on the chairs. LEE is content, pleased, the world has changed in his favour.

End of scene.

Week Five

SCENE ONE

Lights up on the pub on quiz night. MELISSA, WOODY, BUNNY and LEE. LEE is looking cool, well dressed, maybe an expensive and tasteful jacket.

MABEL: Final round, ten questions left of the Grand Super League knockout final in week five of the White Horse pub quiz league. The 'Staff Of Life' are currently on thirty-nine, like me they just can't get to forty, and 'My Dad's a Drug Addict' are in the lead on forty-one.

MELISSA: Two ahead. We can afford to get one question wrong.

LEE: We're not gonna get any questions wrong.

MABEL: After the quiz it's 'Hull's Got Talent'. I'll be dedicating a song to my fourth husband, Flanagan, he was one half of a pair of Siamese twins, with his brother, Alan. So as a memorial to our first night of passion I'm gonna sing 'our song', which was very special to the three of us. The old Hollies classic 'He ain't heavy, he's my brother'.

(*Beat.*) That's later, right now, the final round. Question one, which medically approved painkilling drug is extracted from the seed of the opium poppy?

BUNNY: Oh I know this one…oh it's er…oh…what's it called?

WOODY: Morphine.

MELISSA writes it down.

LEE: How does heroin differ from morphine?

WOODY: Diamorphine is heroin.

LEE looks at BUNNY. No eye contact from BUNNY, he's unaware of the thought.

MABEL: Question two, who said 'erotica is using a feather, pornography is using the whole chicken?'

BUNNY: Oh, I know this…oh, whatshername…er…

MELISSA: Yes, it is, it's a woman.

LEE: Can we help?

MELISSA: It's a woman, a novelist.

WOODY: Enid Blyton.

LEE: Enid Blyton wouldn't know what pornography was.

WOODY: Have you not read *Five Go Dogging*?

MELISSA: South American. Damn! *(Beat.)* Got it. Isabelle Allende.

LEE: You're brilliant.

WOODY: I wanna talk to you Melissa. Business.

MABEL: Question three.

MELISSA: OK, maybe now's not the best time.

MABEL: Stalactites and stalagmites. Now, what I want,

She sings the first two lines of 'Wannabe' by the Spice Girls.

Which ones go up?

WOODY: Tights come down. Mights go up. Stalagmites.

MELISSA: You've got a filthy mind haven't you?

WOODY: Oh yeah. I'm interested in the Old Fruit Market development. Have you got any units left?

MELISSA: Two. A restaurant, and a small live/work space.

WOODY: It's the restaurant I want.

MABEL: Question four. Who said to whom, two points, 'Don't bother washing darling, I'm coming home'.

MELISSA: Got it.

She writes.

MABEL: I'll give you a clue cos –

MELISSA: NO!

MABEL: Oh, she knows it. No clues then.

LEE: Who said that then?

MELISSA: *Ne te lave pas chéri. J'arrive.* Napoleon to Josephine.

LEE: I like you.

MELISSA: Have you run a restaurant before?

LEE: A cake shop.

WOODY: This would be Hull's first dedicated stand-up gig.

LEE: Every top ten town needs a permanent comedy venue.

WOODY: Cabaret-style tables, bar, simple food so they can eat and laugh at the same time. Hummus, olives, sun-dried tomatoes. That kind of shit.

MABEL: Question five.

BUNNY: This is the final. Can we concentrate please?

MABEL: What is the name of the tube that joins the kidney to the bladder?

WOODY: The Piccadilly Line.

BUNNY: Oh I know this! Oh, what's it called, er…the er…

LEE: Urethra?

BUNNY: Not urethra, it's ur-et-er. I know cos mine gives me gyp.

LEE: If we'd gone to Zürich and had you put down we wouldn't have got that.

WOODY: I've got the finance in place, I'm ready to go.

MELISSA: Would you be the manager?

LEE: Excuse me, he's an artist.

WOODY: I'd be the compere. I'd hire a chef.

MABEL: Question six. Other than Hull City, what are the other two professional sporting teams with the nickname the Tigers?

BUNNY: Oh, I know this one, er…oh…

LEE: Bangladesh, cricket?

WOODY: No, Leicester Tigers, rugby union. And Cass.

MELISSA: Who?

WOODY: Castleford. Rugby League.

MELISSA writes.

MELISSA: We're doing well.

WOODY: Proper gigs on a Friday and Saturday with international stand-ups.

MELISSA: A business can't succeed on two days a week.

WOODY: Open Mic try-outs on a Thursday, comedy workshops for up-and-coming Hull comedians during the week. Daytime.

MABEL: Question seven.

BUNNY: Shutup and concentrate will yer!

MABEL: What is Gene Cernan best known for?

WOODY: First man ever to fuck a polar bear.

LEE: The last man on the moon.

WOODY: Well, what do you think?

MELISSA: *(To LEE.)* You know it?

LEE: Yeah. But Woody meant what do you think about the restaurant?

MELISSA: A business can't run on three days a week.

WOODY: But comedy is my dream, my passion.

MELISSA: Passion is the first ingredient in most bankruptcies.

WOODY: Alright, but listen, I've got a trump card –

MABEL: Question eight. What is the largest organ in the body?

BUNNY: Oh, I know this…er…it's er…oh, she's asked it before…

LEE: The liver?

BUNNY: No.

WOODY: The onions?

MELISSA: I think it's the skin.

BUNNY: That's it! The skin.

LEE: Is that an organ? *(To MABEL.)* Is this a trick question?

MABEL: No. But I might be lying.

MELISSA: I'll put skin.

WOODY and LEE both shrug their shoulders.

Look at you both! Woody, Lee. Neither of you are interested. I'm trying to win here.

WOODY: Mabel.

MELISSA: Mabel? She's your trump card?

WOODY: Pub quiz with Mabel Tuesday nights and 'Hull's Got Talent' with Mabel, Wednesdays.

MABEL: Question nine. Who said: 'In spite of everything I still believe that people are good at heart'?

LEE: Dad?

BUNNY: No idea.

MELISSA: Got to be ironic.

LEE: It'll be someone who has gone through a lot of suffering.

WOODY: Pauline Prescott.

LEE: Be a writer who survived the Holocaust, or –

MELISSA: – Yes! Who wrote that diary? Hid in a cupboard. Little girl.

BUNNY: Anne Frank.

MELISSA: It's a guess, but it's a good guess.

MELISSA writes.

WOODY: I thought I'd call it the Laff Caff?

MELISSA: No. The Comedy Café.

LEE: That's classy. I'd go there. I wouldn't go to the Laff Caff. You're worth every penny we pay you.

WOODY: Can I come and see you tomorrow and do the deal?

MELISSA: Yes. Come to the Hull Advance offices and I can introduce you to Camilla.

LEE: Camilla?

MELISSA: I'm leaving Hull.

MABEL: The last question in the grand final. What does 'the Taliban' mean?

BUNNY: Lee?

LEE: 'The students'.

MELISSA writes the answer down.

MABEL: That's the end of the quiz. Hand in your answer sheets. Five-minute break and we're straight into 'Hull's Got Talent'.

BUNNY: I think we've won son.

LEE: I'm sure we have.

WOODY: Is that what Taliban means. Students?

LEE: Yup.

WOODY: Why don't we send our students to fight the Taliban? Save money, they'd live off Newcastle Brown and jam sandwiches. And they'd win the war. They'd grind the

Taliban down with party-related sleep deprivation, and confuse the fuck out of them by nicking all the road signs.

BUNNY: You could put that in your act.

WOODY: Yeah, brilliant. I'm writing material without trying.

BUNNY: Are you nervous about doing your stand-up?

WOODY: No. I feel like I'm about to turn from grub into chrysalis, break out and shed me old skin, and be reborn as a God-like thing of great beauty.

LEE: Or you might be shit.

WOODY: There is that, yeah.

LEE: You're leaving Hull?

MELISSA: I've been head-hunted. I'm going to lead the regeneration of North Tyneside.

LEE: They've already got an iconic footbridge haven't they?

MELISSA: One can't have too many iconic footbridges.

LEE: I'll miss you.

WOODY: I'm gonna go outside, prepare for me act by doing some breathing exercises with a cigarette.

WOODY leaves. LEE takes the answer sheet up to MABEL at the bar.

MELISSA: Has something happened? That I don't know about?

BUNNY: Aye. Lee's moving out to South Cave. Gonna open a flower shop with his Janet.

MELISSA: They're back together again?

BUNNY: Aye. It's been a bit of a scratchy marriage theirs. I don't like her. They had the boys early and then they made a stupid decision together.

MELISSA: What was that?

BUNNY: He had the snip didn't he.

MELISSA: A vasectomy?

BUNNY: Aye. Now she wants a girl of course.

MELISSA: I see.

BUNNY: His Jamie's going to Pocklington. That's a private school. I don't know where the bloody hell the money's coming from, but I don't care either, I've got me own problems.

LEE returns to the table.

MABEL: The 'Staff of Life' finished on forty-eight points.

BUNNY: We've won this.

MABEL: 'My Dad's a Drug Addict' are the league champions with fifty-one points!

Cheers.

Can we have a representative from the team to collect the trophy please.

MELISSA stands, LEE stands.

MELISSA: Sit down Lee. That trophy's mine.

MELISSA goes up to collect the trophy.

LEE: What's all that about?

Applause as MELISSA raises the cup above her head. She returns to the table holding the trophy.

LEE: You alright?

MELISSA: I'm going. Camilla is interested in pub quiz. I'll send her along next Tuesday. I'm taking this with me. Because I've earned it.

She turns and is gone. Tight spot on MABEL, alone now, BUNNY and LEE gone. We are now in a cabaret.

MABEL: 'Hull's got Talent'! What a bill we've got for you tonight. There's a young lass from Sutton Park who's gonna swallow a live swan. No? You're gonna *follow* a live song. That's karaoke love, that's Wednesdays. Shame, I like a good swan-swallowing act. There's Graham from Ings

Road whose unique talent is that he can mend things quite quickly. Have you brought your own things in to mend or are you gonna mend stuff the audience throws at you? You've brought in some badly smashed-up nick nacks of your own. I can't wait. With a line up like that you wonder why anyone bothers living in London. To kick us off it's South Cave's very own Lenny Bruce, Woody, who tonight is gonna do his stand-up for the first time –

(*Singing.*) '…ever I saw your face
I thought the sun shone out your arse.'

(*Speaking.*) Aye well, we've all made that mistake after fifteen tequila slammers.

Ladies and Gentlemen, the future of British comedy – Woody!

WOODY takes the stage. Very still, face giving nothing away, pure Buster Keaton.

WOODY: Being tall has its advantages. I went for an interview, on Tuesday half past ten, for a job as a lifeguard. She said 'Can you swim?' 'I said 'No, but I can wade out a fuck of a long way'.

– Women flirt with me cos they think I must be built in proportion. Let me tell you, if I was built in proportion, I'd be twenty-four foot seven.

– Driving's not a problem. I can drive any car with a sunroof.

– I'm heavy as well, eighteen stone. I refuse to sit on wicker furniture. I don't want to die with a twig up me arse.

– Went to the doctor this morning, new doctor, never met him before. He said, 'Your problem, Mr Woodhouse, is that you're paranoid'. I said, 'How can you say that doctor, you've only just met me'. He said, 'On the contrary, I've been watching and following you for years'.

End of scene.

SCENE TWO

BUNNY's flat. BUNNY is laid out on the sofa. LEE gets out a hyperdermic needle, and starts preparing a shot. This involves placing the heroin powder in a spoon and heating the spoon from below with a cigarette lighter. He then fills the hyperdermic needle. This is all done skilfully.

BUNNY: What you got there?

LEE: Your pain relief. Are you watching, cos in the future, you're gonna have to learn to do this for yourself.

BUNNY: I was gonna have a little burn.

LEE: This is better. Take some of this, you won't feel no pain, and me mam won't show, and even if she does you'll be pleased to see her. It's that good. This stuff is better than Beta Interferon.

BUNNY: Do you know what you're doing with that needle?

LEE: Yeah. I've been on the front line Dad. First time, it'll make you sick Dad. After that, it'll be brilliant. You're gonna stop thinking about Switzerland, and enjoy life.

BUNNY: I don't like being sick.

LEE: You'll be sick first time. Then, your body will develop a tolerance for it and you won't be sick. You'll be dreaming. You'll be floating down a warm river on a warm raft on a warm day.

BUNNY: What is it?

LEE: Diamorphine. It's a painkiller.

BUNNY: Let me read the packet.

LEE: There isn't a packet. You alright? Do you want to try it?

BUNNY: I'll try anything. Are you sure you know what you're doing with that needle?

LEE: Dad? What am I?

BUNNY: You're army trained.

LEE finds a vein, and injects BUNNY.

Slow to black.

THE END

PITCAIRN

Characters

Mutineers

FLETCHER CHRISTIAN

NED YOUNG

MATTHEW QUINTAL

WILLIAM MCKOY

WILLIAM BROWN

JOHN ADAMS

Polynesian Women (their 'husbands' in brackets)

WALUA (MATTHEW QUINTAL)

TE'O (WILLIAM MCKOY)

MATA (NED YOUNG)

MI MITTI (FLETCHER CHRISTIAN)

TE LAHU (WILLIAM BROWN)

FASTO (OHA/JOHN ADAMS)

Polynesian Men

MENALEE

HITI

OHA

Marines and Officers

CAPTAIN PIPON

CAPTAIN STAINES

CALVERT (MARINE)

MAGEE (MARINE)

PRATT (MARINE)

Set

Pitcairn Island. A fist of volcanic rock thrusting out from an expanse of Pacific. It is not a welcoming island. The Pacific crashes against sheer cliffs which rise hundreds of feet from the sea. No sense of a beach, nothing is gentle.

The playing area is the fertile plateau above Bounty Bay. Up stage is a cliff top beyond which is a sea and sky horizon.

Stage right, and high, is a cave, an eyrie. A path to the eyrie snakes down to the playing area.

Pitcairn was first performed on 22 August 2014 at the Chichester Festival Theatre with the following cast:

TE LAHU	Lois Chimimba
QUINTAL	Samuel Edward-Cook
FASTO	Vanessa Emme
HITI	Eben Figueiredo
MI MITTI	Siubhan Harrison
TE'O	Saffron Hocking
NED YOUNG	Ash Hunter
KHAN MENALEE	Naveed
MATA	Cassie Layton
WALUA	Anna Leong Brophy
FLETCHER CHRISTIAN	Tom Morley
JOHN ADAMS	Adam Newington
WILLIAM MCKOY	Henry Pettigrew
OHA	David Rubin
WILLIAM BROWN	Jack Tarlton

Director	Max Stafford-Clark
Designer	Tim Shortall
Lighting Designer	Johanna Town
Composer	Adam Pleeth
Choreographer	Orian Michaeli
Sound Designer	Emma Laxton
Casting Director	Gabrielle Dawes CDG
Associate Director	Tim Hoare
Assistant Director	Jake Smith

PROLOGUE 1

1814. A clearing surrounded by trees. Enter a group of English marines with muskets cocked, ready, casually nervous. There is a basket of collected coconuts. CAPTAIN PIPON and CAPTAIN STAINES follow.

PRATT: This island's got life sir. Look, someone's gathered these here coconuts.

PIPON: And someone made the basket.

PRATT: Oh aye. That kind o' thinking'll be how you made officer.

MAGEE: I'll wager I'll find a rum tree in a minute.

CALVERT: It's a damned paradise!

PRATT: Shh!

Silence.

Wood smoke sir.

STAINES: You can hear wood smoke?

PRATT: Smell it sir.

CALVERT: We're on the village.

STAINES: Company! Consider! Fletcher Christian has nothing to lose, he knows he will hang. They were young men when they took the Bounty, so they're old now, yes, but not too old to fight. Not all the men were active mutineers so no firing, except in self-defence.

MATA appears, she has a musket raised. MATA wears a large wooden cross around her neck. She is seen by the Marines but not the officers.

Our aim is to secure the men, alive, and return them to court martial –

CALVERT: – Sir?!

STAINES: I doubt they still have powder but if they have had peace in this garden of Eden then their reserves may yet be plenty.

MATA: Yoo kah pahs!

STAINES: Lord Almighty?!

MAGEE raises his musket.

PIPON: No firing!

MATA: Wosing yourley doon?

PIPON: *(To STAINES.)* It's not English.

CALVERT: It is sir. 'What are you doing?'

PIPON: We wish to speak with Fletcher Christian.

The other women now appear. They are all either pregnant or carrying babies at the breast. All have wooden crosses around their necks.

MAGEE: Strewth!

STAINES: Greetings! English! Friendly!

PIPON: Magee! Stop pointing that musket!

STAINES: Where are your husbands?

TE LAHU: Es wuhn man.

CALVERT: Is one man.

STAINES: What is this man's name?

TE LAHU: Adam.

PIPON: Fletcher Christian, is he dead?

MI MITTI: Titreano?

CALVERT: *(To PIPON.)* Titreano is the name they gave Christian on Tahiti sir.

MI MITTI: Ai ka wes Titreano –

MATA and FASTO pull MI MITTI to the back of the group.

TE LAHU: – *(Louder.)* Titreano dead uz hatchet long time.

CALVERT: *(Pedantically.)* Christian has been dead as a hatchet for a long time, sir.

PIPON: I've got the measure of it now thank you Calvert.

Enter a middle-aged man, though looking much older with wild hair and a sun hat obscuring his face. He is carried by four women in a kind of sedan chair arrangement. He has a Bible on his lap. They put the sedan chair down.

MUTINEER: *(Cockney.)* You come all this way to hang me then have yer lads!

STAINES: Not summarily.

PIPON: Captain Philip Pipon. HMS Tagus.

STAINES: Captain Thomas Staines. HMS Briton.

MUTINEER: John Adams.

PIPON: Your rank?

MUTINEER: AB.

STAINES: Your ship?

MUTINEER: H.M.A.V. Bounty. Welcome to Pitcairn's Island. Fasto! Wickles for everyone. Jump to it girl! And summat to slake the thirst of these officers!

PIPON: Calvert! Take the company through to the village.

MUTINEER: They'll spoil you. Aye.

PIPON: How much might they spoil them?

MUTINEER: You got an imagination son. Na! They're all God fearing. I learned 'em all in the way of the book ain't I.

The marines follow the women off. MUTINEER, PIPON and STAINES are left alone.

STAINES: You are the one remaining man on the island?

MUTINEER: Aye. What of Bligh? Does he live?

PIPON: He does.

MUTINEER: I said he'd make land! God Bless Him! That morning on the Bounty, I were in me cot, and I come up when all Bedlam broke out. Bligh sees me and sends me back down to get his breeches, to cover his modesty, which, being loyal and innocent of all schemes, I did. Is he here? Bligh?

STAINES: No. He has another commission.

MUTINEER: Joseph Banks and the breadfruit?

STAINES: Yes.

MUTINEER: Kaw! Bligh loves that damned bread fruit don't he?!

STAINES: What happened to the Master's Mate, Christian?

MUTINEER: Has there ever, in the history of all England, been a more unfortunate man? Eh? A gentleman of Westmorland, an officer, he coulda been an ornament to his country but in them first six months on Tahiti the Lord tempted him with his fruit and like Adam in the Garden he didn't have no chance, and he left the righteous path of the Lord and turned to Venus.

STAINES: Lust?

MUTINEER: I think he thought it were love, the two are easily confused. Not being quarter deck meself I never got near enough to be sure.

STAINES: But he's dead? Fletcher Christian?

MUTINEER: Over twenty year back. Aye, a terrible gripe, laid all the lads low.

PIPON: All but you.

MUTINEER: I'm blessed with me father's blood, the only thing he ever give me worth having. He was a waterman on the Thames, and picked up every disease the devil's invented, and never had a day in bed. Aye, a gripe laid all the lads low, until one day the sun comes up and I was the only man standing. That were twenty year back. By my reckoning I'm forty-nine. I know, I look older, that's the women.

End of scene.

ACT 1
SCENE 1

A clearing on the plateau. The sound of dogs barking. MATTHEW QUINTAL leads the men in singing Shantyman style, improvising lines as he goes. On each Haul Away! they take a step back, which brings them slowly on to the stage. Hauling the rope are WILLIAM MCKOY, JOHN ADAMS, MATTHEW QUINTAL and the Polynesians MENALEE, OHA and the boy HITI. HITI wears a union jack flag as a kind of toga. The Brits are tattooed with Polynesian style tattoos and all look to have gone a bit native with shell necklaces and the like. QUINTAL is the most extreme – he wears only a loin cloth. FLETCHER CHRISTIAN is high in the eyrie, he's writing, working on what looks like a document, or a speech. The team are hauling a sled laden with valuable goods recovered from the Bounty. The women run on and off to the bathing pool, but return to the fire as a base as the food is being prepared there. There is the consistent background noise of dogs barking from below.

QUINTAL: *In South West England I was born*

ALL: Heave away! Haul away!

QUINTAL: *To Tahiti round Cape Horn*

ALL: We're bound for O Tahiti
Haul away you rolling King
Heave away! Haul away!
All the way you'll hear me sing
We're bound for O Tahiti

QUINTAL: *On that isle met a native lass*

Some laughter, some yeahs!

ALL: Heave away! Haul away!

QUINTAL: *Her body's shaped like an hour glass*

More laughter.

ALL: We're bound to O Tahiti

QUINTAL: *I shook her up I shook her down (More laughter.)*

ALL: Heave away! Haul away!

QUINTAL: *There's none like her in Deptford town*

ALL: We're bound to O'Tahiti
Haul away you rolling King
Heave away! Haul away!
All the way you'll hear me sing
We're bound to O'Tahiti

Enter WALUA, TE'O, TE LAHU, and MATA. QUINTAL drops the rope and goes over to WALUA for a grope and a kiss.

NED: *(Off.)* McKoy! What's the damned problem?!

MCKOY: Our shanty man's got a prick for brains!

QUINTAL: Get us some water you little coney! Go on! Damn it, I'm beat, bone tired.

The girls run off, QUINTAL sits and leches after them, gets a wave from WALUA.

MCKOY: Yous won't need rocking to sleep tonight then.

QUINTAL: I'll find some blood for that one.

Enter NED YOUNG. He is wearing an officer's jacket.

NED: You can sit when the work's done Quintal.

QUINTAL: I'll sweat as much as any land-owning squire in England, and no damned long pelt of a blackamoor bitch is gonna lash me on me own island.

They square off. The rope starts to slip.

ADAMS: Oi! She's slipping down.

QUINTAL stands his ground so NED takes up some of the rope.

NED: McKoy, call us a shanty.

QUINTAL: *(Singing.) That bastard Bligh he lashed me twice!*

ALL: Heave away! Haul away!

QUINTAL: *They'll lash me no more in my life*
I'm bound to Pitcairn's Island

ALL: Haul away you rolling King

Heave away! Haul away!
All the way you'll hear me sing
We're bound to Pitcairn's Island

The work is done. The sled secured. The girls come back with water. The men sit and drink. MATA gives HITI a half coconut. He is smitten. He drinks the milk walking forwards for direct address, and fourth wall-breaking engagement with the audience.

HITI: I was surfing on my island, Tubuai, my island called Tubuai, not Tahiti. I am from Tubuai, not Tahiti. Understand? Do you understand? Where am I from? *(Tubuai.)* Which is not? *(Tahiti.)* You are intelligent and will be wealthy. When you grow up. With many pigs. Surfing is my favourite thing. We Polynesians invented surfing, and swimming. I saw three trees where the sky meets the sea. I know it is the three masts of an English ship because when I was a small small boy King Toote came to my island *(Tubuai.)* Who is King Toote? *(Captain Cook.)* Yes, very clever. You will be wealthy when you grow up with many pigs. And King Toote touched my head with his hand, and did like that with my hair. Like that. So when I saw the trees I ran down to the beach. My island..?..*(Tubuai.)* has a beach, white, beautiful, not like here. Only one good thing about Pitcairn, no flies.

MATA walks by teasing him. He places his hand on his penis. Just placed, no frottage.

Two good things about Pitcairn. No flies and Mataohu. She makes me hard. She's seventeen. I'm fifteen. Mmmm. The ship was called His Majesty's Armed Vessel Bounty, but no flag. It was not King Toote it was Titreano. In English Fletcher Christian, but we say Titreano. Can you say Titreano? *(Titreano.)* Beautiful. You will be wealthy when you grow up with many pigs. Titreano had a coat with iron buttons. We don't have iron on my island, it is wonderful, iron, I love it.

He points up to FLETCHER CHRISTIAN.

Titreano made me his taio, which is blood friend until death. He gave me porter to drink, which tastes like piss, and makes you sick, very good. He then give me an iron button, look, beautiful, but no jacket, not yet. Maybe soon. Titreano gave me a job on The Bounty as an AB which means 'nearly a God'. I asked my mother if I could go sail away with Titreano and her advice was 'always kill the fish before you eat it'. What do you think that means? I had no idea, so here I am now on Matakitereangi, but because I am now English, I will call it Pitcairn. Not Pitcairn Island, you don't say England Island do you, no, just Pitcairn.

QUINTAL: Where's my dog Alex Smith? A country squire needs a damned dog for his dirty acres.

ADAMS: All them dogs is locked in the chart room. Ain't nofin to do wi' me.

QUINTAL looks up at CHRISTIAN who is scanning the horizon.

QUINTAL: If Bligh turns up here with a Man O'War, we could defend this island.

MCKOY: That stinking Jesuit's dead and rotting in hell.

NED: Wouldn't surprise me if he's back in Deptford right now, fitting out a prison ship with manacles for seven.

ADAMS: Six.

QUINTAL: 'Cause you was sick in your hammock, want yer? Slept right through the whole watch didn't yer? Woke up in the morning to a new captain.

ADAMS: Aye, that's it.

MCKOY: You're as tarred as any of us Alex Smith, and Bligh he seen you too, aye.

QUINTAL: I heard him whisper your name as he climbed into the launch. 'Alex Smith', 'Alex Smith'. He was stowing your name away ready for the Admirals.

ADAMS: I'll be alright then 'cause Alex Smith ain't my name.

QUINTAL: Reckless Jack that's your name!

MCKOY: If you're nae Alex Smith who are ye? Bonny Prince Charlie?

Enter William BROWN. BROWN is carrying a notebook. He is dressed not as a seaman, but as a gardener.

BROWN: Mister Young, sir! Wonderful news!

QUINTAL: You've found some more women?

BROWN: I thought it unsupposable, but this land has been populated before! The land was farmed, and is planted with many different species –

OHA and MENALEE address the women, ignoring the mutineers.

OHA: *(To the other Polynesians.)* Their gardener is saying what I was saying on the ship, our people have lived on this island here before.

MENALEE: This is the lost island of Matakiterangi?

The Polynesians gather round. Excluding the English.

MCKOY: Oi! Mammu Mammu!

QUINTAL: Speak English!

NED: Menalee, what is all this excitement?

MENALEE: Owuz folk back afore.

OHA: Plenty marae, yus ken?

MENALEE: Marae. Stone, stone, stone, stone.

NED: A temple?

MENALEE:/OHA: Eyeuh!!

BROWN: There's breadfruit, coconuts, yams, plantains, two different types of banana and the Mulberry tree for cloth. We can make clothes!

QUINTAL: I got no plans to wear no damned clothes.

BROWN: Where is Mister Christian?

NED: On his watch.

NED indicates where CHRISTIAN is and BROWN heads off to tell him the news. Enter MI MITTI, tall and superior, she's just bathed.

QUINTAL: Eh up lads! The Queen's coming. Stand to attention. Mine already is! Strewth, look at that, she gets me all venereal. I'm gonna tup her, if it takes my last breath.

NED: Quintal, I'll counsel you to leave Christian's girl alone.

QUINTAL: Go wipe. And I'll counsel you Ned Young not to build your house too near me. I don't want to keep you awake at nights.

NED: And what is it that might disturb me?

QUINTAL: The sound of my balls slapping again' her arse.

NED walks down and joins MI MITTI. He sits.

NED: Mi Mitti, I see you found a bathing pool.

MI MITTI: Eeyeuh! No flies.

NED: You must be on your guard against Mister Quintal.

MI MITTI: I am ra'atira. He knows he cannot speak to me.

NED: He considers all the rules are now rewrit, and I'm afraid the fact of you being high born will not constrain his behaviour.

CHRISTIAN approaches.

NED: *(To CHRISTIAN.)* This is the last sled. The ship is voided.

CHRISTIAN: What of the boats?

NED: The jolly boat and the canoe are hauled and secured above the tide.

CHRISTIAN: Have the people had their ration?

NED: Not yet.

CHRISTIAN: Hold it back.

NED: I can't control them, and now that the work is done they will want to take their pleasures with the women.

CHRISTIAN: No! The 'House' must sit tonight, and sober.

NED: The Lords or Commons sir?

CHRISTIAN: The Lords and Commons as one. I plan to open the meeting by taking off my uniform. I will place it on the fire, and then ask you to take off your tunic and do like wise.

NED: I know of no successful society that does not have some vestige of hierarchy.

CHRISTIAN: This levelling is more painful for us. The men are trading the short, brutal, scurvy-ridden life of an AB for a cottage in Arcadia.

NED: With respect sir, you and I are not equal in sacrifice. Your family were already bankrupted and their lands on the Isle of Man taken in lieu before you could have your portrait painted. This contrasts with my fortune on St Kitts which is intact.

CHRISTIAN: Brutal.

NED: Now is the time for truths. Before your Parliament of the people further depletes, by enclosure, what little of the earth is left to me.

CHRISTIAN: I count it a blessing, that my family were bankrupted before my portrait was painted. My mother might forget me more easily.

NED: Mine must suffer, I have two portraits.

CHRISTIAN: Don't speak of this with my wife. She naturally presumes that as an officer I'm heir to a fortune.

NED: She will find your ideas of equality difficult.

CHRISTIAN: Perhaps, but the division between quarter deck and forecastle cannot continue.

NED: Why not?

CHRISTIAN: Because this island is a new leaf. Why foul it with tradition?

NED: Easy to say when you've lost your fortune.

CHRISTIAN: Your fortune may be extant on St. Kitts, but you will never see it again. You will see a rope sooner.

NED: So what are the principles of this levelling?

CHRISTIAN: Reason and individualism. Our age has gifted us with thinkers that have shown us a rational approach to life and nature, allowing us to question faith and tradition. Spinoza –

NED: – A Jew?

CHRISTIAN: He was excommunicated from the synagogue –

NED: – so a nobody and a Jew.

CHRISTIAN: God did not give us Pitcairn? I found it by reason, by charts, by science!

NED: I prayed every night.

CHRISTIAN: You know the truth. There was no celestial hand.

NED: What of God, here?

CHRISTIAN: Imagine life without the clergy!? When we were in Tenerife I discussed with a French officer, a prisoner on The Daffodil, and he told me that there is a movement to raise the third estate, the serfs, and this thinking comes from the aristocracy! He said that in his lifetime he expected all men in his country to be equal.

NED: They'd still be French. We are both gentlemen, I expect no less from the division of this island than you.

CHRISTIAN: And I will have no more than any man.

NED: Then I will take my reduction in good heart.

CHRISTIAN: Such gloom! We have everything we need!

NED: We have no physician.

CHRISTIAN: Are you ill?

NED: Not yet.

CHRISTIAN: We shall live better here than on rations. Ned, one last order, before we abdicate all authority, we must have the dogs killed. Their barking will betray us.

NED: They can't be heard in Deptford.

CHRISTIAN: If a ship arrives, they'll give us away.

NED: Quintal won't take kindly to the killing of his dog.

CHRISTIAN: What is his mood?

NED: Foul. As ever.

CHRISTIAN: I blame myself, for Quintal.

NED: Are you mother or father?

CHRISTIAN: When the pressed men ran, Bligh sent me out to recruit, under oath not to disclose our destination. I found McKoy and Quintal in a tavern. I couldn't sway them, initially, and then I said the word.

NED: Tahiti.

CHRISTIAN: Since Cook Tahitian girls have ousted mermaids in every sailor's imagination.

A scream as QUINTAL starts urinating in front of the girls.

NED: And yet from today, Quintal is my equal?

CHRISTIAN: And not just Quintal.

NED: There is someone lower?

CHRISTIAN: The natives.

NED: *(Laughs.)* This is scoptical!

CHRISTIAN: You, yourself, as a quadroon, are one quarter native.

NED: And three quarters English gentleman. Do you have plans to enfranchise the women?

CHRISTIAN: Ned, I'm not mad.

NED: I no longer know what to expect. What was revolutionary yesterday, today is Tory policy.

CHRISTIAN: Muster the crew and the chiefs at dusk on the log there, in this clearing. This will be our Parliament.

NED: There will be violence if the men perceive their station undercut. Put your equality proposals before the crew alone, and let them decide.

CHRISTIAN: *(He considers.)* Very well. But kill the dogs first.

CHRISTIAN turns and goes to the fire and gets himself some food and water. The men disperse. The women are gathered around the fire. A pot is cooking. MI MITTI, TE LAHU, WALUA, TE'O, FASTO and MATA.

NED: Rum and pleasures will be delayed this evening!

QUINTAL: Go wipe your arse! Walua! Girl! I'm gonna dock you all the darkmans!

WALUA giggles.

NED: No drinking! There are decisions to be made. At the log. Sober. On the bell! Hiti!

QUINTAL exits. HITI comes over.

HITI: Aye sir!

Ned Because of your brave and constant service Titreano has promoted you to 'Midshipman', which means 'at God's right hand'. This tunic is yours.

NED takes off his naval tunic and gives it to HITI, who puts it on, it's way too big.

HITI: Tank yoo sir!

NED: The dogs are locked in the Bounty's chart room. Go back down to her, and –

HITI: – her? Who her?

NED: A ship in the English navy is a she, a her, because like a woman if you look after her, she'll look after you. It'll make sense when you're older.

HITI: Aye, aye, sir.

He hands over a key.

NED: Kill the dogs.

HITI: Ah like em dogs.

NED: Hiti, when a sailor says 'aye, aye sir' what does it mean?

HITI: First cum aye mean him ken di order, uderwun aye mean him gonna do it.

NED: Thus. Kill the dogs!

HITI: Aye, aye, sir!

NED: And when you've done it, show me your thumb, like this.

NED demonstrates a thumbs up.

That means all is well.

HITI tries a thumbs up, but does it with both thumbs.

NED: We don't use both thumbs or we'd fall over the gunwale –

HITI: – one hand fe me, one hand for the ship.

NED: Good, you're learning. Both thumbs up is reserved for the most brilliant thing, the most fantastical event. Go on!

HITI: Aye, aye sir.

HITI runs off, but stops to stare at MATA. She walks down stage for direct address.

MATA: That's Hiti. He's only a boy. Fifteen. Watch what he does. *(Beat.)* He stares at me. He'll touch his dick in a minute, watch.

A couple of beats of staring from HITI and then he touches his dick.

These English sailors, their cocks are poxy. They are not circumcised. Urgh! And how can I describe their breath? You know what a dead shark's arse smells like? Yes? You, I'm talking to you. Yes. So it's about twice as bad as that. Why do we sleep with them then? For these.

Holds up a nail.

Nails. Girls, hands up, who would sleep with a sailor for a nail? Two nails? *(There's always one.)* Most of you ladies would say 'no'. But on my island there is no iron. A nail for us is a miracle, a piece of the sun. So the question you girls should ask yourselves is, 'would I have sex with a stranger for a piece of the sun'. Ah! One night I fell asleep on The Bounty with Ned Young. Titreano woke him and they went up on deck. I followed, silently, a few paces behind. I saw my Ned and Titreano, they did this together, they took their knives and they started cutting through the rope of the anchor, which is really thick, as thick as, an arm. You! Raise your arm.

She mime saws through the audience member's arm.

And they sawed and sawed and when it was cut the rope slipped into the lagoon, and The Bounty started to drift and I saw that there was a boat ahead with men rowing and it was pulling us out of the reef towards the open sea. Yes, we were being stolen, like chickens, like goats, stolen away, our lives stolen, never to see Tahiti again.

NED: Hiti!

HITI: Aye, aye sir!

HITI runs off. NED exits.

TE'O: I'm starving. I could eat a whale.

MATA: So do we now eat separate from the men again, like on Tahiti.

FASTO: Yes! It is tapu!

TE'O: I like eating with the men, they're funny.

MI MITTI: We are Tahitian women, we don't eat with the men. It is tapu.

WALUA: We're not on Tahiti!

MI MITTI: We must not lose our traditions, or we lose ourselves.

FASTO: What are the rules?! It's so confusing!

WALUA: We're English now!

TE'O: Yes. We were four months on the ship. All our traditions are lost. We are no longer Tahitian. And I don't care. I like being English.

MI MITTI: No. A ship is only temporary but this is permanent, and we can restore our traditions, and live in the right way, here.

TE LAHU: No. We must return to Tahiti. We can do this, we have The Bounty.

FASTO: Mi Mitti, your Queen is happy here. Don't speak to your Queen like that!

MI MITTI: This island has everything.

TE LAHU: Except my children.

MI MITTI: You can have more children here. With Mister Brown.

TE LAHU: You volunteered, to sail with Titreano. I didn't. I was stolen. What will be a home to you, will be a prison to me.

TE'O: I didn't like Tahiti. It was all rules, rules, rules.

MATA: And mosquitoes.

WALUA: And we have white husbands, that's good isn't it? We'll have white children. Te'o is pregnant.

TE'O: Yes, my blood hasn't come.

They make a fuss of TE'O.

TE LAHU: For the sake of this unborn child. We must find a way back to Tahiti. For there can be no future here.

TE'O: No! My baby is English.

MATA: Why do you fear for the future?

TE LAHU: During our journey here I watched Titreano.

MI MITTI: You watched my husband?

TE LAHU: He has lost his authority.

MI MITTI: He sailed The Bounty, he found this island!

TE LAHU: We all sailed the ship.

MI MITTI: He read the charts.

WALUA: Can you read their sea charts?

TE LAHU: Of course not.

TE'O: Stop farting out your mouth then.

They laugh.

TE LAHU: When McKoy shot that chief, the one that stole the jacket, at Purutea –

FASTO: – they are all thieves on Purutea.

MATA: We were outnumbered, we could have been torn limb from limb.

TE LAHU: But what did Christian do to punish McKoy? Lash him, beat him, kill him? No! He turned his back and walked away. Titreano has no authority. And a people without a leader will get lost.

TE'O: Alright, don't go on about it.

MATA: We can live here, but we need to know how to live.

WALUA: We're English now, we married them!

TE'O: Yes, and this is a part of England.

TE LAHU: On Tahiti Mi Mitti is Ra'atira, our Queen, on Tahiti. I am Arioi, I make performances, on Tahiti. And you are the Manuhane, the people, of Tahiti. But we are all cast away now, we are all nothing now. Prisoners, slaves, we are living in oblivion, at the edge of the world, divided from our people by the ocean, washed up on a lost island, like fish bones.

WALUA: I'm sick of listening to you, you whining turd.

MATA: Is this England or is this Tahiti.

TE'O: My man refuses to call me Te'o, he calls me Mary.

FASTO: He can't pronounce Te'o?

They laugh.

TE'O: Mary is the name of the English God's wife.

FASTO: What's the English god's name then?

TE'O: God. Just God. Like that. God. He doesn't have a name. They just call him God.

MATA: That's like having a boat and calling it Boat.

TE LAHU: They lack imagination.

WALUA: Quintal calls me Sarah. Which was his mother's name in England.

TE LAHU: Did he used to fuck his mother then?

They laugh.

WALUA: He calls me Sarah, because he loves me!

TE LAHU: Oh mummy, mummy, Sarah, oh mummy, oh, oh, oh!

WALUA clips TE LAHU and they start fighting. Uproar. The others break it up.

WALUA: At least I've got a proper man for a husband not a freak.

TE LAHU: I didn't choose him.

WALUA: What were you doing at the party then?

TE'O: Collecting nails.

They laugh.

TE LAHU: I was not collecting nails.

MATA: You are Arioi, you were there to dance.

TE LAHU: I was stolen.

They laugh.

TE LAHU: *(To MI MITTI.)* You were married to Titreano on Tahiti. My question is, did you know their plans? Did you help them plan our abduction?

FASTO: You cannot ask such a question of our Queen.

MATA: Te Lahu is Arioi, that is her job, to ask strange questions.

TE'O: Yes! Answer Te Lahu's question.

MI MITTI stands and walks away.

TE LAHU: Our Queen betrayed us.

FASTO is crying. NED enters and rings the bell.

FASTO: I hate it here. Everything is wrong!

TE LAHU: From this day Mi Mitti is not my Queen.

TE LAHU walks away from the group. NED rings the bell, politely. QUINTAL is by the bell singing and drinking.

NED: *(To QUINTAL.)* I said, no drinking.

QUINTAL: Go wipe your catastrophe, sir.

(Singing.) Shanty man, oh! shanty man
(*Burps.)*
Who's got a berth for a shanty man.
Sing you a song of a world gone wrong
and we got no use for a shanty man

QUINTAL rings the bell manically. Singing as the men gather. NED Young, WILLIAM MCKOY, MATTHEW QUINTAL, WILLIAM BROWN, and JOHN ADAMS. Enter CHRISTIAN.

CHRISTIAN: Mammu! Mammu!

MCKOY: We havenae had our ration yet sir!

CHRISTIAN: Let us, as a priority, consider the future of the rum ration.

MCKOY: I vote to double it!

OTHERS Hear, hear! / Aye!

CHRISTIAN: Half a pint a day for each man will last us but one year.

BROWN: And we are here forever.

QUINTAL: McKoy reckons he can distill, we got the copper out the ship.

MCKOY: I was apprenticed to a distillery as a bairn sir.

QUINTAL: He worked in the bottling shed, emptying bottles.

CHRISTIAN: I am hopeful that life here might offer alternatives to drunkenness as a distraction.

QUINTAL: I've had half a pint of rum, a pint of white wine and a quart of porter every day of my life since I was fourteen Mister Christian.

CHRISTIAN: Then I apologise to you personally Mister Quintal for having failed to discover an island blessed with a livery tavern.

BROWN: You've done very well finding this land Mister Christian, but I've seen the charts I don't think it's Pitcairn.

CHRISTIAN: The Admiralty have charted Pitcairn incorrectly.

The men know the importance of this and cheer loudly.

Yes! We are twenty-five two south and one hundred and thirty west. Captain Carteret was out by three degrees.

QUINTAL: What a wanker!

Further cheering.

CHRISTIAN: Three degrees is not invisible. We need to be constant in our vigil. If Bligh has made land –

QUINTAL: I should have blown the bugger's brains out.

ALL Aye / yeah / for sure / grumbles.

CHRISTIAN: So we keep a watch night and day from the heights. That was my last order. I shall no longer be burdened with the responsibility nor shall I claim its privileges. Our ranks are equal, I am henceforth, Fletcher Christian.

He takes his tunic off and drops it on the grass.

Mister Young? Where is your tunic?

NED: I have bequeathed my commission to the boy Hiti, your taio.

CHRISTIAN: Then we are levelled. I have made mistakes. To consider the many deaths that it has taken to get us to this peaceful place –

ADAMS: – who's died?

NED: The natives killed at Tubuai.

ADAMS: Think of them as animals sir, not men, that way you won't grieve none.

CHRISTIAN: Pitcairn is now our purser.

QUINTAL: Let's hope she's no nip cheese!

CHRISTIAN: The land is fertile, the seas teem with fish, there is fresh water. But that is not our only fortune. How blessed are we to have the skills of the very gardener that Sir Joseph Banks himself chose for the breadfruit expedition, William Brown of Leicester!

Applause/cheers.

MCKOY: Give that man a woman now!

CHRISTIAN: Bill McKoy. No British colony should want for a Scot!

QUINTAL: You mean, no British colony should want for Scotch.

CHRISTIAN: Bill McKoy may not be guild, but I have never seen a finer white iron man!

Cheers.

CHRISTIAN: We have no books, but I'll wager Mister Young has read any author you care to name. His instruction will be our instruction.

Cheers.

Alexander Smith. Pitcairn is an island nation, seamanship will be much in demand.

ADAMS: I am not Alexander Smith sir.

MCKOY: Who are yee then man?

QUINTAL: Oliver Cromwell.

ADAMS: As it is writ in the parish, my name is John Adams.

QUINTAL: You'll always be Reckless Jack to me.

NED: Why did you sign as Alex Smith?

ADAMS: My father, also John Adams, was pressed and then deserted a man o' war and took the meat with him, sir.

The men are giggling.

NED: And signing with Bligh as John Adams might alert the Admiralty?

ADAMS: I thought they might hang me by mistake.

MCKOY: They'll hang yee as John Adams, Reckless Jack or Alex Smith.

QUINTAL: Aye, they'll hang all three of you.

ADAMS: I gave Bligh his breeches, to cover his modesty. He noted that.

QUINTAL: I wish you had gone in the damned launch. I'd have a bigger garden and two wives.

CHRISTIAN: Mammu! Mammu! Matthew Quintal. A seaman with a refreshing directness of manner. Without this man I could not have found the strength to take the ship.

Cheers.

CHRISTIAN: We have all the essentials for this challenge.

NED: Wait. You have not spoken of yourself.

BROWN: Aye.

NED: All successful nations boast a man of vision, whose disciplines can raise the common people above their instinctive predilection to savagery. On this isle we shall want for culture, and those of us that have been exposed to the refinements of the opera, concerts –

QUINTAL: – you, you mean.

NED: Yes. I hope that as an expert observator of the stars you might share that passion with us all. The night sky is the only theatre we can attend.

CHRISTIAN: I shall. To govern ourselves we need a polity that will serve *us* rather than King, Court, or Church. The kelson of our society shall be equality, founded on the love of our fellow man. We have as yet not one edict written down, we have only the natural law of men living in extremis. Let our needs be our guide, and let us eschew the sophistry of Europe. We need a title for this parliament. Might I suggest, 'the court of Yarning'.

QUINTAL: 'Yarning?' Like telling a story?

MCKOY: Bligh lashed me fae yarning.

CHRISTIAN: Bligh saw yarning as revolution. This our yarning court is the Parliament of our revolution!

BROWN: These words sound rather grand to me sir and I approve.

MCKOY: Do we take nae heed of God?

CHRISTIAN: It is as if we find ourselves at the beginning of time. Man and Woman in a natural state. Let Tahiti be our model where men live without a sense of vice, without prejudices, without disputes. Born under a beautiful sky, nourished on the fruits of the earth which is fertile without tillage, ruled by patriarchs rather than kings, knowing no other god but love. There is no equivalent paradise in Christendom.

QUINTAL: Amsterdam? 'Cept the women charge.

The men laugh. CHRISTIAN struggles on.

CHRISTIAN: We are men, that is enough, our moral sense is innate. We do not need God to be good.

NED: And if all else fails I have the Bounty Bible.

MCKOY: Do we's get to vote on everything?

CHRISTIAN: We are nine men in number, so we should never be locked.

QUINTAL: We ain't nine men.

MCKOY: We're six.

CHRISTIAN: Oha, Menalee and Hiti are men.

ADAMS: The Indians?

QUINTAL: Go wipe!

Uproar.

BROWN: The natives' skill in horticulture is superior to ours, they know how to fish these waters, and Oha, is my taio, my brother for life.

MCKOY: If you goes ahead and makes the natives equal sir –

CHRISTIAN: – it will not be my decision, the Yarning court, this meeting –

QUINTAL: – will they be given land?

CHRISTIAN: Naturally. The division of the island would be into nine parts.

Uproar.

QUINTAL: One of them's a damned boy!

MCKOY: He don't even have a woman.

QUINTAL: And who will work our land?

BROWN: The natives are free men, not slaves.

QUINTAL: You took them on to work the damned ship, not to be masters over us.

MCKOY: We can't divide the land nine ways, there's nae enough.

BROWN: You are presuming enclosure.

NED: It would be a very English comedy to see the garden of Eden sprouting fences.

BROWN: The pigs can run wild, like us, they have nowhere to go. And we could consider the island common land, and work it equally.

ADAMS: No. I want my a plot of land, and I'll fence it off, and I'll put my damned name on it.

QUINTAL: Which name are you gonna use?

Laughter.

NED: Let's vote.

MCKOY: What are we voting on?

CHRISTIAN: The proposal is that the three Indian men will be equal yarners with equal land rights, each man taking one ninth part of Pitcairn. All those in favour of this proposition raise your hand.

CHRISTIAN raises, as does BROWN. No one else. There is laughter.

CHRISTIAN: Ned, Menalee is your taio, that means he is your brother. Is your brother not your equal?

QUINTAL: I don't have a taio. I think that's all Tahitian arse wipe.

CHRISTIAN: *(Fired up.)* We came south for the breadfruit, cheap food, to perpetuate and make more profitable a serfdom which we would disavow within an English shire but which we allow to flourish in the Americas.

QUINTAL: What's he on about?

BROWN: Slavery.

CHRISTIAN: We can manumise these men. If they are free we are free. We will vote again tomorrow.

MCKOY: Until ye gets yer preferred result!?

CHRISTIAN: This is too important!

NED: We need to decide the fate of the Bounty.

QUINTAL: She's gotta burn! Damn it! If the navy find the island, they'll see her. If she ain't there, they'll pass on, as there is no natural landing.

MCKOY: And they wouldnae expect us to burn her.

BROWN: Because that would be madness. I'm not a mutineer, so I do not fear the navy.

QUINTAL: They'll hang you Brown, not for mutiny, but for knowing me.

BROWN: After a year or so, we might feel the need to explore. There may be a plant, or tree we need. I think we should keep her.

Enter TE LAHU from upstage. She stands some way off and listens.

MCKOY: Hey, look, that Te Lahu's listening to us. She's trouble.

QUINTAL: I'll knock some sense into her later.

Laughter.

NED: John Adams?

ADAMS: I ain't got nothing to fear from the Admiralty. I'd keep her.

NED: If the navy find Pitcairn they'll come ashore for water. Ship or no ship. And as a gentleman I quite like having my own ship.

CHRISTIAN: This island will satisfy all our wants but one.

MCKOY: Whisky?

CHRISTIAN: We do not have sufficient women.

ADAMS: One each is enough.

QUINTAL: Speak for yourself.

CHRISTIAN: Hiti will need a wife.

QUINTAL: His balls ain't dropped.

CHRISTIAN: An island, which for us is a paradise, will become for him a prison.

QUINTAL: We can't risk our necks so's some Indian kid can have a tumble.

CHRISTIAN's head drops.

CHRISTIAN: Within two months we visit Tahiti and invite further female volunteers.

NED: Why such specific timing?

CHRISTIAN: I set Bligh adrift on the twenty-eighth of April 1789, nine months ago. My calculations are that if he has made land –

MCKOY: – Bligh is fish food.

CHRISTIAN: – I know Bligh and I promise you, he lives! The earliest a navy Man O'War will dock in Tahiti will be one year from that day. That gives us three months.

QUINTAL: That ship must burn, it's as good as a pin in the Admiralty map!

MCKOY: Burn her!

NED: The proposal is 'we retain the Bounty'. All in favour?

CHRISTIAN, BROWN, ADAMS and NED raise their hands.

NED: That she should burn?

MCKOY and QUINTAL raise their hands.

NED: The vote is four to two, we retain the ship.

QUINTAL: No! My damned neck is at stake! *(Re BROWN.)* He won't swing! And he won't swing, so's why does they get a vote?

CHRISTIAN: Because he is a fellow Yarner!

QUINTAL: Damn your Yarning court!

Enter HITI, still wearing his newly acquired tunic which is now covered in blood.

BROWN: My God, the boy is injured! What is it?

QUINTAL: He ain't injured.

MCKOY: What blood is this yer little devil?

HITI looks to NED. QUINTAL sees this, and looks to NED, and then CHRISTIAN.

QUINTAL: Shhhh! Quiet! Listen.

They listen to the silence.

QUINTAL: The dogs. They're not barking. The little bugger's killed the dogs. Have you killed my dog?

HITI: Aye, aye, sir.

QUINTAL: Who told you to kill my dog?

HITI: Mister Young tell him me, Titreano tell him Mister Young.

QUINTAL looks at CHRISTIAN.

QUINTAL: You told him to kill my dog?

QUINTAL goes to the fire pit and takes a burning stick, and heads off down stage right.

MCKOY: Yer didnae trust us to vote the right way on the dogs then Mister Christian. Eh?

MCKOY goes to the fire and he too picks out a burning stick, and heads down to the Bounty.

CHRISTIAN: Rather I had no faith in my power to persuade you.

NED: We can stop them!

CHRISTIAN: Today possibly. Tomorrow?

NED: If they burn the Bounty this island is a prison.

CHRISTIAN: And our sentence a life sentence.

The remaining mutineers walk down stage and watch the Bounty burn. The light fades and the glow of the burning Bounty dominates. They are joined by the women and the native men, all lit by the burning Bounty. Some of the women cry. HITI steps down stage for direct address.

End of scene.

ACT 2
SCENE 1

The Bounty burning at night, segues into a new morning.

HITI: *(Direct address.)* Everybody did nothing, only watching. The women crying watch, the men sit holding their heads in their hands like stones, and watch. Me, Hiti, Midshipman, I didn't watch, I ran down the path screaming, 'that is my ship, my English navy ship, don't burn my ship!' But Mister Quintal he punched me in the mouth. That shut me up double quick. I lost one tooth and one tooth is now wobbly. This one, can you see, it is loose. I can't eat meat on this side. Only fruit this side, meat the other. My mother had a saying 'good days are life, bad days are history'. And this story I tell you today is the history, not the life, I don't do every day, that would send you to sleep, which would be dangerous because some of you are standing up, so the next bad day, the next history day, is today, one year later. I was collecting crayfish, they're easy to catch, and fat, you just have to be quick, and I am quick. Like that. See. That's quick. And I am standing in a rock pool, staring into the water, a wave will make the water bubble, and you stand still wait for it to calm. When the water cleared I saw the face of a woman staring at me. And I was so scared I couldn't scream, just opened my mouth like this, oh, oh, oh, and my mouth like this, oh, oh, oh. And the water around my knees is blood. She is dead.

Women screaming. HITI runs up to the eyrie where CHRISTIAN is staring out to sea. Enter OHA carrying the wet and bloody body of Paurai. She wears good leather English boots. Enter NED.

NED: John Adams' wife?

OHA: Eeyeuh!

TE'O: Paurai! She's dead.

Enter TE LAHU.

TE LAHU: At last she has stopped crying.

Enter CHRISTIAN and everyone except ADAMS and MCKOY.

NED: Adams' wife.

CHRISTIAN: Where did you find her?

OHA: Hiti him see her down ted side.

MENALEE: She was crying all day long today.

TE LAHU: She cried all day every day.

QUINTAL: English!

CHRISTIAN: She must have slipped collecting eggs.

NED: Or leapt.

TE'O: Na! Es storle. Her no leap leap!

QUINTAL: Pushed?

CHRISTIAN: We must cancel today's yarning.

NED: Hiti. Get Mister Adams.

HITI goes off. MCKOY arrives.

MCKOY: Paurai? Adams was sick of her. The wee lass was always bawling.

CHRISTIAN: This is not the time for speculation. Mister Adams does not know she's dead.

BROWN: He knows she's dead.

CHRISTIAN: Why do you say that?

BROWN: Because he's not here.

Enter ADAMS and HITI.

ADAMS: *(Beat.)* Them's my boots. Give 'em here.

HITI takes her boots off and gives them to ADAMS.

We got a yarning at midday, to talk about the hole in my fence. I say we meet now, we're all here. And we can add to the business some talk about which woman I'm gonna be getting now that this one's dead.

ADAMS walks to the log and sits. The women take Paurai's body away.

CHRISTIAN: It doesn't seem right.

MCKOY: We's all here now.

QUINTAL: I wanna know if Reckless Jack pushed her off!

ADAMS squares up to QUINTAL.

QUINTAL: Come on then. I'll rip your head off and shit down your neck.

BROWN: Let us yarn, like gentlemen.

NED: The business today was to be the dispute between Mister Christian and Mister Adams over a fence. However, the tragic events –

ADAMS: – I'm not letting up on my fence on account of the death of an Indian.

BROWN: Your wife.

Some laugh.

ADAMS: I can't go another day with an 'ole in my fence.

QUINTAL: Did you push her?

NED: It is alleged that Mister Christian threatened to shoot Mister Adams' sow.

CHRISTIAN: If his sow were to break through the fence and on to my crops, yes.

QUINTAL: *(Prodding ADAMS.)* You pushed her didn't you?

NED: Whose fence is it?

ADAMS: The fence is mine, the hole is his.

Laughter.

NED: *(To ADAMS.)* Why don't you mend the fence?

ADAMS: My fence ain't the problem, the problem's his hole.

Laughter.

NED: Mister Christian, is it your hole?

CHRISTIAN: My goat made the hole.

QUINTAL: So it's your goat's hole?

Laughter.

CHRISTIAN: My goat made a hole in his fence, yes.

NED: Ergo the hole is your responsibility. Surely it is your task to repair it?

ADAMS: If he touches my fence I'll kill him!

Laughter.

CHRISTIAN: This is the nub! On Tubuai I had this man clapped in irons for whoring ashore contrary to my orders. He has never forgiven me that. Adams raised a musket at me, over his fence.

NED: Did you threaten Mister Christian with a musket?

ADAMS: Aye, I did and I'll do it again, if his goat comes through that hole he tutored her to make.

BROWN: *(To ADAMS.)* Why do you not splice the hole?

ADAMS: I'll mend his hole but I want a consideration for the labour.

NED: Ah! Your price?

ADAMS: I want for candlenuts.

NED: *(To CHRISTIAN.)* A basket of candlenuts?

QUINTAL: Or he'll shove you off the cliff.

CHRISTIAN: Agreed.

NED: *(Writing.)* And recorded. The second item of business.

ADAMS: I can't live here without a woman.

QUINTAL: If it's a woman you want, go to Nottingham.

CHRISTIAN: What a different situation this might be if we had a two hundred and fifteen ton schooner which could reach Tahiti in a month.

MCKOY: Why disnae Reckless Jack take Fasto off Oha?

CHRISTIAN: Because Oha is a man not a beast!

MCKOY: Aye, but Oha spends all day on the mooch.

QUINTAL: You got to start him to get him on his feet.

CHRISTIAN: You whip Oha?

MCKOY: Every time you turn around the man's back on his arse.

CHRISTIAN: Oha is high born, he's a chief!

MCKOY: Aye, that's why you have to start him.

NED: Mister Brown, can you apply your intellect to this conundrumical dilemma.

BROWN: If Mister Adams were given Te'o's daughter, Scully –

ADAMS: – she's a year old!

QUINTAL: She'll be on the reds by thirteen, if not afore.

MCKOY: Yous'll have tae beat your meat for thirteen years man!

Laughter.

QUINTAL: I know Reckless Jack, you won't agree to that, you're a right mutton monger, ain't yer.

ADAMS: I want Mareva or Fasto. I prefer the look of Fasto.

QUINTAL: All cats are grey, when the candle's out.

CHRISTIAN: Mareva is married to Menalee and Fasto to Oha. They both have husbands!

ADAMS: Ask them two girls what they want. I'll wager they choose an Englishman over a slave any day of the week.

CHRISTIAN: So if Fasto is given to Adams then Mareva has to whore herself to three men?

QUINTAL: Aye, that could work.

MCKOY: It's nae hardship for them Indians to share a woman.

ADAMS: And I'm Christian ain't I. God said go forth and multiply. I can't do that on me own now can I?

BROWN: The two native marriages have not produced children. Mister Christian has a child, Quintal a son, and McKoy's woman is carrying again.

NED: Are you saying that the native couplings will ever be barren?

BROWN: These girls can volunteer a miscarriage through violent massage. There is no desire, within the native women who are married to native men, to produce.

CHRISTIAN: *Because* the child will be born a slave!

ADAMS: Aye, that's my point.

NED: *(To BROWN.)* Mister Brown, what population do you think our island can sustain?

BROWN: Many many more than we. Perhaps ten fold.

NED: Who is your preferred wife?

ADAMS: Either of them'll do.

QUINTAL: Damn you! I thought it was love!

NED: Might I suggest we draw straws.

CHRISTIAN: *(Exasperated.)* The drawing of straws?! For a woman?!

NED: It will avoid covetousness, a good thing in God's eyes.

NED picks two straws.

Fasto, the short straw. Mareva, the long straw.

QUINTAL: You got them the wrong way round.

NED: Choose John.

ADAMS chooses.

NED: The short straw. Fasto.

QUINTAL: Woo! Lucky girl.

NED: Fasto. Step forward!

CHRISTIAN: I'm disgusted.

CHRISTIAN exits to his eyrie. MI MITTI follows. FASTO and OHA step forward.

NED: Fasto. The Yarning court has decided that you are to be wife to Mister Adams.

FASTO takes a step forward, almost keen, but is held by OHA.

OHA: Ay es ra'atira! Chief! No man tek woman fe me disday!

QUINTAL raises his musket at OHA.

QUINTAL: Let that girl go or I'll blow your damned brains into the ocean.

OHA assesses his situation. MCKOY draws a knife. He lets FASTO go. She skips to ADAMS.

ADAMS: Stand behind me girl.

OHA: Ay es ra'atira no manuhane! Ay no born fe dig dig yoo groun!

OHA turns and runs into the woods. The situation relaxes.

NED: *(Standing.)* McKoy, do we have any leg irons remaining? Or have you formed them all into hoes?

MCKOY: I'm working on them now.

NED: Then stop the work. I fear, we're going to need them for their original purpose.

End of scene.

ACT 2
SCENE 2

Up in the eyrie cave. CHRISTIAN is standing, keenly looking through the telescope. His log book is beside him.

MI MITTI: Titreano, my husband, are you crazy?!

CHRISTIAN: I voted against!

MI MITTI: This yarning yarning! What are you always talking about? In England, does King Toote have one vote and all the English manuhane have another one vote?

CHRISTIAN: Another vote. Not another one vote. And don't repeat words. We wouldn't say yarning yarning or siki siki.

MI MITTI: I am not learning English now, I am asking you what kind of chief you are?

CHRISTIAN: To answer your question. In England Captain Cook would have a vote, yes, and the English people would not. So, in that regard, Pitcairn is in advance of England. And I am proud of that.

MI MITTI: What are you looking for with the telescope? You have trouble here today, and you are looking out to sea.

CHRISTIAN: I thought I saw a ship.

MI MITTI: There is no ship, there will be no ship, we are nowhere. Your heart is in England.

CHRISTIAN: I think about my mother, and the pain that my actions must have brought her. You understand the importance of honour.

MI MITTI: Your mother in England will not die with a knife across her throat. Your wife on Pitcairn might. You must be a big man now, and kill Oha.

CHRISTIAN: I cannot kill men that have done me no wrong!

MI MITTI: Oha will have to kill you! You took his woman away. You must kill him first! Why did you not kill Captain Bligh? Have I married a little man!?

She is gone, descending. CHRISTIAN looks on. She passes NED ascending.

NED: I sent Menalee after Oha. He might take the canoe. I am proposing that we burn it.

CHRISTIAN: Why not? Burning is established as the solution to all problems.

NED: We could let him take, he'd die at sea, and that would solve one problem.

CHRISTIAN: We need the canoe.

NED: You should've seen Fasto take the hand of Adams? Keen! Adams, a common man to her is the conjunction of Apollo and Achilles.

CHRISTIAN: We are all gods in their eyes.

NED: Add to this the natural licentiousness of their women.

CHRISTIAN: The marriages of the men and their chosen women have been recognised. That should decrease the incidence of venereals.

NED: But increase the incidence of adultery.

CHRISTIAN: Is there adultery?

NED: All the men find Mi Mitti attractive –

CHRISTIAN: – my wife! –

NED: – But Quintal presses.

CHRISTIAN: He wouldn't dare.

NED: He understands that Mi Mitti is ra'atira. He knows her only choice –

CHRISTIAN: – was between you and I.

NED: Yet Quintal is uniquely excited by, what might be called, the general levelling.

CHRISTIAN: Thank you my friend. I will bear it in mind.

NED: You had promised to enthrall me with the theatre of the stars.

NED turns a page in CHRISTIAN's star log.

CHRISTIAN: You will see no ascent of Venus, here, or in your lifetime. They arrive in pairs, eight years apart, but separated by one hundred and twenty years. It's a rare entertainment.

NED: With an extravagant interval. I wouldn't wait for the second act.

CHRISTIAN: Venus is not the only show in town. My calculations promise a total eclipse of the sun. And it's not all amusement Ned, my calendar is sound and I can now divine the position of each planet and the moon to a specific day.

NED: I'm impressed.

CHRISTIAN: Reason. Muster the men.

NED descends. HITI arrives.

HITI: Titreano! Es storle? Yoo tek wife off fe Oha?

CHRISTIAN: The yarning court made a decision, not I.

HITI: Him chief semuz King Toote!

CHRISTIAN: Hiti, have you seen Quintal talking to my wife?

HITI: Aye, wan time an unuduwan time.

CHRISTIAN: I want you to tell me if he approaches her. And what is her reaction.

HITI: Ay gwen in dem wood wid di long eye.

CHRISTIAN: No! I am not asking you to spy on them. Just let me know if they speak. Go on then, off you go.

HITI doesn't move.

What is it?

HITI: Ay wan woman.

CHRISTIAN: You're too young.

HITI: No! Wan dawn, uderwan dawn, ha unuderwan dawn.

CHRISTIAN: Every dawn, yes, what do you do every dawn?

HITI: Ay hide me in di big one iron tree yonder, down ted side.

CHRISTIAN: I know it. Where the women bathe.

HITI: Aye, aye! Owuz women no ken ay is in di tree.

CHRISTIAN: You hide? They don't know you're in the tree.

HITI: Eeyeuh! Ay see dem. Me feelin' big fe Mata in me heart.

CHRISTIAN: Hiti, some advice. Mata is very pretty, yes. And she is Ned's wife. And don't try and grow up too quickly, you might not like it when you do.

End of scene.

ACT 2
SCENE 3

OHA and MENALEE in the woods hiding.

OHA: Don't look at me. You should not even look at me. I am ra'atira, a chief, high born. You are manuhane, you should not be able to speak to me even. And yet I have had to share a woman with you, a manuhane.

MENALEE: Yes, that must be very difficult for you. But it is a great honour for me.

OHA: Everything is different here. But I must have a wife!

MENALEE: Yes! You're a chief. You can have any woman you choose. Titreano has deceived you. His promises to you of land, and wealth are like the wind.

OHA: On Tubuai I had many women.

MENALEE: He makes you work the land. Which is stupid. Stupid because you've never worked, and you're all fat, which is how it should be. Your job is to eat.

OHA: Every night since I was thirteen I have had a woman. One night I had seven women. All sisters. Ah, yes. A great great night.

MENALEE: Titreano has made the manuhane ra'atira, and the ra'atira manuhane. I don't understand why anyone would want to turn the world upside down.

OHA: Night is day, and day is night.

MENALEE: I left Tahiti because he promised me my own farm. And when we arrived here my heart lifted.

OHA: You're a farmer, you understand the soil. I don't.

MENALEE: No, you're useless.

OHA: Useless?

MENALEE: I mean, you're not a farmer, and I have to do half your work.

OHA: The land would be easier to work if it was mine.

MENALEE: I'm a slave twice over. Once to them and again to you. Which is a great honour.

OHA: I have a plan.

MENALEE: Take the canoe?

OHA: Why leave such a plentiful island? With so many women.

MENALEE: Ah! Kill the English?

OHA: There are enough women here for me to live like a chief, and you would have Mareva for yourself.

MENALEE: But I cannot kill Ned Young. He is my taio.

OHA: Taio! He cannot be your taio, he's not one of us.

MENALEE: I can't kill my taio. I could kill the others, and you kill my taio!?

OHA: So be it.

MENALEE: We have no muskets.

OHA: You, walk into the village and take a musket, and bring it to me. Say you are going hunting for a pig.

MENALEE: Very clever. Good! Tomorrow I will say that I need a musket to hunt a pig.

OHA grabs him, shakes him.

OHA: You are hunting pigs for me *today*!

MENALEE: Today?

OHA: Today!

MENALEE: Today!

MENALEE bows before OHA, and exits.

End of scene.

ACT 2
SCENE 4

NED YOUNG is on BROWN's ground. BROWN is working sorting cuttings.

NED: Look at this! William, you have turned the Garden of Eden into… Norwich.

BROWN: What do you want Ned Young?

NED: Does Pitcairn have yeast?

BROWN: McKoy begs me for yeast every day for his distillery. He's using a sugar beet mash and failing with it.

NED: For want of yeast?

BROWN: Yeast and an education.

NED: I am not in league with those two.

BROWN: Do you have your own distillery?

NED: Look man! Pitcairn's yeast is not your yeast.

BROWN: It is, and I am its jailer. To have Quintal and McKoy unfettered with an endless supply of alcohol would be suicide for us all.

NED: I am ill. I need yeast for an essay at a cure.

BROWN: I don't believe you.

NED: My father considered it to be a blight in my African blood. Mata found me on the floor, faint.

BROWN: I know of no medicines that depend on yeast.

NED: You will not hoard power on this island! We, are all levelled, thus your knowledge is my knowledge. And, my life is at stake!

BROWN: Your life?

NED: Aye, my life.

BROWN: Do you swear to keep the knowledge from McKoy?

NED: I do.

BROWN: *(Beat.)* The root of the ti tree.

NED: Thank you.

NED turns and leaves.

You're a feculent beast aren't you Brown. Ugly as sin itself. In the whole of your life you couldn't get a woman to even look at you, until you beached on Tahiti. Whence you filled your boots. For six months. I watched you. Lucifer in a permanent tumble. Pitiful.

End of scene.

ACT 2
SCENE 5

MATA direct address, but with TE LAHU preparing to dance.

MATA: Te Lahu is Arioi. Arioi are human, not god, but special. On Tahiti we carry the Arioi about the place, so that they don't have to touch the floor. On Tahiti Arioi nail clippings, hair and shit is sacred. The Arioi live in bands of about fifteen to twenty men and women and their job is to give surprises from village to village and we must feed them, for they are not allowed to work. Do you have this in England? Performers who don't work in the fields, and the workers have an obligation to feed them if they do performances? You do? What are they called? On Tahiti the men of the Arioi they can make you laugh with just their penises. They pull the skin and their two stones about to make shapes, like a canoe, then like a dog, or two chickens. One Arioi I saw made his penis look like an old man with no teeth. It stayed with me for many days. Most of the Arioi surprises are about sex. My favourite surprise is called 'fishing'. There is a short bit about fishing at the beginning but very quickly everyone is having sex in the boat, and there is no more fishing after that. I have seen Te Lahu perform the fishing surprise, and she was brilliant. At the end she had two men in her, one in the front hole, and one in the back hole, and they lift her off the ground and carry her into a canoe. No hands! Ha, ha! Yes! It was really funny and everyone laughed. Te Lahu is the only Arioi on Pitcairn so she performs her surprises alone. I think we're ready to start.

TE LAHU performs her dance. Essentially it illustrates OHA's predicament, once a chief now a slave, being beaten, to the ground, gets up, beaten to the ground, gets up, beaten to the ground, gets up, beaten to the ground. And then sharpening his axe ready to kill his oppressors. The women gather and join in with the chorus. MENALEE provides percussion.

TE LAHU: *(In Tahitian.)* Why does the black man sharpen his axe?
Why does the black man sharpen his axe?
To kill the white man,
to kill the white man

ALL WOMEN: *(In Tahitian.)* Why does the black man sharpen his axe?
Why does the black man sharpen his axe?

To kill the white man,
to kill the white man

CHRISTIAN: Mi Mitti, translate for me please.

MI MITTI: Why does the black man sharpen his axe, to kill the white man, to kill the white man.

She walks away. He ponders, then rings the bell. Enter MCKOY.

CHRISTIAN: McKoy! Manacles! Bring your musket too!

MCKOY: Aye, aye, sir.

MCKOY heads off. QUINTAL and ADAMS arrive.

QUINTAL: What is it? A ship?

CHRISTIAN: No! Quintal, Adams, arrest Menalee and Hiti.

QUINTAL: Aye, aye sir.

QUINTAL exits. ADAMS drags MENALEE over. Enter MCKOY with manacles which he strings around the tree.

ADAMS: We got to kill all the native men now.

CHRISTIAN: We'll do no such thing! You'll take direction from me!

ADAMS: By whose authority.

CHRISTIAN: Necessity itself!

Enter QUINTAL abusing HITI.

QUINTAL: Go on, you dog, move!

CHRISTIAN: Fetter them!

QUINTAL: Aye, aye sir.

CHRISTIAN: Ned, keep the women back.

QUINTAL: *(To TE LAHU.)* Oi! Stand off!

QUINTAL clips TE LAHU round the ear.

CHRISTIAN: McKoy! Get these women back!

MCKOY: Aye, aye sir!

MCKOY shoos back the women who stay and watch. MI MITTI stays watching CHRISTIAN and he plays to her, to prove his leadership.

CHRISTIAN: Menalee!? Does Oha have a musket?

MENALEE: Ay no bin see no musket wid him.

HITI: Titreano mi taio! Yoo no ka kill me! Mi taoi!

CHRISTIAN: I will not let you be harmed. *(To MENALEE.)* Where is Oha?

MENALEE: Kah wah!

QUINTAL kicks him in the groin.

QUINTAL: Speak the truth you damned dog!

CHRISTIAN: How do you know he has no musket? You must have spoken with him. Where is he hiding?

QUINTAL punches him. CHRISTIAN seems happy with that.

NED: Menalee, you may be my taio, and I love you like a brother, but if you are in league with Oha I will kill you myself.

MENALEE: Him yonder ted side. Him wan me join him. Fetch him muskets.

MCKOY: We got to kill these two now sir, then we form a vigilante and hunt down the black laird.

CHRISTIAN: *(To MENALEE.)* No. Release Menalee.

BROWN: Aye, aye.

WILLIAMS releases MENALEE.

CHRISTIAN: Menalee, this is a test of your loyalty. The prize is your life. Take this bowie knife, this musket –

Objections from the men.

– he has no lead, it is not a threat to us. Offer up the musket to Oha, take him some food, as a deception, as proof of your friendship. And when his guard is dropped, kill him.

QUINTAL: Oh aye, I like this!

MENALEE: Ay tek him musket an' wickles. Him turn back. I kill him bignayf.

CHRISTIAN: But! If the sun sinks behind the hill, and you have not returned with word that the task is completed, I will kill the boy Hiti.

HITI: Mi am yous taio Titreano!

NED: How do we know he's killed Oha?

CHRISTIAN: Menalee is a man of his word.

MENALEE: Ay gwen do dis fe yoo Titreano.

QUINTAL: Don't lie you devil, you'll do this 'cause you love your own life.

MENALEE is freed. He turns to go.

NED: *(Playing to MI MITTI.)* Wait! When you return, having killed Oha, deliver your word to Mister Christian, for you are a man of your word, but deliver Oha's head to me.

MENALEE: Him tete?

NED: As proof of the task completed.

ADAMS: And his hands. To be sure.

QUINTAL: Damn your blood Adams! We don't need his hands, we'll have his head!

NED: Go!

MENALEE exits.

CHRISTIAN: We muster again at sunset. Back to your houses, lock your doors, secure your muskets.

The men disperse. Except ADAMS and NED. CHRISTIAN exits to his eyrie.

NED: *(To ADAMS.)* You've started a war John Adams.

ADAMS: Some folk take things the wrong way.

HITI: Please sir! Some water.

NED: Of course.

NED goes to fetch water.

HITI: Will dem kill me?

NED: I'll not let them.

MI MITTI walks past NED. NED looks after her. She makes eye contact. HITI sees this.

NED: Mi Mitti? I would counsel against bathing whilst Oha is at large. It is not safe. Go home. Let your husband protect you.

MI MITTI: My husband is not at home.

MI MITTI exits. HITI and NED watch her go. After a pause, NED follows.

End of scene.

ACT 2
SCENE 6

MENALEE in the woods.

MENALEE: Chief Oha! It is me! Menalee!! I have brought you some food!

OHA appears with a musket raised pointing at MENALEE.

You've got a musket?!

OHA: I stole it from Mister Brown's house.

MENALEE: Good! So now we have two muskets. I have an axe too.

OHA: Why would they give you a musket and an axe?

MENALEE: They're crazy. The musket is to kill you and the axe is to chop off your head. Don't worry, I'm not going to. I've got some food here.

OHA: Do you have any meat? There is fruit out here, but no meat.

MENALEE: I've got plenty of meat. Ha! They gave me that as well!

OHA: Where is Hiti?

MENALEE: Hiti will join us after dark. By tomorrow we will have three muskets.

OHA: Tomorrow will be a great day.

MENALEE: Let us eat.

OHA: Were you followed?

MENALEE: No, no, they are stupid men. They didn't think of following me.

OHA: Come, I have a place to hide, it is shaded and we can eat and sleep.

OHA turns his back and walks off. MENALEE pauses, and then follows him.

End of scene.

ACT 2
SCENE 7

MI MITTI and NED.

NED: I was concerned for your safety.

MI MITTI: I don't believe you.

NED: What other motivation could I have?

MI MITTI: You're a man.

NED: And you are married, to my leader.

MI MITTI: You remember. You have a wife.

NED: Mata is young, yes, and pretty but she is manuhane

NED sits, invites her to join him.

MI MITTI: I can't sit with you.

NED: Au contraire. You can sit with me. You sat with Captain Cook, you told me that once.

MI MITTI: King Toote was ra'atira.

NED: Captain Cook was manuhane. He became ra'atira, through learning and position.

MI MITTI: Born manuhane, die manuhane. Born ra'atira, die ra'atira.

NED: Not in England. Your husband is a perfect example of this phenomenon, but in reverse. Titreano, was born aristocracy, ra'atira, but, as you know, became manuhane. His brother played ducks and drakes with the family fortune.

MI MITTI: What is ducks and drakes?

NED: When you throw pebbles across the water and they bounce, and sink, forever.

MI MITTI: Titreano brother threw their money into the sea?

NED: Metaphorically. In truth drink and gambling. Has he not told you this? Their family have nothing. Even I have more. My inheritance on St. Kitts is intact. A sugar plantation ten times the size of this island.

MI MITTI: So Titreano has lied to me?

NED: Omitted to mention.

MI MITTI stands, distressed.

What is it?

MI MITTI: I cannot sleep with manuhane.

MI MITTI turns to leave. NED stands.

NED: I thought you knew. I feel terrible, as if I have betrayed a confidentiality. I beg you, say nothing of this to him.

MI MITTI runs off.

End of scene.

ACT 2
SCENE 8

HITI is manacled.

HITI: Will this history day be the last day of my life? I had never thought one could see the sun move, it moves so slowly, taking twelve hours to get from there to there. Often I watched the sun and it doesn't move, you take your eyes off it and make play or work, and then you look back and it has moved, but never when you look at it. The sun always waits until you turn your back. And then it skips across the sky like a mouse. But that day I looked at the sun and I could see it moving, slowly yes, slowly, but moving, moving towards night and the end of my life.

Enter MATA.

MATA: Hiti? Water?

HITI: Please! Yes!

She gives him water and walks off.

HITI: Did you see that?! She gave me water! Why did she give me water? If she hated me she would not give me water. So at least she doesn't hate me. And she called me Hiti. By name. I think she did. Did she?! Oh my God, she must love me! I love her name, her full name is Mataohu. I love to say it. Mataohu.

Enter CHRISTIAN. He looks at the sun. He rings the bell. Others begin to gather.

HITI: No kill me! Titreano. Ay bin di best damned good Midshipman. Yoo kah kill me, ay yoo taoi!

The sun goes down over the hill.

CHRISTIAN: I am fully aware of my social obligations as your taio. Onerous.

One by one people gather. QUINTAL puts a knife under HITI's chin.

QUINTAL: How do you want to die yer little Snacker? Knife or lead?

HITI: Lead. Yoo be quick.

MCKOY: We'll waste nae lead on a little devil like you.

QUINTAL: Can we burn him?

MCKOY: Aye, I ain't never seen a man burn.

QUINTAL: We lack for sport.

CHRISTIAN: Whatever we do with the wretch it will not be for your amusement.

Enter MENALEE carrying OHA's head by the hair. Everyone gathers.

HITI: Aaaaaaghhh!

QUINTAL inspects the head.

QUINTAL: It's definitely Oha's head. I reckon the chief is dead sir.

Laughter. MENALEE approaches CHRISTIAN still holding the head by the hair.

MENALEE: Titreano! Yoo see!? Ay es servant to yoo. Semuz brother!

CHRISTIAN: Out of my sight!

NED: Good work Menalee.

CHRISTIAN: McKoy! Release the boy!

MCKOY releases HITI. He runs to CHRISTIAN and hugs him. MENALEE turns to NED, approaches him. He puts the head on the ground before him.

MENALEE: Mister Young. Yoo mek me fetch him head.

NED: I commissioned this horror in the service of society in the hope that it will furnish us with a lasting peace.

CHRISTIAN: Go now, back to your labours, gather your wives and children and sleep peacefully knowing that there is no further threat to you.

The people disperse. CHRISTIAN turns to make the long ascent to his eyrie, as he does so he turns to MI MITTI, who turns her back on him. CHRISTIAN walks up the eyrie. MI MITTI approaches NED. NED grabs her hand. They kiss. CHRISTIAN does not see this. HITI does.

End of scene.

INTERVAL

ACT 3
SCENE 1

The women meet on the yarning log. TE LAHU, FASTO, TE'O, WALUA, MATA, and FASTO. MI MITTI is not there. They are animated. FASTO is being comforted. They are speaking Tahitian.

MATA: *(Direct address.)* Tahitian people, we like eating, and so we have a lot of fat people, and we like surfing, but our favourite thing is sex. We have sex everywhere, on the beach, outside, on the roof, and we don't care if anyone is watching. If people start throwing things then we might say something but that never happens. Young people go into the hills in a big group for days and do nothing but have sex with each other. It is a good way to make friends. Do you do that? And we have mahu. The Mahu are men but dress as women, talk like women and walk like women. They can tuck their penis inside themselves, make it disappear, look more like a woman. Do you have mahu? On Tahiti a wife can sleep with her husband's brothers and also his taio, and his honoured guests. Taio means best friend. Do you do that in England? It is good, but you have to be careful who you marry, and if you're clever you sleep with all the brothers first. Yes, we love sex, but one thing we don't allow is rape.

FASTO: *(Crying.)* Quintal –

WALUA: – my husband, what did he do to you?

FASTO: – He found me collecting birds eggs, on the cliffs, and he forced me.

TE LAHU: He raped you?

FASTO: Yes.

Uproar.

TE LAHU: Mammu! Mammu!

WALUA: What did you do, show him your tits!?

TE LAHU: Mammu! Mammu!

FASTO: Rape is tapu.

TE LAHU: On Tahiti it is punishable by death.

WALUA: Or you can give meat to the family.

FASTO: No! It is always death!

Uproar.

MATA: *(To WALUA.)* Fasto is not alone. Your man has forced me three times.

WALUA: You?! You horny bitch. I don't believe it.

TE LAHU: Mammu! Walua. Do you know your man does this?

WALUA: Quintal, is a good man. He has given me children.

FASTO: These things would not happen on Tahiti!

WALUA: *(To MATA.)* You should cover your tits up.

TE LAHU: No Tahitian will ever find happiness on Pitcairn.

WALUA: English women wrap up their tits.

FASTO: I want to go back to Tahiti.

TE'O: I don't.

WALUA: Me and Te'o, we're happy here. We have English husbands.

TE'O: Land.

WALUA: Children.

TE LAHU: We can return to Tahiti.

FASTO: We have no ship.

TE'O: Even if you had a boat, you don't know where Tahiti is.

TE LAHU: Titreano has The Bounty star reader. He can find Tahiti. But I saw him standing on the cliff yesterday. Where Paurai jump.

TE'O: Pushed.

TE LAHU: I hid, said nothing, he looked down at the stones below.

TE'O: Ned Young is pumping his wife.

WALUA: That baby of hers will be black.

FASTO: He loved Mi Mitti too much.

TE'O: Mi Mitti is nothing special.

WALUA: She walks about Pitcairn like a queen.

FASTO: She is a queen.

WALUA: I know.

FASTO: What do you mean then?

WALUA: What I mean is, who does she think she is?

FASTO: She thinks she's a queen.

WALUA: I know.

TE'O: You're an idiot.

WALUA: You keep your tits covered up.

TE LAHU: Does anyone know if Titreano is eating? Mata?

MATA: Why would I know?

TE'O: Because your husband is pumping his wife!

WALUA and TE'O laugh.

TE'O: Has Ned stopped sleeping with you?

MATA: Yes. He says I am manuhane and he is ra'atira.

WALUA: So who are you having sex with then?

TE'O: Stay away from McKoy or I'll kill you.

MATA: Te Lahu, do you think Titreano is suicidal?

WALUA: How long can a man go without a tumble?

TE LAHU: Titreano is our only chance of leaving Pitcairn. We need to protect him, like a child. From both himself, and from Ned Young and his friends.

FASTO: Te Lahu, you are arioi, I am scared, what will happen to us?

TE LAHU: Your man will kill your man, and your man will kill your man, and your man will kill my man.

MATA: What about Hiti?

WALUA: You like Hiti?

TE'O: You could have Titreano girl!

WALUA: How do we protect Titreano?

TE LAHU: We kidnap him.

NED and JOHN ADAMS approach. NED has his Bible.

MATA: Arrgh! Shit!!! Bible class!

TE LAHU stands.

TE LAHU: I am going to dance. You do their stupid book class, look stupid, like happy slaves, but inside be strong, we are taking control.

NED and ADAMS discuss that morning's class. TE LAHU slips away.

NED: They confound me John.

There is an artful fart amongst the women. They all giggle.

See! Our Lord creating the world in seven days doesn't impress them half as much as an artful fart.

ADAMS: Give 'em the miracles like grapeshot. Who could not be swayed by Christ walking on water?

NED: Our women! They all surf. This morning I thought I'd try the demon possessed mute.

ADAMS: No! The *blind*, demon possessed mute. That's better.

NED: Why?

ADAMS: 'Cause he's blind. As well as being demon possessed. It's more of a miracle then ain't it?

NED: A miracle is a miracle. Let's continue with the old testament. Solomon. At least they'll find the violence entertaining.

FASTO: Yourley tardey!

NED: Yes, sorry. Good morning ladies. Today Mister Adams is going to talk about the wisdom of Solomon. John.

ADAMS: Aye, King Solomon was really clever. He was the wisest man in Christendom.

NED: It wasn't called Christendom at that time John.

ADAMS: No? Why not?

NED: Christ hadn't yet been born.

FASTO: Woz Soloman good surfer samuz Christ?

NED: Yes. He was the surfing champion of all Judea.

SOME WOMEN: *(Very impressed.)* Ah!

ADAMS: Solomon had seven hundred wives.

FASTO: Him pump dem all?

NED: Each of his wives got satisfaction by him, yes, once a week.

TE'O: Na! Him pump one hundred times wuhn day?

ADAMS: *(Looks to NED, gets a nod.)* Yes.

FASTO: Him mus' him have balls semuz coconuts!

ADAMS: Yes. He did.

NED: And yet his wisdom was more remarkable than his –

TE'O: – coconut balls?

They laugh.

NED: Tell the ladies about his remarkable wisdom John.

ADAMS: One day there was a dispute. Two women was claiming to be the mother of the one little babby.

FASTO: Wa' not di true mother kill di thief woman?

ALL: Eeyeuh! Yes!

ADAMS: Mammu! Solomon says 'I'll chop the babby in two and you can have half each'. See?

Beat. NED's head drops.

FASTO: Him stupid. Di bebe would die.

NED: He knew the real mother would protect her child, and save its life by giving it to the imposter. Which she subsequently did.

WALUA: So di true ma give di bebe te di thief woman?

SOME: No. / Aue! / Eeyeuh! *(General confused groaning.)*

FASTO: Dat be stupid as chopp di bebe up in pieces!

NED: Solomon had no intention of dividing the child.

WOMEN: *(Realisation.)* Ah! / Oh.

Enter TE LAHU. She performs a dance. MATA rings the bell.

WALUA: Eeyeuh!

FASTO: Arioi dance!!

MATA: Surprises!

All the men arrive except MENALEE. Enter MI MITTI, she is very pregnant. During the dance everyone gathers, drawn by the women cheering. TE LAHU charts MI MITTI's relationship with FLETCHER CHRISTIAN, illustrated by a white dildo, and then her seduction by NED, illustrated by a black dildo. TE LAHU mimes the nine month gestation of the child, and then gives birth to a black aubergine, which cries like a baby. The women scream their applause. A silence falls, and all look to CHRISTIAN.

CHRISTIAN: *(To MI MITTI.)* My wife. I thought you were resting. The child is imminent.

MI MITTI: I came to see the Arioi dance.

CHRISTIAN: And you women, what are you doing sitting around? Is there not cloth to be made?

FASTO: We am learn 'bout King Solomon.

CHRISTIAN: From John Adams and Ned Young? The first can barely read, and the second elects himself a prophet to the women.

NED: Why do you libel me?

CHRISTIAN: Your life is a libel on the commandments!

NED: Which one of the ten?

CHRISTIAN: Thou shalt not commit adultery!

ADAMS: That's not the first commandment.

CHRISTIAN: I don't have to start at the beginning you damned feculent inbred!

QUINTAL: Adultery ain't so bad, here, is it?

BROWN: I didn't think you were one for the book Mister Christian.

CHRISTIAN: We do not need a book to be civilised! I accuse Ned Young of adultery with my wife!

QUINTAL: A duel!

MCKOY: Swords or pistols?!

ADAMS: Ned Young would swear on the Bible and his innocence will be proven.

CHRISTIAN: That book means nothing to him. It is exclusively an alternative authority to me, to my yarning court, to what I could have built here. It allows him to reject my every innovation.

NED: Who twixt you and I talks most like a prophet? 'My every innovation'; 'alternative to me' 'my yarning court'. These are megalomaniac phrases worthy of Bedlam.

CHRISTIAN: I am not mad!

QUINTAL: Also heard in Bedlam!

CHRISTIAN: To be consumed by reasonable fury is not to be mad! This girl, who took my heart; upturned my world; transformed me from gentleman to rover; from officer to dead man; from sceptic to supplicant; for whom I took a ship, and cast my captain, my family, and my reputation to the sharks. This girl! With whom I fell into a fever of hope that transformed all the ill and pestilence of the world into dreams of a different future in Arcadia. This girl! I taught her English, she taught me Tahitian, I made her my wife, and I swore to worship her with my last breath. It seems this girl has betrayed me with this man, Ned Young, who, on the wooden world of the ship, I counted as a gentleman, an officer and a friend. But he, with only words, traduced me, diminished me, and then stole away the purpose of my days. I may not yet be mad, but I will never love again, and am condemned, by my proximity, as we all are approximate to each other on this fist of rock, to forty years of torment as witness to their cooing. I would rather spend my next forty years put to the rack. Mister McKoy build me a wheel!

MI MITTI: Titreano, you deceived me!

(To them all.) On Tahiti he told my father, the king –

QUINTAL: In English you damned bitch!

MI MITTI: – Him say he high born, but truth is him family has no land, no houses, no wealth.

QUINTAL: I said –

CHRISTIAN: Let her have her say.

MI MITTI: Him lie to me, and him lie to you the night he sailed from Tahiti. It is I who has been betrayed, insulted, and disrespected.

MCKOY: What d'yer say to them? Yer speak English! Come on!

MI MITTI: Him family not ra'atira, them manuhane!

Grumblings amongst the Tahitians.

CHRISTIAN: Why in this land of plenty, where we could all have too much, are you still fettered by prejudice? God made no social divisions. 'When Adam delved and Eve span, where then was the gentleman?'

ADAMS: You ain't a believer, so don't go enlisting God's wisdom.

CHRISTIAN: Those words were written by a man.

ADAMS: Who?

BROWN: The preacher John Ball. Leader of the Peasants' revolt.

CHRISTIAN: We are born equal, the only divisions are of our own invention! Ha!

ADAMS: What's funny?

CHRISTIAN: But it should come to this! We had this island! This virgin leaf of vellum! So perfect a sanctuary, and what have we done with it? We have stained it, soiled it with our traditions both English, and Tahitian.

TE LAHU: Youwuz talk talk fe dis man samuz dis man an' dis man samuz dis man. Wot bout de woman?

CHRISTIAN: Women?

TE LAHU: Ah wuken too. Yowuz plenty ground, yowuz plenty goat, me none.

QUINTAL: You're a woman!

TE LAHU: Ay ken dat cock brain!

QUINTAL advances but is held back by MCKOY.

CHRISTIAN: Your husband, Mister Brown, has an equal share of the island. So you are equal.

TE LAHU: Wosing me ground?!

CHRISTIAN: Your husband's land is your land.

QUINTAL pushes TE LAHU back.

BROWN: Can we return to the matter in hand and not be distracted by the fantastical. Ned Young. You stand accused of a serious crime.

NED: I am innocent of these charges.

CHRISTIAN: Thou shalt not bear false witness!

BROWN: Ned, would you swear on the book?

NED: Without hesitation.

BROWN takes the Bible from ADAMS. He steps forward, and holds it before NED.

BROWN: Place your hand on the book.

NED does so.

Er… Let me think how to word this.

CHRISTIAN: Have you lain with my wife?! Have you soiled this woman with your foul seed?!

BROWN: Thank you. Er…what he said.

NED: No. I have not.

CHRISTIAN: Ha! On the Bible!!
(Mainly to ADAMS.) And when that whore's child is born black you will take a minute to consider this day.

CHRISTIAN turns and exits to his cave.

QUINTAL: The sport's over lads. Back to work!

The men disperse. BROWN collars a somewhat reluctant WILLIAMS and they follow CHRISTIAN up to the eyrie, this is seen by NED. The women disperse. HITI throws a banana at MATA.

MATA: Why are you throwing fruit at me little boy?

HITI: Do you want to go fishing? With me.

MATA: No. Why would I?

HITI: To get some fish.

MATA: *(Laughing.)*

HITI: It's fun. We can swim. I know a pool that gets hot.

MATA: I haven't eaten yet.

HITI: No, don't eat. You shouldn't eat and then go swimming, you might drown.

MATA: That's why I said no, to fishing, with you.

HITI: I know you love me. You brought me water when I was chained. You don't have a husband now.

MATA: You're a boy.

HITI: Me heart feels full for you.

MATA: You're boiling over are you?

HITI: Yes I am. I'll catch a whole basket of fish for you. Mata, I promise.

MATA: Where is this hot pool?

HITI: Near Paurai drop off.

MATA: Let's go then big man.

HITI: Aye, aye.

She walks off, he's shocked, but turns to the audience and gives a double thumbs up, and runs off.

End of scene.

ACT 3
SCENE 2

CHRISTIAN in his eyrie with BROWN.

CHRISTIAN: Have you come to offer me your wife?

BROWN: No, my loyalty, and an idea.

CHRISTIAN: The yarning court is the mortar and the men the pestle to crush all ideas.

BROWN: You know that Quintal raped Fasto?
And yesterday he lashed Menalee and rubbed salt in his wounds.

CHRISTIAN: For sport?

BROWN: What other reason could there be.

CHRISTIAN: Then it is excused, for it is sport we lack!

BROWN: We should kill Quintal. And McKoy.

CHRISTIAN: This is your idea? A man of your intelligence.

BROWN: Think of it like we're a crop and we have a blight. You'd cut it out.

CHRISTIAN: Do you propose a fair trial? Or something more summary.

BROWN: We kill them in their sleep. You are my captain. My only hope. I fear for my own skin. Quintal and McKoy are not the sum of our troubles. Menalee has a musket, hidden away. He intends to kill us all, the English men.

CHRISTIAN: How do you know this?

BROWN: Mareva, Menalee's wife, told Fasto. He might spare Ned Young. Because he is taio to him. And Ned and Adams are close because of their faith so that is three men. And we are three.

CHRISTIAN: Two surely.

BROWN: Three. Hiti, your taio, would be faithful.

CHRISTIAN: Yes, he would. Why do wish to align with me?

BROWN: I have no desire to live under the cosh of the Bible.

CHRISTIAN: This hill is defendable. The cave a redoubt.

BROWN: We should supply it. Meat, water, powder.

CHRISTIAN: We could start at first light. Give me your hand.

BROWN proffers his hand, but it turns into hug with CHRISTIAN sobbing.

End of scene.

ACT 3
SCENE 3

MI MITTI, heavily pregnant, and NED at MI MITTI's house. Dark.

NED: I have offered Menalee my wife, and Brown's gardens if he kills Brown. We can populate this island how we wish, and deliver the paradise of our imaginations. As Queen, who would you be without?

MI MITTI: I keep all women.

NED: For contrast. None matches your beauty.

MI MITTI: I can no be Queen alone.

They kiss, and move into an embrace.

Go through the roll. I can no live with Quintal.

NED: I know how to reduce Quintal. What of McKoy?

MI MITTI: McKoy is a pig. Drink at sunrise, drink all day, drink at sunset. What kind of fool is this?

NED: He's Scottish. But even drunk he's a fine white iron man.

MI MITTI: Them anchors, them all nails now. What we need him for?

NED: He mends the hoes.

MI MITTI: And threatens owuz lives.

NED catches his breath, sits suddenly, holds his chest.

Wosing dat? You siki?

NED: Nothing. I've not eaten today.

NED: William Brown?

MI MITTI: His face disgusts me. That scar.

NED: Scrophula. We call it the King's Evil. Brown is invaluable, as a horticulturalist.

MI MITTI: Owuz gardens are all grow grow. I can no look at him.

NED: The boy Hiti? We must have some men to work the land.

MI MITTI: Hiti is taoi to Titreano. Him must take revenge. You has Menalee as a slave.

NED: And Adams. Now, all rests on the timing. Shakespeare's tragedies take an age, and audience and hero succumb to the delays. Racine would have this done in a day, and that day must be tomorrow. Tahitian women can induce an aborsement of a child, can you also bring forward parturition?

MI MITTI: Titreano no teach me teach me word?

NED: Birth. The birth of your child as a part of the plan needs to be tomorrow.

MI MITTI: Eeyeuh! Owuz women make baby come when ready, and ready now.

NED: Tomorrow then, at first light. All the women would attend your labours, and would thus neither be able to defend their husbands. The sound of your pains, if artfully increased, might hide, or explain the other work. Tomorrow.

NED turns to go but faint and dizzy, steadies himself.

MI MITTI: Again. You siki? You have him gripe?

NED: No. It's nothing. I'll eat at my house.

MI MITTI: Don't leave me alone.

NED: I need to alert John Adams, to God's work, and his part in it. I will spend the night with you.

End of scene.

ACT 3
SCENE 4

CHRISTIAN's cave, night. BROWN, CHRISTIAN and HITI. BROWN is priming muskets. Provisioning, building defences.

CHRISTIAN's eyrie. CHRISTIAN and HITI.

CHRISTIAN: The opposite of taoi is enemy.

HITI: Owuz no word.

CHRISTIAN: We English do.

HITI: Wosing?

CHRISTIAN: Enemy.

HITI: Enimi.

CHRISTIAN: Ned Young is my enemy. And Menalee is his taio. My enemy's taio must be my enemy.

HITI: Eeyeuh!

CHRISTIAN: And yet you sleep at Menalee's house.

BROWN: That must end. Now.

HITI: Eeyeuh!

CHRISTIAN: Sleep in the woods tonight. Do you like Mata?

HITI: Mata? Mataohu. Mmmm. Her es goodahn!

CHRISTIAN: She will be your wife. Your tiro.

HITI: Mi tiro!? Mataohu! Wo dis?

CHRISTIAN: There will be a war. You, me, and Mister Brown, we fight together.

HITI: What day dis war begin?

CHRISTIAN: When we choose.

BROWN: Take this. It is primed.

BROWN gives him a musket.

HITI: Yoo wan me kill him Ned Young?

CHRISTIAN: Kill my enemy, yes. Ned Young, John Adams, and Menalee.

HITI: Disday?

CHRISTIAN: Tomorrow. Wait in the woods. Listen for musket fire and then advance upon them from behind their lines. There will be glory, and for you –

HITI: – Mata?

CHRISTIAN: Yes.

HITI runs off.

CHRISTIAN: Not yet two years in the Garden of Eden and we have a civil war.

BROWN: We will benefit doubly from their deaths. Two women would become available. Or do you wish to spend the rest of your life a widower, living in a cave, staring out to sea, seeing Bligh in every cloud.

CHRISTIAN: At night I have the stars, and yes, Bligh's imminent return is enough to fill the day.

BROWN: Bligh is dead sir.

CHRISTIAN: No, no, no! He lives! No finer navigator has ever been born. He's on the ocean now, headed this way, with a following wind. He comes to hang me! *(Beat.)* Don't look at me like that! I am not mad. That is reason. I know the man and I have done my calculations.

BROWN: Running down mutineers is not a job for Bligh. It's a task for a post captain, a man o' war and fifty marines.

CHRISTIAN: Yes, you're right.

BROWN: Bligh and Banks'll be back out after the bread fruit.

CHRISTIAN: Thank you. A sobering thought.

BROWN: In the morning, I'll harvest some yams, and plantains. Then we'll be provisioned.

End of scene.

ACT 3
SCENE 6

Dark. HITI asleep in a tree. He has a musket with him. Enter MATA.

MATA: Hiti!

HITI: Wa dat?! Ay ha' musket. Ay no freud te use him!

MATA: It's me. Mata!

HITI: What are you doing out here in the woods?

MATA: I could ask the same of you.

HITI: There will be a war tomorrow. And I am hiding.

MATA: I found you.

HITI: Yes, how did you find me here? This my secret place.

MATA: The pool where we bathe every morning is just there, and every morning you hide in this iron wood tree and watch us.

HITI: You know about me hiding in the tree watching you bathe?

MATA: Yes.

HITI: Oh no.

MATA: I knew you would be here.

HITI: So you came looking for a kiss then?

MATA: I'm scared. Mister Ned has spent all night priming muskets, and he told me that tomorrow I must be tiro to Menalee.

HITI: Ned Young has given you to Menalee as tiro?

MATA: I would rather die than have that fat bull on top of me every night.

HITI: I want to be your tiro.

MATA: You're a bit young for me

HITI: I make you laugh. And there's no one else.

MATA: Titreano has no wife.

HITI: You must want Titreano more than me.

MATA: No. He's sad. Crazy.

HITI: He is my taio, you mustn't speak like that of him, but yes, I agree, he is too crazy to be your husband. You need a young, funny, normal man like me.

MATA: Can I sit with you?

HITI: Yes, climb up.

She does.

MATA: Hold me. I'm scared.

HITI snatches a kiss.

Don't be so quick. We've got all night.

They kiss. The night sets in dark.

ACT 4
SCENE 1

Lights up. Sunrise. NED is standing outside MCKOY's house. He is suffering from a mild tachypnea – rapid breathing. Not a cough, but the rapid breathing breaks up his speech. QUINTAL's house is next door.

NED: Mister McKoy! *(Breaths.)* It's me, Ned Young! Is anyone home! McKoy, it's me, Ned Young!

Enter HITI, swaggering in like a man.

HITI: *(Direct address.)* Surfing is for little boys. I can smell her on me. Strange. The smell, that was a surprise. I thought it would be sweet, but it's not, it's like a plant you find, deep in the roots of a tree. Rub the leaf, stain your fingers. Wash and it is still there. I like it. Do you remember that good days are…life, bad days are…history. The next history day, the next bad day, is today, dawning bright, and beautiful, the first day of my life as a man.

WALUA comes out.

NED: *(Surprised.)* Mrs Quintal?

WALUA: Wut a way you?

NED: I thought this was McKoy's house.

MCKOY comes out, and fondles WALUA.

MCKOY: It is.

NED: Have you exchanged wives?

Enter QUINTAL.

MCKOY: I was gyte with the horn last nite but mine wouldn't let me tup her so Quintal had tae lend me his.

NED: How utilitarian.

QUINTAL: You're grinding Christian's girl so go wipe your arse.

MCKOY: Aye, at least what we does is above board.

QUINTAL: You're out of breath fellah. Hey girl, get him some water.

WALUA goes off and gets water.

MCKOY: It's nae that hot man.

NED: It's a fever, I get, the only inheritance I will ever see.

Enter TE'O bandaged across the head, she is whimpering.

NED: Mrs McKoy, you're injured?

TE'O: Him bit dis wun ear off.

MCKOY: Aye, she wouldnae let me, so I skelped her one –

NED: And bit her ear off?

MCKOY: Dinna fash yersel with her singing.

WALUA returns with water.

QUINTAL: Sit yourself man, and slake your throat with that.

NED: Brown told me that you are having no success distilling from sugar beet.

QUINTAL: What's it to you?

NED: I've been drinking rum longer than either of you. My wet nurse on St. Kitts gave me a thimble every night.

MCKOY: We have nae yeast.

NED: I can help, in exchange for a supply.

QUINTAL and MCKOY exchange glances, nods.

MCKOY: Aye, that's braw.

NED: Mister Brown tells me the root of the ti tree has yeast.

QUINTAL: The ti tree?

NED: The root. There's an abundance of ti trees on the western side, near the waterfall.

MCKOY starts to gather up the still etc.

MCKOY: That's my day decided then.

NED: I'd join you. But I'm on a hog shoot with Adams.

MCKOY: Yee nae fit to hunt man.

NED: Needs must. If you hear musket fire, that's us, not Bligh and a company of marines.

QUINTAL: *(To MCKOY.)* Are we sleeping out?

MCKOY: Aye, man, I'm not hauling that machine there and back for no purpose. And we got tae find the roots, and boil up a mash. That's more than a day.

QUINTAL: Oi! Te'o, wrap us some meat up will you, yer sweet little skate!?

TE'O goes in.

NED: I'll come out and find you tomorrow. Equipped with a cup.

NED walks off.

End of scene.

ACT 4
SCENE 2

TE LAHU, TE'O and FASTO, climb the path to CHRISTIAN's eyrie. CHRISTIAN is armed.

CHRISTIAN: Stay! Show your arms!

TE LAHU: Owuz women come fe get you come see di bebe.

CHRISTIAN: She's had the child?

FASTO: Eeyeuh!

CHRISTIAN: I heard nothing. No cries of labour.

TE LAHU: *(Beat.)* Mi Mitti woz baby mother afore.

CHRISTIAN: It may be easier second time, but not that easy.

TE'O: Him little little boy.

CHRISTIAN: A boy?

TE LAHU: Es him white boy.

ALL Eyeugh!

FASTO: Mi Mitti...she wan talk fe you.

TE'O: Her heart big fe you.

FASTO: Yoo gwen come see dis bebe.

CHRISTIAN: Where is Ned Young?

FASTO: Him feelun siki siki disday. Fiva has him in his grip.

TE'O: Him na wan see di baby.

FASTO: He ken di baby white.

CHRISTIAN lowers his muskets and walks towards them, through them, and on down the slope. TE LAHU pushes FASTO up into the cave, whispers something in her ear. TE LAHU follows the party down.

End of scene.

ACT 4
SCENE 3

At NED's house. ADAMS and NED. NED's health is now moving towards an Acute Chest Syndrome Crisis caused by his Sickle Cell Anaemia. The symptoms of this are tachypnea (rapid breathing) and dyspnea (breathlessness). He does not have a cough, but does have chest pains, of a pulmonary nature, not heart.

NED: Did you sleep well last night John?

ADAMS: Grand. Aye. I had me supper, and a tot of rum, said me prayers, then I give her one, and that were enough to send me off.

NED: I'll put it in the log.

ADAMS: Ha! I'd rather you didn't!

Rapid breathing from NED. He hangs on to the table.

Sailed with a darkie had this off Malagasy.

NED: I pray he lived?

ADAMS: For a day.

NED: I hope you gave him a Christian burial?

ADAMS: We chucked him overboard.

NED: Did you see Mister Brown.

ADAMS: Aye, he's in his gardens. He give me a wave.

NED: Which tells us what John?

ADAMS: That he ain't in the right mood for a Christian massacre.

NED: So their attack might come tomorrow? But we can better defend ourselves by using time to our advantage.

ADAMS: Attack before they are prepared?

NED: As General Wolfe surprised the French at Quebec. Prime this John.

Enter MENALEE.

MENALEE: Yo rah nah! Me taoi!

NED: Maita'i. Brown is in his gardens. Engage him in conversation. When you have his confidence, use the hatchet.

MENALEE: You sikie sikie?

NED: *(Angry.)* Never mind me! Avoid the musket, excepting necessity.

ADAMS: Bring us his head.

NED: Do you understand?

MENALEE: I ken good. Kill him Brown. Wa bout Titreano?

NED: Mister Christian is in his cave. Which he can defend.

MENALEE: Mi feart fe Mister Quintal. Ay freten.

NED: Quintal and McKoy will be west and over the ridge. Consumed.

MENALEE: Wosing Mata. Me tiro! You kah say wosing place she be?

NED: She's on Pitcairn. Somewhere. And she's yours. Now go.

MENALEE: Aye, aye.

MENALEE leaves. NED is breathing rapidly, and is in full tachypnea crisis.

ADAMS: Can God see us now? Indoors?

NED: He can see indoors.

ADAMS: And we're not doing wrong in his eyes?

NED: The Bible says that those who live by the false prophets of drink and licentiousness shall meet with swift destruction.

ADAMS: Which gospel is that?

NED: One of the early ones.

End of scene.

ACT 4
SCENE 4

A still is set up with the copper coil running through a waterfall. QUINTAL and MCKOY are both intent on watching the distillation. One drip comes through.

MCKOY: There's a jill.

QUINTAL: Jill my arse, it's like a Persian faucet!

MCKOY takes the cup from the still. QUINTAL snatches it from him.

Give it here yer damned arseworm!

QUINTAL sniffs it, pulls a face, not at the smell but at its obvious strength.

No sea too rough, no muff too tough!

He swigs it down.

MCKOY: What's it taste of man?

QUINTAL: Jesus! It's terrible.

MCKOY: Can you drink it?

QUINTAL: We got no choice do we, you damned sheep biter!

QUINTAL snatches a drink of water. A distant musket shot is heard. They freeze in fear.

MCKOY: Bligh?

QUINTAL: Ned Young hunting pigs.

MCKOY has a cup now, he sniffs, doesn't like the smell.

Come on man!

MCKOY takes a gulp.

Here, you'll need water, or you'll lose your tongue.

MCKOY swigs some water.

MCKOY: Ach! It's just the damnedest thing that any man slung down his neck.

QUINTAL: Jesus!

QUINTAL holds his cock and staggers around.

MCKOY: What is it man?

QUINTAL: It's gone straight to me romantics. God man, you've made a potion for the venereals!

MCKOY takes a bite of fruit, a cucumber or something.

MCKOY: Christ! Do you need the fruit or nae!?

QUINTAL: I've ne'er felt like this. I could fuck a tree.

QUINTAL walks off holding his cock.

MCKOY: Where you going man!?

QUINTAL: I'm gonna find mesel a good looking tree.

End of scene.

ACT 4
SCENE 5

Indoors at NED's place. ADAMS and NED. NED is kneeling on the floor, breathing rapidly, holding his chest. Technically, medically, he is mid Acute Chest Syndrome and is under pulmonary strain and also suffering rapid heart – tachycardia. ADAMS stands over him.

NED: I can't slow my heart!

ADAMS: You know this well then?

NED: On St Kitts. In the Africans.

ADAMS: I always said you're no quadroon. You got more than a touch of the tar brush then, you got their blighted blood an'all.

NED: Punch my chest, here. You will outlive me John, so listen good. The women are the real task. Do not let them imagine a world where women have advantage, for if they can imagine it today, they might have it tomorrow. And what would that mean for us John?

ADAMS: Dunno er…dunno.

NED: Slavery.

ADAMS kneels and punches NED's chest. Enter MENALEE bloodied, carrying the basket covered with a bloodied cloth.

MENALEE: Yoo siki siki! Water!

ADAMS: He's got water. It ain't no use.

MENALEE puts BROWN's head on the table.

MENALEE: Mister Brown! See!

ADAMS: You've blown his damned brains clean out the back of his head.

MENALEE: Ai. I like him good Mister Brown.

NED is on his knees, holding his chest, breathing rapidly.

NED: Get that head out of my sight!

MENALEE: In war owuz folk lash up dead man head on dem belt.

He ties the head by the hair on to his belt.

Where be Mata? My tiro? She come here?

ADAMS: I ain't seen her.

MENALEE: Titreano come down fe top, come see Mi Mitti an' di bebe.

NED: She's had the child?

MENALEE: Mus do.

NED: Have you seen it?

MENALEE: No.

NED: In the cave Christian was safe, but not now. You know what to do?

MENALEE: Aye, aye. Ay kill him, bring yuz him head. Mata me tiro disday, aye aye!

NED: Yes, she is yours!

MENALEE exits. ADAMS sits at the table. NED chest pains, breathless.

ADAMS: That's a fair churchyard cough you got there sir.

NED: I'm dying John. Pitcairn will be yours. For God.

End of scene.

ACT 4
SCENE 6

Outside MI MITTI's house. The women enter with CHRISTIAN amongst them. TE LAHU trips CHRISTIAN.

MI MITTI: Kneel!

CHRISTIAN: Where is my wife?

They jump him and manacle him, he puts up a fight.

What is this?

TE LAHU: Yorley mek boat fe us, we sail big water.

FASTO: *(Wielding the sextant.)* Yorley come fe us, point one way, point anudderone way.

CHRISTIAN: I am no use to you without the star charts.

TE LAHU: We got all yus papers.

FASTO: We don't have to speak your stupid language any more.

CHRISTIAN: What did you say?

TE'O: Owuz women no kah speak arsewipe English no more disday!

TE LAHU: Youz stole stole us fe Tahiti. Fe mi children.

Enter MI MITTI.

CHRISTIAN: Where's my baby? It's black isn't it. Where's Ned Young?

MI MITTI: Him siki siki.

TE LAHU: Our Queen. Come speak to me.

They go out of earshot of CHRISTIAN.

Where is the baby?

MI MITTI: Dead.

TE LAHU: The baby died?

MI MITTI: Ned Young lied to me. He is sick, and he knew he was sick.

TE LAHU: These English lie, to get what they want.

MI MITTI: It is as if they they don't know that it is not possible to lie on an island. Perhaps England is so big that it is possible to lie, and not be found out.

TE LAHU: I hate them.

MI MITTI: My father was confused by their ships, their iron, their muskets. So he made them gods, and set them high above us, when there is nothing they have that we ever wanted or needed.

TE LAHU: Are you with us then now.

MI MITTI: It is my obligation to return to Tahiti and destroy everything English, every nail, every mirror, every piece of jewelry. No one will be allowed to even talk about the English and we will attack any ship that comes into the bay!

Enter HITI and MATA. HITI is armed with a musket.

HITI: What have you done with Titreano!?

TE'O: He is our prisoner.

HITI: No! He is my taio!

TE LAHU raises her musket at HITI.

TE LAHU: I will shoot.

HITI drops the musket. FASTO picks it up.

TE LAHU: We're running the island now. The Women.

TE'O: *(To MATA.)* Are you and Hiti tiro now then?

SOME Oooh! / ha, ha. /

WALUA: Where did you do it?

TE'O: In his tree!?

Laughter.

FASTO: Why is Hiti sitting here? He's not a woman.

TE'O: Aye, piss off. Sit over there with your taio.

HITI moves to near CHRISTIAN.

TE LAHU: We must decide what to do with the other men.

FASTO: Kill them!

WALUA: Don't be stupid.

TE'O: Who would build the boat?

TE LAHU: If we all live here, in one house, we can kill the men, we can pull down the other houses and use the boards to build a boat.

WALUA: You're not pulling down my house!

TE LAHU: Mammu! Let us discuss the men first, one by one.

HITI moves and sits with CHRISTIAN.

TE LAHU: Shall we spare John Adams to help build the boat.

TE'O: I'm not going to sea in a boat built by an idiot.

TE LAHU: Mister Adams, your husband, do you want to speak for him?

WALUA: Is he an idiot?

FASTO: Yes.

TE'O:/WALUA: Kill him!

FASTO: If you kill him will I keep the gardens?

TE LAHU: That is all determined by how we decide to live.

FASTO: No! No one is taking my gardens from me!
I married an Englishman.

TE'O: What happened in the past doesn't matter now.

TE LAHU: Do you want to work your gardens alone?

FASTO: Yes! They are my gardens.

TE LAHU: We can have one big garden and share the labour.

FASTO: I own the land from the aute forest to Brown's fence and when I die it is my children's.

WALUA: I thought you wanted to go back to Tahiti.

FASTO: I do but whilst the boat is being built, or if the boat sinks.

TE LAHU: The best man to build a boat would be McKoy.

FASTO: A drunk.

TE LAHU: A blacksmith. Te'o, he is your husband.

TE'O: I never want to see him again. He bit my ear off.

FASTO: And he is taoi to Quintal, who must die.

WALUA: Why do you want to kill my man?

FASTO: He raped me.
Kill them both!

WALUA stands.

WALUA: No! He has given me children. I love him.

WALUA exits running.

TE'O: If we kill all the men, what do we do for sex?

MATA: We will have three men!

FASTO: Titreano, Adams and Hiti.

TE LAHU: Sex for them is a payment for good work on the boat.

TE'O: Hiti?

FASTO: Hiti is a man now!

ALL: Eeyeuh! / Ah yes! / That's clever. / Of course!

MENALEE steps forward, musket raised. He has BROWN's head tied to his belt by the hair. The women stand and wield their muskets.

TE LAHU: Stop!

MENALEE: Mata! Girl. You're my tiro now. Ned Young has given you to me.

HITI: No! Mataohu is my tiro.

HITI steps between him and MATA. MENALEE fires on HITI who is hit, and falls dying. TE'O fires. MENALEE is hit, falls and drops his musket.

MENALEE: Te'o. You shot me?!

TE'O: I did. Mareva is your wife, not Mata.

MENALEE: My mana is gone.

MENALEE dies. MATA is left holding HITI who is dying.

MATA: Hiti! Hiti! Talk to me!

HITI: I can see you. Touch me.

MATA kisses his lips.

We were together, once. Only once, but once. Yes?

MATA: Yes. It was beautiful.

HITI: My mana is gone now.

MATA: No! Hiti! Don't close your eyes. Hiti!

He dies.

TE LAHU: His mana has gone to the gods.

ALL: *(As a respectful chant.)*
Let his mana play with the gods
Let his mana kiss the gods
Let his mana be a god

FASTO: His mana has gone.

Enter JOHN ADAMS unarmed. TE LAHU points a musket at him.

TE'O: Yoo kah pahs!

ADAMS: I heard the shots. I want my wife. Fasto.
(To FASTO.) Go home girl.

TE LAHU: Yoo no tumble her disday!

ADAMS: I'll tumble my wife whenever I likes and I don't have to beg your approval. What is this?

TE LAHU: All Pitcairn groun es ours disday.

ADAMS: By what right?

TE LAHU: Fe musket.

MATA: Owuz women got all muskets.

ADAMS: No you aint, I got one back at my house.

TE LAHU: Te'o! Quick! Go and get Adams musket.

ADAMS: Oh bugger!

TE'O: No. I'm scared. I'm not going on my own.
I don't know where Quintal is.

TE LAHU: Sit yorley arse on ground!

TE'O: Or yoo gwen fetch yorley balls in yon water?!

ADAMS sits.

ADAMS: *(To CHRISTIAN.)* What are you doing?

CHRISTIAN: I have to build them a boat. And you're to help me.

ADAMS: Are you enslaved?

CHRISTIAN: I am.

TE LAHU chucks a set of manacles at ADAMS on the ground.

TE LAHU: Yorley put iron on foot now!

CHRISTIAN: And so are you.

TE LAHU: *(To ADAMS.)* Wosing your taio, Ned Young?

ADAMS: Aye, he's badly. Breathing like a leaking bellows.

FASTO: It's true, I seen him. He's lying on the mud outside his house.

TE'O: What do we do?

TE LAHU: We need to control all the muskets. Then tomorrow we will hunt down Quintal and McKoy. Fasto, and Te'o get Adams musket and bring Ned Young here. Bind him, make him secure.

FASTO: We have no more manacles.

TE'O: We could nail him to a plank of wood.

MI MITTI: He would want to die like his god, on a cross.

TE'O: Yes, it would be really funny!

TE LAHU: No sentiments! No sympathy! These men enslaved us!

MATA: So why do you want to keep him alive?

TE LAHU: He can work the star machine.

TE'O: But we have Titreano for that.

TE LAHU: If Quintal kills Titreano, and we have killed Ned Young, then we are lost.

TE'O and FASTO exit. HITI stands and walks to the front of stage for direct address.

HITI: Now it is unusual for the narrator to be killed in the middle of his own story?! But that is Pitcairn. Everything is different on Pitcairn. There are no rules. But at least I did not die a boy. I knew love, and died a man. But I do not know what happens next so I will sit and watch the next history day with you.

HITI sits in the audience.

End of scene.

ACT 4
SCENE 7

MCKOY by the waterfall. Asleep, dead drunk. Enter WALUA, with a child at her breast.

WALUA: *(Shouting loud.)* Matty! Ay got wickles!

She kicks MCKOY awake.

Bill McKoy! Wa sing yourley doin!? Wosing be my man Quintal?

MCKOY: Arghh! Strewth!

WALUA: Ay bring yoo pork an' egg.

MCKOY wakes.

MCKOY: Yous a fine braw lassie, Walua. Come here yer bonny wee bundle.

MCKOY makes a grab at her, she fights him off.

WALUA: Gwen wipe! Ay no wan no bedtime working. Ay got di bebe on di tit.

MCKOY sits up.

MCKOY: Agh! Jesus! My damned heed!

WALUA finds a cup of rum.

WALUA: Yoo mekking rum eh?

MCKOY: Aye. It's damned powerful. Here.

He offers her some. He drinks it instead.

WALUA: Ay no wan rum disday. Us women come fe kill yoo disday. Us women ha' all musket. Wa bin my man?!

MCKOY: *(Shouting.)* Quintal! *(Holding his head.)* Jesus. What of Christian?

WALUA: Titreano him live on.

MCKOY: You got sweet wee dugs Walua.

MCKOY fondles her breasts. WALUA whacks him really hard.

WALUA: Kah foo yoo cock like wood so early disday?

MCKOY: The brew. It fires yer Venus.

WALUA: Eeyeugh!?

MCKOY: Aye, it makes your ready for loving.

WALUA: Gimme.

MCKOY gives her a drink.

Agh!

MCKOY: Here, a wee shot of fruit calms it!

She snatches a bite, swallows.

WALUA: Ay like it damn good. Es hot! Unuderwun gimme!

MCKOY holds it back.

MCKOY: If you let me have a wee feel.

WALUA: Yoo be quick?

MCKOY: Aye.

MCKOY starts to grope her, she puts the baby aside, and climbs on top of her. Enter the women from both sides holding muskets and axes/knives. MATA is not with them. MCKOY grabs WALUA as a shield.

TE'O: Us cum fe to kill yoo disday.

MCKOY: Te'o?! You're my damned wife!

TE'O: If ay be yoo wife, who dat den?

Enter QUINTAL. MCKOY turns sees him. WALUA frees herself.

QUINTAL: You damned black bitches!

WALUA: Matty! Dey gwen kill yoo disday!

FASTO fires, misses.

QUINTAL: Aye, there's a knack to them old navy canons.

QUINTAL runs off.

TE LAHU: Let him go.

The women turn again to MCKOY. He drops to his knees. MCKOY is surrounded. The women close the circle. No one seems to want to make the first move. MCKOY assesses the situation, and reaches for the bottle.

MCKOY: A last dram!?

TE LAHU: Kah.

(TE LAHU kicks the cup over. MCKOY is tragic, desperate for the drink.)

MCKOY: Argh! Yous a lang shanked black witch, yous!

The women start to close in. We don't see him killed.

End of scene.

ACT 4
SCENE 8

CHRISTIAN and ADAMS are guarded by MATA with musket. NED YOUNG's hands are nailed to a plank, a single plank, not a crucifix. He is on his knees. He lives yet. ADAMS is feeding him water. The breathlessness and chest pains continue.

NED: God bless you John.

ADAMS: I'd pull them there nails out but that bitch won't let me.

MATA: Nuff! Nuff! Yus fe working build boat now disday!

NED: I need shade, John, please.

ADAMS: Aye, but me chain lacks the length to –

MATA: – Last time! Last time!

CHRISTIAN: So you will die like Christ.

NED: It's the only blessing in all this hell.

CHRISTIAN: You don't know, you might rise on the third day.

NED: My soul shall be content with Heaven.

CHRISTIAN: Heaven might be full. And your 'sins to good works' ledger won't balance, not if your God's been watching.

ADAMS: God forgives.

CHRISTIAN: God does but I don't. What about the Holy Ghost? Does he forgive?

NED: Why do you torture me with this rhetoric!

CHRISTIAN: I always think of him as a cantankerous old bugger.

NED: He is God, part of the trinity.

CHRISTIAN: God the Father, God the Son, and God the Holy Ghost. You'd think there would only be one God in a montheistic religion.

ADAMS: He's on his last breath man, don't give him doubts now.

NED: I have no doubts John!

ADAMS: *(To MATA.)* He needs some shade, can I move him?

MATA: Speak Tahitian! You stupid cunt rag!

ADAMS: What did she say? You speak their tongue.

CHRISTIAN: She said – I like you Reckless Jack, you're my favourite.

ADAMS: Aye? I seen her admirin' me. I could give her one. She's a ripe little doxy. If I weren't such a good Christian. And in chains. Ah forget it.

NED: Press my chest John. My chest!

ADAMS puts his foot on NED's chest.

NED: That helps, it helps.

CHRISTIAN: You have two toes missing. On your right foot.

ADAMS: Aye.

CHRISTIAN: What happened to them?

ADAMS: I got one in a pearl case back in Hackney, I dunno where the other is.

CHRISTIAN: I mean't, how did you lose them?

ADAMS: In that Bethnal Green Poor House of mine, one of them come at me with an axe. Aye, they was unreasonable fierce was our nuns.

CHRISTIAN: You deceived Bligh then, both in name and condition?

ADAMS: Bligh knows about the toes. He made me run the length of the dockside. It didn't slow me down, so he took me on.

CHRISTIAN: Will you be missed in England John Adams?

ADAMS: I'm an orphan, ain't I. London's glad to see the back of me. You, your mother'll be weeping before your portrait every day.

NED: He has no portrait. Help me John! Water!

TE LAHU and MI MITTI enter.

ADAMS: He's dying! You're his damn wife, you ripe little bitch!

TE LAHU: Don't talk to them.

CHRISTIAN: Taking orders now my darling?

TE LAHU: Speak Tahitian!

MI MITTI: Te Lahu has not lied to me. She is the spirit of Tahiti so I follow her.

Enter the other women, except WALUA. TEO carries MCKOY's bloodied head.

MATA: Whose head is that?

TEO: McKoy, my husband.

TE LAHU: Quintal lives.

MATA: Why do you keep McKoy's head?

TEO: His land is mine, I have his head!

MATA: We agreed not to divide the land.

ADAMS: Someone's lost their head.

CHRISTIAN: McKoy. Te'o will use it as proof of her inheritance.

ADAMS: Aye, I seen that on Tahiti. Skulls on sticks outside the houses.

CHRISTIAN: The English have titles and deeds, and pay lawyers. They have their ancestors' skulls, and don't pay lawyers. We could discuss which is the better system.

ADAMS: Damn these chains!

CHRISTIAN: You don't like being enslaved by women then John?

ADAMS: If the Lord had wanted women to rule o'er men He woulda give 'em some particular advantage like, I dunno, longer arms.

CHRISTIAN: Longer arms?

ADAMS: Aye, or something equivalently useful.

CHRISTIAN: These women are like you Ned, they like their theatre! They're staging a passion! And you have the lead!

NED: I'd rather this than your fate. They'll drag you back to Deptford and string you from the yard arm and let you rot like a mole on a fence as a message to every tar in England.

ADAMS: They wouldn't hang me.

NED: They should hang you twice. Once for the mutiny and once for the levelling that led to this carnage.

CHRISTIAN: I have made mistakes. But I now know that the natural condition of man is violence, lechery, drunkenness, greed, suspician and hate. And there is a lesson learned – that man's free will needs an authority greater than that of a mere yarning court of mortal men. Maybe I do need God.

NED: Pitcairn! I die!

NED dies.

ADAMS: He's gone I think. He's right though. You ain't a man of God.

CHRISTIAN: God does not need to exist in order to be useful to me.

End of scene.

ACT 4
SCENE 9

WALUA is on the cliff top with her child suckling at her breast. She puts it down in the grass.

WALUA: *(A scream. A second scream.)*
Mi Mitti has milk. You will not want for milk. Your daddy gave me this on Tahiti years ago. Look, it has never changed, it is as constant as my love for him.

She ties the nail around the baby's neck.

It is iron. A piece of England. You will grow to be like a nail, strong and rare, like an Englishman.

Baby cries.

Don't cry, someone will come.

Enter MATA, FASTO, TE'O all wielding muskets. WALUA starts backing to the cliff.

FASTO: Where's Quintal?

TE'O: Walua! What are you doing?!

WALUA: I have just fed the boy. Mi Mitti has milk.

TE'O: No! We are going home, in the boat, you will come with us.

FASTO: We're going back to Tahiti.

TE'O: Walua! Come away from the cliff!

WALUA: I was happy here.

WALUA throws herself off the cliff. MATA steps down stage for direct address.

MATA: We all know that good days are life, and get forgotten, and only bad days, history days, are remembered. That day, Menalee killed Brown, and the boy Hiti; Te'o killed Menalee; the women killed McKoy and Ned Young; and my friend Walua threw herself off the cliff. Ever since this rock of Pitcairn rose from the sea there has never been a more history day than this day.

HITI: Mata! Mata! I'm here!

MATA: For the next two months Fletcher Christian and John Adams, in chains, built the boat, and we women worked together fishing and farming, looking after the children. It sounds idyllic, but the mad dog Quintal was still at large. Imagine that. I want you to try and imagine that. Living on a small island, one English mile by two miles, with a mad dog on the loose.

HITI: Mata! I'm here!?

MATA: Sometimes in the night I thought I heard Hiti calling me.

HITI: Yes!

MATA: And I lay awake imagining a life with him.

HITI: Yes! Oh Mata'oha!

MATA: But it scared me. Pitcairn will not make me mad. The next history day is the day we launch the boat.

End of scene.

ACT 5
SCENE 1

The boat is built. A bright sunny day. CHRISTIAN and ADAMS, guarded by FASTO, and MI MITTI whose attention is divided between guarding them and pushing the baby in the crib. FASTO is asleep. CHRISTIAN looks to the heavens.

CHRISTIAN: What are we now? Two hours before midday?

ADAMS: What does time matter?

CHRISTIAN: Time is everything. The work's done, I'll get on with the caulking. What do you think? Will she float or will she founder?

CHRISTIAN: She'll founder.

ADAMS: No! With the hull caulked she'll be a fair little jolly boat. But we must caulk her good. Ten coats, ten more days. Why spoil the boat for a ha'peth of tar.

CHRISTIAN: No. We sail today, it has to be today.

ADAMS: Are you mad? It's not caulked, she'll sink.

CHRISTIAN: Don't give me away, or death's your portion.

ADAMS: Oh, I get it, you want the boat to sink. You got a scheme eh?

MI MITTI takes FASTO's pistol and approaches CHRISTIAN with it, at the same time as holding the baby. ADAMS sees her advance.

ADAMS: Mister Christian. Your wife's got herself a musket. And is aiming it at your head.

CHRISTIAN turns around.

CHRISTIAN: You would kill me?

MI MITTI: I want. I want.

CHRISTIAN: You can't. That would not serve your people. I can use the sextant. Kill me when we get to Tahiti. The musket is threatening, but that picaninny is the real violence.

MI MITTI shows the baby more deliberately.

MI MITTI: Ned loved me good. Like a man. You love me like a boy.

CHRISTIAN: Hurt on hurt. Pile it on. I have no feelings left.

MI MITTI: Ned kiss me good. Sweet.

CHRISTIAN: That's his profession. He's a coster monger of kissing.

MI MITTI: Ned love me long. Yowuz quick quick.

CHRISTIAN: You can't make me feel. I'm numb.

MI MITTI: I wash you away. Completely.

CHRISTIAN: Where's Thursday, our son? Who's looking after him?

MI MITTI: He is dead to me.

CHRISTIAN: He's too young to run wild. Will you take him in the boat?

MI MITTI: He is a dog now. Dogs run wild.

CHRISTIAN: What will your father do, to me, when I get you home.

MI MITTI: He will kill you with a knife.

CHRISTIAN: I didn't lie to him when I said that I am ra'atira. I am.

MI MITTI: You no ground in England.

CHRISTIAN: No land, no. But my blood is aristocratic, ra'atira. But I have nothing and that is not uncommon. The gambling debts of second sons ruin many a noble family, but it doesn't make them any the less noble.

MI MITTI: This I don't understand, how –

CHRISTIAN: – yes! This is our real failure, to dove tail our cultures, to understand, to sympathise instead of allow incredulity to wash away our love.

MI MITTI: Work. No talking.

CHRISTIAN: Give me your chisel.

CHRISTIAN takes ADAM's chisel. MI MITTI raises the musket. CHRISTIAN places it on his little toe of the right foot. With an intake of breath and a swift blow from the malet he chops off his toe.

CHRISTIAN: Aaargh!

Swiftly he does the same to the next toe.

ADAMS: What are you doing man?!

CHRISTIAN: Aargh!

The girls come forward.

ADAMS: You cut your toes off!

FASTO starts to care for him, with water, and dressings.

ADAMS: You lost your damned senses man!

QUINTAL appears out of the woods. He is wearing nothing but a loin cloth. He carries a bottle in one hand, a knife in the other. He grabs MI MITTI from behind. She screams. Loudly. He uses her as a shield during the next, wielding a knife.

ADAMS: Have you been drinking?

QUINTAL: I promised meself I'd dock this doxie afore I die. Got yer manacled eh Reckless Jack? Sick of your sermonising?

QUINTAL stabs him.

QUINTAL: – that'll shut you up your damned soul driver.

ADAMS is dead.

(To CHRISTIAN.) In all your puff did ye ever meet a more complete idiot?

CHRISTIAN: Never. Is that alcohol? I could use some.

QUINTAL: You don't want to drink this, it'll make you hard, and if they don't give you a woman you'll go mad. But you're mad already.

QUINTAL throws him a bottle. He then forces a kiss on MI MITTI, she screams, so he thrusting a rag in her mouth. CHRISTIAN pours the alcohol on his wounded foot. It stings. He wails.

QUINTAL: What the hell you done with your foot man?

CHRISTIAN: An accident. With a chisel.

QUINTAL: Them's the self same toes that Reckless Jack had missing. I know you, you're scheming.

QUINTAL mounts MI MITTI, penetrates. CHRISTIAN watches.

QUINTAL: Argh, yes. What are they keeping you for then?

CHRISTIAN: Navigation. Back to Tahiti.

QUINTAL: Clever. Giss it here! Giss it!

CHRISTIAN gives him the bottle and he swigs away as he thrusts. Enter TE LAHU with musket and encircles QUINTAL at a distance.

Don't fire! Eh! I gots your queen under here.

TE LAHU: No musket fire!

QUINTAL: Let me finish. A tumble ain't a tumble without a finish. Is it? Then you can do your worst.

Suddenly TE'O dives in and whacks him on the head with the musket. Then all the women pile in. It is a frenzied, seemingly endless attack during which we can see QUINTAL use all his strength to fight the women off, at one point standing with three women clinging to him beating him down. The frenzy continues until he seems dead, knives sticking out of his back. The women step away. Suddenly he rises to his knees.

Aargh! You damned black bitches! I'll see you in hell Fletcher Christian. After Pitcairn, it'll be a dove.

He dies.

TE'O: His mana is gone.

CHRISTIAN: We should give these men a Christian burial and offer their souls to God.

TE LAHU: God es storley, storley, storley. Es no white man god.

CHRISTIAN: It is true that at one time, blinded by conceit, invincible, lord of all I surveyed, I could not see Him, obscured as He was by mine own brilliance. But he has shown himself to me. He sent the Angel Gabriel to comfort me last night.

TE LAHU: You loy!

TE'O: Wot wickles you cook up for him?

CHRISTIAN: He'd already eaten. He told me that God did not make Eve to rule over Adam.

TE LAHU: Es storley!

CHRISTIAN: Here in his first creation, the garden of Eden. Yes, this island, Pitcairn, was the first garden. That's what Gabriel told me.

TE LAHU: Yorley loy loy loy.

CHRISTIAN: I am not lying. The Angel Gabriel told me that God is going to sink the boat. If we try to leave, and He will turn the day into night. He will place a great stone over the sun.

TE LAHU: We sail disday, now, disday! Is di boat complete.

CHRISTIAN: The work is finished.

MATA: Es done, es good disday.

TE LAHU: Load the boat. Put all those provisions in. And the fishing lines. The sextant, the charts. We must make the most of the light. Come on!

TE'O: We are scared!

MATA: Titreano is saying that their god will sink the boat.

TE'O: Their god will take the sun away and every day will be dark.

FASTO: Go wipe! The boat is finished, we can leave today.

TE'O: All their God stories are shit!

MATA: What about their god's son rising from the dead.

TE'O: I rise from the dead every morning.

MI MITTI: Titreano himself does not follow the English God. Many times he told me of his certainty that the Bible was a story written by men to control other men.

TE LAHU: – Mammu! That is an end to this talk! We have a task. We are going home. Let us carry the boat to the water.

The women lift the boat. It starts to get dark as the moon begins to pass across the sun.

TE'O: It's getting dark!

MATA: It is the middle of the day.

FASTO: It is like Titreano said. Their God has placed his hand over the sun!

Bedlam, screaming and prostrating towards the sun. CHRISTIAN *watches. And drops to his knees and begins to pray. During his prayer he encourages the women to join him, and stop their wailing and running around.*

CHRISTIAN: Let us pray! Everone! Pray with me!

O Lord our heavenly Father almighty
and everlasting God, who safely brought
us to this Eden accept now our unfeigned prayer

(To TE LAHU.*)* Kneel!

We now supplicate ourselves to thy Glorious Majesty, offer Thee our thanksgivings and beg for Thy Gracious Protection.

We most devoutly thank thee for our
preservation & are truly conscious that
only through thy Divine intervention we have been
saved from certain death at sea.

CHRISTIAN has a crafty look up at the sun, to see how the eclipse is progressing. It's in its third act so he too proceeds to the third act of the prayer.

Everyone repeat this after me. Loudly, so He can
hear! In English!
From this day forward

ALL: From disday.

CHRISTIAN: I promise to live my life.

ALL: Ay promise 'o live mi life.

CHRISTIAN: In accord with Thy Commandments

ALL: In cord wid di Command.

CHRISTIAN: As described by your instrument Titreano

ALL: As decribe by yoo instrument Titreano

CHRISTIAN: Who shall be known as Adam.

ALL: Who be ken by Adam.

CHRISTIAN: We, obey! Return us to the light!

ALL: We obey! Return us to di light!

The scene ends in the dark.

End of scene.

EPILOGUE

Lights up on CAPTAIN PIPON and CAPTAIN STAINES sitting on a log. STAINES is studying papers, books, the Bounty log.

STAINES: I can't find a John Adams on the Bounty roll.

PIPON: Perhaps he didn't sign as an AB.

STAINES: I've been through the full complement, quarter deck and forecastle.

PIPON: Any Londoners?

STAINES: There's an Alexander Smith.

PIPON: Ah! Bligh describes an Alexander Smith. Two toes missing from his right foot. 'To be spared. There was no room in the launch.'

Enter CHRISTIAN carried in a sedan chair by four women.

STAINES: We can't find you on the Bounty roll.

CHRISTIAN: I signed on as Alex Smith. My father, John Adams were a thief, known to the navy, so for Bligh I had myself invent a clean name, Alexander Smith. A loyal man to Bligh I were. I fetched him his breeches that morning to cover his modesty. He'll have that writ down if I know Bligh.

PIPON: No, he doesn't mention that.

STAINES: We'd like to inspect your right foot.

CHRISTIAN: Aye.

CHRISTIAN proffers his foot. One of the women take his boot off.

PIPON: What happened to your toes?

CHRISTIAN: I got one in a pearl case back in Hackney, I dunno where the other is.

PIPON: Thank you.

CHRISTIAN: Has Bligh writ me down as a rebel?

STAINES: No. 'To be spared. No room in the launch.'

PIPON: Never in these islands have we seen such a healthy, happy and devout colony. You have claimed this island for the King and its people for the Lord and you are its worthy governor.

CHRISTIAN: You don't want me 'ead then?

STAINES: You're a free man. Free to come with us, back to England.

PIPON: Or free to stay. It is your choice.

CHRISTIAN: What would I return to? What's my reputation?

PIPON: John Adams is not known. England only knows Christian.

CHRISTIAN: And what do they say of that unfortunate wretch?

STAINES: The ideas of the age, the revolution in France, the passing years have developed a wealth of sympathy for the men, antipathy for Bligh, and elevated Fletcher Christian to lion.

CHRISTIAN: Lion?

STAINES: That's the pamphlets, the chop houses and the people.

PIPON: Not the Admiralty.

CHRISTIAN: They'd hang Christian if he were alive?

PIPON: They would.

CHRISTIAN: There's one of the women Te Lahu would like to go back to Tahiti, she has children there, and never had none here.

STAINES: Certainly.

CHRISTIAN: I will stay. Til death. My family is here. And, as you can see, the Lord has a full slate of work for me.

THE END.

GREAT BRITAIN

Acknowledgements

I'd like to thank all who helped me in researching and writing this play. In particular I owe a great debt to Clive Coleman who is often cited as the story consultant but he should be credited with much terrific 'additional material'. David Yelland, once the editor of *The Sun* gave his time and opinions generously. I also owe another ex-*Sun* editor, Kelvin MacKenzie, several rounds of drinks. The cast and creative team made many original contributions and fixes. Andrew Caldecott's legal notes were essential, and his unsolicited dramaturgical interventions were not ignored.

But particular credit should be given to Nick Hytner, who held his nerve by rehearsing this play in secret, and opened it, without the benefit of previews, immediately after the court verdicts in the Operation Weeting phone hacking trial. His job, as Artistic Director of the National Theatre, is partly to consider the state of the nation, and I was happy to make a contribution in fulfilling this obligation.

Characters

Press and their roles at the start of Act 1

PAIGE BRITAIN
late 20s or early 30s, Journalist

GARTH
40s, O'Leary Business Executive

WILSON
late 50s, Editor

JACKIE
30s, ex-Page 7 girl, now Picture Editor

TINA
20s, Celebrity Desk

LARRY
50s, Crime Desk

WALLACE
TV column, How Big's Your Telly!

MADDY
40s, Royal Correspondent

MARCUS
30s, Investigative Reporter

GEMMA
30s, Foreign Desk

HOWARD
50s, Senior Journalist

THE LEGEND
(Billy Cain) 68, Sports Desk

PASCHAL O'LEARY
60s, Proprietor

VIRGINIA WHITE
New York, New York Editor

Civilians

BORIS TUDOR, 70s

CLARISSA KINGSTON-MILLS, 60s

STELLA STONE
20s, Celebrity

WENDY KLINKARD
30s, Solicitor (in a wheelchair)

Police

DONALD DOYLE DAVIDSON
30s

MAC MACMANAMAN
50s

SULIMAN (SULLY) KASSAM
40s, of Pakistani ethnicity

DI CRAM
30s

Politicians

JONATHAN WHEY
40s

ST. JOHN
30s

DIANE BENDALL
40s

Police, waiters, other press as required.

Set

A fluid, open stage, with use of video wall. The video is used to show the morning's papers, the rivals of *The Free Press.* These are THE DEPENDENT (dependent on Russian Oil Wealth), THE GUARDENER (We think so you don't have to), THE DAILY WAIL, THE EXPECTORANT, THE REAR VIEW. The video wall is also used to show TV, and filmed scenes.

One recurring set is the newsroom of *The Free Press* which has at least two very large flat screens.

Great Britain was first performed at the National Theatre, Lyttelton Theatre, London on 30 June 2014 with the following:

Press

Paschal O'Leary, Proprietor Dermot Crowley
Wilson Tikkel, Editor Robert Glenister
Garth Ellerington, Finance William Chubb
Paige Britain, News Editor Billie Piper
Virginia White, New York New York Jo Dockery
Hunter Dixon, News Ross Boatman
Howard Woolf, Features Nick Sampson
Billy Cain (Legend), Sport Iain Mitchell
Larry Arthur, Crime Robert Calvert
Wallace Gee, Showbiz James Harkness
Jackie Spence, Pictures Jo Dockery
Tina Ursal, Celebrity Sarah Annis
Maddy Fitzpatrick, Royal Barbara Kirby
Gemma Charles, Foreign Kellie Shirley
Thierry Picq, Intern Miles Mitchell
Jimmy the Bins, Freelance Ian Hallard
Marcus Hussein, Freelance Scott Karim

Police

Commissioner Sully Kassam Aaron Neil
Asst. Commissioner Donald Doyle Davidson Oliver Chris
Mac Macmanaman, Head of PR Andrew Woodall
DCI Cram Joseph Wilkins
DI Da Costa Jo Dockery
Sergeant Ojo Miles Mitchell
Nicola, Crown Prosecution Service Harriet Thorpe

Politicians

Jonathan Whey, Conservative Leader Rupert Vansittart
St John, Spin Doctor Ian Hallard
Diane Bendall, Labour MP Maggie McCarthy

Civilians

Wendy Klinkard, Solicitor Kiruna Stamell
Jasper Donald, Cricketer Joseph Wilkins
Boris Tudor Nicholas Lumley
Clarissa Kingston-Mills, PR Consultant Harriet Thorpe
Stella Stone Kellie Shirley
Stella's Dad Nicholas Lumley

Stella's Mum Harriet Thorpe
Babs, Stella's friend Sarah Annis
Kieron Mills James Harkness
Bodger, Private Detective Robert Calvert
Stevie, Private Detective Rupert Vansittart
Felix, Royal Protection Squad Ian Hallard
Jonas, Security Joseph Wilkins

On Screen
TV Anchors Paapa Essiedu, Debra Gillett, Niky Wardley
TV Reporters Rosie Armstrong, Cassie Bradley, Matthew Lloyd Davies, Eleanor Matsuura, Daniel Millar, Samuel Taylor, Ross Waiton
Select Committee Chairman Jonathan Dryden Taylor
Archbishop Tony Boncza

Other parts played by
Jonathan Bailey, Lucy Bailey, Charlotte Bevan, Lewis Boulcher, Colin Burnicle, Abby Cassidy, Gunnar Cauthery, Richard Charlton, Victor Correia, Daniel Debono, Samantha Evans, Luke Gray, Colin Haigh, Lenny Henry, Claire Hughes, Robert Killalea, Nigel Lindsay, Raphael Lowe, Tom Lyons, Fran Miller, Anna Nightingale, Natalie Pryce, Alan Richardson, James Roxburgh, Russell Saunders, Matthew Scott, Olivia Vinall, Brian Walters, Daisy Watford

Director Nicholas Hytner
Designer Tim Hatley
Video Design 59 Productions
Lighting Designer Neil Austin
Music Grant Olding
Sound Designer Paul Arditti
Company Voice Work Kate Godfrey
Staff Director Alex Brown
Story Consultant Clive Coleman

For 59 Productions:
Creative Director Leo Warner
Animation Director Zsolt Balogh
Senior Assistant Designer Akhila Krishnan
Animators Ninoslav Vrana, Dan Radley-Bennett
Assistant Designer Gareth Damian-Martin
Programmer & Associate Designer Nick Simmons
Assistant Programmer & Automation Tracking Dan Murfin
Filming: DoP: Vanessa Whyte
Camera Assistant/DIT: Chris Belcher

Great Britain transferred to the Theatre Royal Haymarket, London on 9 September 2014 with the following role changes:

Press

Paige Britain, News Editor Lucy Punch

Police

Asst. Commissioner Donald Doyle Davidson Ben Mansfield

Prologue

SCREENS: A TV commercial for *The Free Press* pushing its staples i.e.: bingo, union jacks, tits, bold headlines, football, horoscopes, How Big's Your Telly etc. The recent front page scoop of FONT FIDDLER featuring a vicar and a photo of a tattooed rent boy dominates.

'Your fabulous fun, *Free Press* is busting out this week with celebrity gossip, find out who's sorting out who. Fifteen pages of *Free Press* footie, and 'is your Vicar on Gaydar?' Look him up in our UK COTTAGING VICARS PULL OUT SPECIAL. All this for 30p, less than a pot of paprika and twice as hot!'

London. The street outside the entrance to The Free Press *offices, indicated by bold signage declaring 'The Free Press' on a red background, and in smaller letters 'O'Leary Media International'. Above the entrance is a banner poster advertising the paper featuring bingo, union jacks, tits, bold headlines, football, horoscopes etc. Enter PAIGE BRITAIN.*

PAIGE: I love this paper. It's end of the pier; it's 'naughty but nice', like knocking the VAT off for cash; it's full of half-naked girls, and chopped up prostitutes, and pop star's drugs, and footballers' wives. It's my England. As a kid, it never failed to make me feel a little bit horny. Not so horny that you have to sort it out, but, you know, that pleasant, itchy, 'glad to be alive' horny. One time, on the Pembroke Road, Bristol, I was maybe thirteen, when I realised that Dino was going to wrap my chips in the *Guardian.* Aaaargh! I leaned over the counter and grabbed his arm, and screamed 'No! No! No! Stop! Not the *Guardian*! I want something to read!' Ironically my first job was at the *Guardian.* I didn't last two days, my revulsion was physical. Rows and rows of journos knocking out sanctimonious, liberal propaganda about tax dodging, multi-national corporations, seemingly unaware that Guardian Media

Group registered multiple companies in the Cayman Islands to dodge as much tax as possible. Woah! Looks like you guys didn't know about that either!? Isn't it a wonderful thing, free speech.

Act One

SCENE ONE

The open-plan newsroom of THE FREE PRESS. A placard hangs from the ceiling – TRUTH, BEAUTY and JUSTICE. Two TV screens upstage, one showing 24-hour BBC news and one 24-hour Sky news. Upstage a cut out of Terry, a thirty-ish man with a fag, a pint, and a leer, looking at a copy of THE FREE PRESS open at a topless model page. Adjacent a cut-out of his wife, Tracy, playing the paper's Bingo – smile on her face. Many desks, all with PCs, and hacks working away or sitting chatting, or taking phone calls.

Enter JIMMY THE BINS, carrying two bin bags which he sells to DICKIE. Having done that he moves on to PAIGE with a Sainsbury's carrier bag containing a laptop. WALLACE is watching Sky TV which is showing a Millwall goal.

WALLACE: Jimmy!

PAIGE: *(Aside.)* This is Jimmy the Bins. Every bin tells a story. Sometimes it's brilliant, sometimes it's rubbish.

JIMMY: Gazza's laptop. He left it in a black cab.

PAIGE: What would Gazza want with a laptop? He can't kick it, he can't drink it, and he can't fuck it.

JIMMY: The *Mirror* have offered me two K.

PAIGE: This is an auction is it?

JIMMY: I gotta make a living.

PAIGE: Three K.

JIMMY: Done.

PAIGE: Dickie! Get someone to clone this hard drive. Tina! Jackie! Ring Gazza, tell him we've got his laptop here. Tempt him in with a photo op with a couple of Page 7 beauties, then take him to lunch, get him pissed, and try and get a picture of him in a canal, drowning.

(GARTH approaches.)

GARTH: How much is this going to cost me?

PAIGE: *(Aside.)* This is Garth, money man, hard man. *(JIMMY hands GARTH an invoice.)*

JIMMY: Cash.

GARTH: We've stopped paying cash.

JIMMY: Waeeurghhh!?

GARTH: Go to Western Union in St. James, take some ID, tell them that Mrs Orla Gilhooley, your grannie, has sent you your birthday money, money transfer from County Offaly.

JIMMY: My gran lives in Australia.

HOWARD: *(Spills coffee.)* Shit!

PAIGE: *(Aside.)* This is Howard. He's been here forever, and he's a man of principle. He says things like –

HOWARD: *(To audience.)* – Journalism is not a profession, it's a human right. There is no journalism in Zimbabwe, Belarus, or North Korea.

PAIGE: *(Aside.)* Which is why I'll be the next editor.

JACKIE: Stella… –

STELLA: Stone.

JACKIE: Stella Stone.

HOWARD: We like your portfolio, very much, Stella Stone.

JACKIE: But could you drop a dress size?

STELLA: Yes.

JACKIE: And have you ever considered breast enlargement?

STELLA: I can't afford a boob job!

HOWARD: We, *The Free Press*, would pay for your operation. Then you reduce that debt to us with every Page 7 that you do.

STELLA: I'd have to work my tits off!

HOWARD/JACKIE: *(Beat.)* Yes.

WALLACE: Hey, look at this.

(WALLACE turns up the TV sound. An image of twin twelve-year-old girls both wearing puffa waistcoat/jackets.)

REPORTER: ' – identical twins, Pippa and Paula Mills, disappeared from their parents' caravan…'

HOWARD: Wallace! Some of us are at work!

(WALLACE zaps down the volume.)

WALLACE: Sorry man, my bad! *(To STELLA.)* Fuck, hello!

PAIGE: *(Aside.)* Wallace writes the TV column 'How Big's Your Telly!?' His life is consumed by the inane, and the ephemeral. One day someone will invent Twitter and make his life complete.

(Enter BORIS TUDOR, a Countryside Alliance type. He approaches PAIGE with a letter.)

TUDOR: Excuse me, I have an eleven o'clock meeting with Howard Woolf. I've come all the way from Tewkesbury. And I'm seventy-three now.

PAIGE: How old were you when you set off?

(Reading.) Dr Boris Tudor, Laburnum Cottage, Badgeworth.

TUDOR: That's me.

PAIGE: *(Re. the letter.)* And Howard wants your story?

TUDOR: Yes, he's very interested in it. I'm not worried about the money.

PAIGE: We're not *Blue Peter*, we don't give badges.

HOWARD: *(On the phone.)* Yes, hello? *(PAIGE stands and ushers him to an interview room.)*

PAIGE: Howard is not in today, but I can take your story. After conference, you and I will go out for a proper coffee.

HOWARD: *(HOWARD approaches, suspicious.)* Hey, is that my civilian? Boris Tudor?

PAIGE: No, that is Gerri Halliwell's osteopath.

GARTH: Gather, gather.

(Enter WILSON followed by GARTH. GARTH has a pineapple in his hand. WILSON is ringing a bell. Andrew Neil is on the BBC.)

WILSON: *(Answers his mobile.)* Yep?

PAIGE: *(Aside.)* Fifteen years ago *The Free Press* was a Labour Party puff sheet, good for nothing but wiping the arses of the TUC, but Wilson took it, and created the modern tabloid. I love him, but he's got my job, knowwhatimean?

WILSON: *(Re. Andrew Neil.)* Who will rid me of this turbulent cunt?! Circulation. Saturday…

GARTH: Down forty thousand.

WILSON: The *Mirror…*

GARTH: Up thirty thousand.

WILSON: I have been summoned by the Paddy, our proprietor to County Offaly. I hate fucking Ireland. It's one great big outdoor asylum. I'll get a bullet in the head or a shelaleigh up the arse. I blame you Dickie.

DICKIE: Why me?

WILSON: 'cause I bent over backwards to purchase your gay vicar rent boy kiss and tell off Clarissa Kingston fucking Mills and I put it on the front page. Cost how much?

GARTH: Fifty thousand pounds.

WILSON: Dickie, you are 'cunt of the month'.

DICKIE: Oh no!

(GARTH writes CUNT across DICKIE's forehead in dry marker pen.)

LARRY: Piddle Hinton vicar deceives wife of thirty years with rent boy in font.

LEGEND: Come on, it's a classic.

WILSON: Jackie? Can you make these nipples look a bit less fantastic.

JACKIE: Why?

WILSON: 'cause some of our readers work in saw mills. Right, who's got what today!? Larry?

LARRY: The Kingston caravan park story. Twelve-year-old twins snatched by a paedophile.

PAIGE: Paedo Parks!

WILSON: Alliteration! And the first hard-on of the day! Two scum go for a pint, and a paedo nicks the kids. It's fabulous! But these TV twats are killing it four times an hour.

LARRY: I'm having my regular lunch with the Met Commissioner tomorrow.

WILSON: Good, get him pissed and suck his truncheon, but get me an angle! Maddy!? What are the Germans up to this week?

MADDY: Princess Anne is visiting Belfast.

WILSON: *(Beat.)* Is she pregnant?

MADDY: She's fifty.

WILSON: I need story! Princess Anne banged up by Gerry Adams, that is a story! Story, story, fucking story! Sport! Football!? Where's The Legend?

LEGEND: I'm here, and it's the cricket season.

WILSON: Fuck that! Our reader, Terry, does he look like an Oxford Blue? No! He's a scaffolder. He's a cunt. He likes football. What've you got?

LEGEND: '66 World Cup hero Tommy Burns auctions his medal to pay his gas bill.

WILSON: If that's a story my prick's a Chinaman! Legend, you were a legend once which is why we call you The Legend.

The best football stories came from you. Mickey Thomas, forged bank notes; Tony Adams, drink-driving; Peter Storey, car theft, forgery, smuggling porn, and running a brothel. I need more stories like that, or go and live in a fucking hospice!

(Enter CLARISSA Kingston-Mills.)

CLARISSA: Morning darlings!

ALL: Fuck off, etc.

WILSON: Oi! Clarissa! Are you invited to this meeting?!

CLARISSA: Willy, sweetheart, you never invite me to anything.

WILSON: That's a 'no' then, so fuck off.

(During the next CLARISSA gives DICKIE an invoice, DICKIE hands it on to GARTH.)

PAIGE: *(Aside.)* Clarissa Kingston-Mills OBE. For services to kiss and tell. She can put you in the papers, if you want to be in the papers, and if you don't want to be in the papers, she can keep you out.

(CLARISSA takes an envelope out of her handbag.)

CLARISSA: I have another story. If you want it.

WILSON: No, you fucked me over with this pufta vicar rent boy bollocks, cost me forty thousand circulation, you're bleeding this paper dry. Go on, fuck off!

CLARISSA: Someone high up in politics is pregnant, someone you wouldn't expect.

PAIGE: Boris Yeltsin?!

CLARISSA: Very well. Buy the *Mirror* tomorrow. Sheekey's some time?

WILSON: I'm banned from Sheekey's!

(CLARISSA has gone.)

HOWARD: Why are you banned from Sheekey's?

WILSON: I took me own sandwiches in. Jackie! Go round the *Mirror*, dressed as a cleaner, and nick the proofs off the stone.

JACKIE: No! I'm not doing that again. Last time they hit me.

WILSON: Tina, go round the *Mirror*, dressed as a cleaner, and nick the proofs off the stone.

TINA: You do it.

WILSON: I can't do it, cleaners are women!

PAIGE: I'll go.

WILSON: See! Wit, commitment, testicles! What else've we got?! Come on!

LEGEND: The great Sir Peter Blane's obituary. Orphan, desert rat, Sussex and England.

WILSON: When have you ever seen an obituary in my paper?

LEGEND: Every day. The same one. Diana, Princess of Wales.

WILSON: Because she sells more papers dead than you ever have alive!

(Enter MARCUS dressed as a geek.)

MARCUS: Dude. Dudes!

PAIGE: Marcus is setting up a sting.

MARCUS: D.I. Gull off *The Bill* likes his sherbert.

PAIGE: Cocaine Cop.

WILSON: Alliteration! And the second hard-on of the day!

HOWARD: Except he's not a cop, he's an actor.

WILSON: Yeah, actor likes sherbert is not a story.

PAIGE: If he agrees to sell Marcus cocaine he's a dealer.

WILSON: Dealer is a story.

MARCUS: Yeah, and this is the new character. The Meek Geek. A computer billionaire nerd, never been laid, never done coke.

WILSON: The Meek Geek? What's that?

THIERY: Assonance.

WILSON: Fuck assonance! Assonance never gave anyone a hard-on?!

HOWARD: The police would call that entrapment.

PAIGE: We're not the police, so it's not entrapment.

WILSON: What do you need Marcus?

MARCUS: A suite at the Savoy.

PAIGE: Go large!

WILSON: Garth, give this twat some money will yer. What else!? Gemma!

GEMMA: Somalia. Another civilian massacre, some very moving pictures.

WILSON: When did you last have a foreign news story in my paper?

GEMMA: 1997. The Burmese democracy campaigner, Aung San Suu Kyi.

WILSON: And what was she doing?

GEMMA: She was wearing a bikini.

WILSON: Exactly! I'm gonna sack you.

GEMMA: Why?

WILSON: 'cause everything you know about journalism could be hidden up a gnat's arse.

(Beat. A change of tone. He rings the bell.)

Alright! The tragedy of this job is that we have to do this *every fucking* day, but let me remind you why we do it. Out there right now a famous, well-loved actor is actively conning our readers. He's married one woman, and he's shagging another. Hypocrisy! Out there, right now, a member of CND is in his garage building a nuclear bomb. Out there, right now at half-past fucking ten in the morning, a back-to-basics Tory MP is paying Miss Whiplash to nail his dick to a wardrobe door. Our democracy floats like an aerated turd on an ocean of filth, corruption and nepotism. And it is only our efforts in exposing the wrongdoing of the rich, the privileged and the powerful that keeps that beautiful fragile floater afloat. Do your duty, England expects, St. Krispin's day, once more into the breach, like greyhounds in the slips, blah blah fucking blah, you know what I mean. What's at stake? The British way of life. Go out there and get those stories. But remember if you don't deliver, I will personally shove this pineapple up your arse. We go off stone at half nine, there's no football!

(WILSON walks off to the Editor's office. Office buzz returns, phones. DR. BORIS TUDOR comes out of the waiting room and approaches DICKIE.)

TUDOR: Excuse me, I had an eleven o'clock appointment with Howard Woolf – why do you have 'cunt' written on your forehead?

DICKIE: Because I'm 'cunt of the month'.

TUDOR: Is that like Page 3?

DICKIE: Fuck off will you.

PAIGE: Dr Tudor.

(PAIGE, slinging her coat on, interjects and sweeps TUDOR away.)

TUDOR: The cunt of the month just told me to fuck off.

PAIGE: Coffee?

(They head for the door. WILSON opens the door to his office. He rings the bell long and mournful. Silence.)

WILSON: *(Quietly.)* Dickie.

DICKIE: Yes boss?

WILSON: Your Piddle Hinton vicar just killed himself.

(DICKIE's head drops.)

PAIGE: *(Direct address.)* That's what we do. We go out there, and we destroy other people's lives. On your behalf. Because you want to read about other people's lives.

End of Scene.

SCREENS: The Free Press headline is FONT FIDDLER ENDS SHAME.

On a TV the Archbishop. 'He was a sweet and godly man, and will be missed by the whole community, not just the young men.'

Also THE REAR VIEW leads on Angela Merkel. MERKEL IS MIRACLE MUM TO BE. (With a photo of Angela Merkel looking stout.)

THE DAILY WAIL = THE DOLE HOLE IMMIGRANTS SEND BENEFITS HOME

SCENE TWO

SCREENS: Location setting on screen. They're in COSTALOT coffee franchise.

TUDOR: Brenda had sent me to Tewkesbury with a list. Items unattainable in Badgeworth. Sausages, juniper berries and an air rifle.

PAIGE: You can't get sausages in Badgeworth?

TUDOR: We have an award-winning butcher, with eczema. Plan A was that she'd ring me, whilst I was driving, and leave the brand and model number on the ansaphone.

PAIGE: Voicemail.

TUDOR: But when I got to Tewkesbury I realised I'd left my mobile phone in the fridge.

PAIGE: Easily done.

TUDOR: I wanted to test the battery under cold conditions. We're going to Scarborough for Christmas. I used a phone box to talk to the Vodafone customer services chap who told me to dial my own number –

PAIGE: – from the pay phone.

TUDOR: Yes, and then press the hash key and enter 3333, which is the factory setting. Suddenly, I am listening to my own voicemail from a pay phone. Meaning that anyone, can listen to anyone else's messages.

PAIGE: *(Aside.)* Kerching!

TUDOR: What if the Muhammadens got hold of this?

PAIGE: Imagine.

TUDOR: I saw the Queen on her mobile in, er…oh what's it called –

PAIGE: – Argos?

TUDOR: No, er…in…

PAIGE: – Morrisons?

TUDOR: – Horse and Hound! These are the default PINs for all the networks. *(He gives her a sheet of A4.)*

PAIGE: *(Aside.)* Kerching and cashback too! *(PAIGE gives money to BORIS TUDOR.)* Me buying the story means it's my story now, not yours. You can't go to the *Daily Mirror* and try and make another two hundred.

TUDOR: Wild horses wouldn't drag me to London again.

PAIGE: And why does Brenda want an air rifle?

TUDOR: It's all she's allowed, now that they've taken her shotguns away.

End of Scene.

(PAIGE walks to her next scene.)

PAIGE: *(Direct address.)* A stranger gives you a superhero's special power, absolutely without a caveat that it must only be used for good. What's a poor girl to do? The business model of my paper is the sale for profit of private information. To do that effectively we must become less like a newspaper and more like GCHQ.

End of Scene.

SCENE THREE

SCREENS: A shop front 'SPY SPY' with on the window of the shop the things they do listed. CORPORATE DATA THEFT, WITNESS INTIMIDATION, POLICE COMPUTER RECORDS, INTRUSIVE VIDEO SURVEILLANCE, DOMESTIC BURGLARY, CONTRACT KILLING.

(She meets up with LEGEND outside Spy Spy. They go in.)

PAIGE: What can you offer me?

STEVIE: DVLA, VAT records, tax records, X directory, hospital, Criminal Records Check, police computer and Bodger can blag anything. Do your Stevie Gerrard.

BODGER: Erm! Hello mate, I been tryna find the balance on me account like, but I lost me card in Turkey like last week, European Cup. Can you tell me the balance like over the phone, like now?

(STEVIE is laughing.)

PAIGE: Knowing how much Stevie G has in his bank account is not a story. Legend, tell these guys what a story needs.

LEGEND: Betrayal, love, hate, tears, loss, anger, sex, crime, and cowardice.

PAIGE: I'm going to show you a technique –

STEVIE: – You, you're gonna show *us* how to do something?

BODGER: *(Laughing.)* We know how to do everything.

PAIGE: Access to mobile phone voicemail.

STEVIE: We're always happy to learn new things.

PAIGE: OK. Legend is going to ring Jasper Donald, the cricketer.

LEGEND: First, I call him on his mobile telephone –

PAIGE: Jasper Donald is with Vodafone. Knowing the network is important.

BODGER: We can blag that.

(LEGEND dials, it's ringing. PAIGE is ready with her mobile.)

PAIGE: When The Legend gets through, I dial the same number.

STEVIE: Which will be engaged.

PAIGE: Exactly.

LEGEND: *(On the phone.)* – hello?! is that Jasper?… *(PAIGE exaggerates her pressing of the pre-dial.)*

PAIGE: Now I dial…

LEGEND: Well done yesterday young man. The ghost of Fred Truman…

PAIGE: … Mine has gone to voicemail.

LEGEND: I do apologise Jasper, when is a good time to ring?

PAIGE: … I press hash…

LEGEND: *(Phone away from mouth.)* Ill-bred youth. He cut me off.

PAIGE: …it offers me a menu.

STEVIE: This why you need two people. It's a double tap.

PAIGE: I choose to listen to voicemail. I'm asked to enter a PIN, which is always the factory setting as no one ever bothers to set their own PIN.

(She dials 3333.)

The Vodafone factory setting is 3333. *(To LEGEND.)* There's a message.

BODGER: Here, here, let me plug it in.

STEVIE: *(To BODGER.)* Record it an'all.

(BODGER connects PAIGE's mobile so they can all listen, and presses record on some kit.)

BEXY-ANNE: *(Distort.)* Yesterday man, you were crunk, and I'm really really soz I got smashed. But you were so sweeeeeet, and sensitive. À la prochaine!

Beep! No more messages.

PAIGE: That's Bex, lead singer of Metal Theft.

LEGEND: Bexy-Anne Blane, the grand-daughter of the great Sir Peter Blane. It was his funeral yesterday.

PAIGE: The lead singer of Metal Theft fucks England's Ashes hero at her grandfather's funeral. Story.

STEVIE: This is fucking Eldorado.

SCREENS: Phone interceptions shown as audio recordings, overlapping etc.

(JANET STREET-PORTER.) It's me, I'm in Waitrose, now, looking at a tin of duck confit, and I can't remember if your mother was sick last time we had confit, was it your mother, or was it your sister, or was it confit. One of your lot was sick last time we had confit, or didn't have confit. I'm giving you ten minutes, you're gonna ring me or your mother's getting tomato soup.

(MALE.) The doctor said it's called tortion. Basically they have to be rehung like chandeliers.

(PAIGE and LEGEND leave the offices of the PIs and are once more in a busy London street.)

PAIGE: Wilson will want to know the source.

LEGEND: Throughout my career I've named all my sources after villages in Northamptonshire, but I've never had a Burton Latimer.

PAIGE: Burton Latimer. Cool. *(Aside.)* It's probably a little bit illegal. And riding a bike without lights is also a little bit illegal, and the police don't do anything about that. They've got other priorities.

SCENE FOUR

SCREENS: THE GUARDENER = MET OFFICERS GUN DOWN BLACK SUSPECT IN SUPERMARKET.

THE FREE PRESS = DEATH IS CHEAP IN LIDL

THE REAR VIEW with a photo of Kassam and the front page THE BLACK DEATH.

THE DAILY WAIL = IMMIGRANTS CAN'T SPELL

(A Metropolitan Police 'grace and favour' flat in Westminster. In full uniform including hat, Sir SULLY KASSAM, British Asian, the Commissioner of the Metropolitan Police is sitting in the middle of a sofa on the edge of the seat. MAC MACMANAMAN mid-sixties, dressed in holiday shorts and deck shoes is prowling. He reads a document. He is PR for the Met. DONALD DOYLE DAVIDSON, 37, uniformed but without his hat on, is Sully's staff officer.)

MACM: We've shot the wrong black guy?

KASSAM: *I* didn't.

MACM: History will record that the first Asian Commissioner shot the wrong black guy. *(Turns page.)* In Lidl.

DOYLE D: Armed Response were looking for an IC6 male with a concealed hand gun.

MACM: Did Elroy Baptiste have a concealed hand gun?

KASASM: – Delroy.

MACM: Is it Elroy or Delroy?

DOYLE D: It's actually Leroy.

MACM: Have you called him either Elroy or Delroy in the media?

KASSAM: Yes.

MACM: Which?

DOYLE D: Both.

MACM: Brilliant. Did –

DOYLE D: – Leroy.

MACM: Did Leroy have anything that looked like a gun?

KASSAM: Yes. He had a carrot in a carrier bag.

MACM: OK. What have we got on him? There must be something, he's black.

KASSAM: Why would we run a Criminal Records Check on the victim?

MACM: If we've shot an innocent black man, we're institutionally racist. If we've shot a black man with a criminal record, we've been heavy-handed.

DOYLE D: He's a vicar. Was a vicar.

MACM: Brilliant. What time is Tim Henman on court tomorrow?

DOYLE D: Two – ish.

MACM: So, three o'clock press conference.

(KASSAM shuffles uncomfortably, takes his hat off. DOYLE D looks at the carpet.) Why are you not leaving? There's something else?

KASSAM: There's a civilian works in diversity education.

DOYLE D: He's threatening a sexual harrassment claim.

KASSAM: Bryn. He's Welsh.

DOYLE D: With a Chinese father. Bryn Wong.

MACM: Is he a whistle blower?

DOYLE D: So far the only thing he's blown is the Commissioner.

MACM: What was the most important thing they taught you at Bramshill?

KASSAM: Er…motivate your senior team –

MACM: No – thou shalt not comfort thy rod with thy staff!

KASSAM: When you get these pips, it's an aphrodisiac.

MACM: I could use the Bill Clinton defence. Monica misheard me. I said 'sack my cook'.

(The doorbell sounds.)

DOYLE D: This'll be DCI Cram. SIO on the twins case.

MACM: Three things!

(MACM goes out into the hall.)

KASSAM: It'll be the dad. It's always the dad.

DOYLE D: We have time-calibrated video footage of him winning the karaoke.

KASSAM: Fuck!

(Enter DI CRAM. DOYLE D stands and shakes his hand.)

KASSAM: Have you found them?

CRAM: Not yet sir. The dad, Kieron Mills, he's not right, he has Asperger's Syndrome, very paranoid about the police, he bit a female officer once.

KASSAM: We've all done that.

CRAM: I don't think he's capable of killing. I don't think he did it. He's very vulnerable, suicide's a possibility, he might do a runner, I dunno, but we need to protect him. He's all we've got.

DOYLE D: What do you need Cram?

CRAM: I want him protected from the press. If Fleet Street turn up, he'll fall over. Ideally, I'd like the whole family locked down on the press side.

MACM: *(To CRAM.)* I can do that, can you?

CRAM: There are no salesmen on my team sir.

MACM: Crap.

KASSAM: You've got what you want, lock up the whole family.

DOYLE D: Down. Lock down.

KASSAM: Sorry, yeah. Don't lock them up, lock them down. You're doing a great job. Anything you need, you know where to come.

MACM: But don't come here. *(CRAM leaves.)*

Three days! You kill a black vicar wielding a carrot; twins get nicked by a paedo; and you fuck a Sino Welshman.

KASSAM: *(Head in hands.)* I am so unlucky!

MACM: You're not unlucky, you're a fur-lined ocean-going fuck up!

KASSAM: Everyone's against me – coppers on the beat, the Mason, criminals. I could clean up this town. Tough on crime, tough on the causes of crime? Crap! If you stop crime, you stop it being caused. One crime is a crime, no crime is not a crime. I could wash the scum off these streets. I didn't go to New York for the air miles. I had a vision out there, zero tolerance. People think I'm gonna be mister cuddly diversity, no! I'm the gay terminator.

MACM: Who knows about Bryn? Does your Martin know?

DOYLE D: Maurice.

KASSAM: It's not been working for a while, me and Maurice. We're splitting up.

MACM: Irreconcilable similarities?

KASSAM: That is homophobic! You need a course Mac.

MACM: I am not homophobic. I'm just not gay.

DOYLE D: What if we create a post, close enough to you for Bryn to feel there's a chance of whatever it is in his head, his vision of life with you, becoming a reality. Community Relations Co-ordinator?

MACM: We've already got three of those.

DOYLE D: Head of LGBT Liaison?

MACM: Great. Kill two birds with one stone. We solve the problem, and look gay at the same time.

KASSAM: That's brilliant. Head of LBGT.

DOYLE D: LGBT. If it sounds like a car you've got it wrong.

KASSAM: See. He was my idea. Cambridge.

DOYLE D: Oxford.

KASSAM: I've heard they're both good.

End of Scene.

SCREENS: 24-hour news and a press conference given by Sully Kassam.

KASSAM: 'Unfortunately, on my watch there have been disproportionately more Afro-Caribbean men shot and killed by armed officers. I'd like to be able to say that just as many white men had been shot accidentally, but unfortunately I can't. Working together with the communities, we will be putting that right in the coming year.'

SCENE FIVE

SCREENS: THE FREE PRESS = STELLA: I LOVE MY NEW BOOBS.

DAILY WAIL = IMMIGRANTS EXPECT FREE HOUSING.

THE FREE PRESS = CRUNK HUNK BUNKS DRUNK PUNK and a picture of Jasper and Bexy Anne Blane.

(A solicitor's office. JASPER DONALD is dressed in cricket whites, and flip flops. He grips a copy of The Free Press. *WENDY has dwarfism and is in a wheelchair.)*

WENDY: So, Jasper, if you insist on buying this seven-bedroomed mock Tudor detached house, with a Greco-Roman pool extension, without 21st-century planning permission, from a known drug dealer, I must insist on you signing a CMA document.

JASPER: What's a CMA document?

WENDY: Cover my arse. To cover your arse I want you to take out indemnity insurance against breaches of planning. Be about two hundred pounds.

JASPER: Go for it. *(JASPER's mobile phone goes off.)*

(On the phone.) Yeah, right!?... Fuck off!

(Turning phone off.) Sorry. We won the toss and we're batting. I bat eleven 'cause I can't fucking bat you know, so I should be alright til this afti, but that's one of the lads tryna tell me we've lost five wickets. Piss take.

WENDY: Anything else? You've been gripping that copy of *The Free Press. (JASPER hands her the newspaper.)*

'Crunk Hunk Bunks Drunk Punk.'

JASPER: Me fiancée read that and dumped me.

WENDY: Have you kissed Bexy Ann?

JASPER: Not French, no.

WENDY: Crunk is a portmanteau of crazy and drunk isn't it?

JASPER: *(Beat.)* Bexy called me crunk in her phone message.

WENDY: Bexy Ann left a message on your phone describing you as 'crunk'?

JASPER: See, her Grandad, kinda taught me everything I know so I ended up doing the whatsit at his funeral.

WENDY: The conga?

JASPER: No. The –

WENDY: – the buffet.

JASPER: – no, where you like big up the dead.

WENDY: The eulogy.

JASPER: That's it. So I did a ...

WENDY: – eulogy.

JASPER: And the following day she left me this voicemail.

(He plays the message.) **'Yesterday man, you were crunk. And I'm really really soz I got smashed. But you were so sweeeeeet, and sensitive. À la prochaine!'**

À la prochaine, what's that? Goodbye in Islam?

WENDY: Have you ever had your mobile stolen?

JASPER: How would I know if I'd had my mobile stolen?

WENDY: *(Beat.)* It'd be missing.

JASPER: You mean, if I didn't get it back. No. Can I sue?

WENDY: Take on *The Free Press* and they'll hound you, and they'll pay people to talk. I don't want to know, but, for example, if you've ever had an STD –

JASPER: – I've got one now, 0161.

WENDY: They'll go through your bins, hide in your garden, they'll destroy you.

JASPER: If I find one of them hiding in the garden, can I kill them?

WENDY: As your solicitor I advise you not to kill anyone kinda generally, anywhere. However, The Human Rights Act gives you a reasonable expectation of privacy which might be enough to nail the bastards. It says here that Lancashire are twenty-three for six.

JASPER: Fuck! *(JASPER exits at pace.)*

End of Scene.

SCREENS: Voicemail interception.

(THE QUEEN.) Philip, I imagine you're sulking somewhere in that awful black cab of yours. I love you, you know I do, but you make it so difficult for one.

(PRINCE CHARLES.) Camilla darling, it's me, I haven't had a bath for a week now. This is what farmers must smell like. I'll be back tonight but only if the bloody Aga's fixed.

SCENE SIX

(The Newsroom daytime. LARRY is managing the screens.)

LEGEND: *(Phone down.)* Jackie, photographer please! Ulrika Jonsson's PR is telling her to leave Soho House in tears in about an hour's time!

JACKIE: Source?

LEGEND: Burton Latimer.

JACKIE: I got it!

(JACKIE gets on the phone to her photographer.)

DICKIE: Jackie, Stella Stone's dad is gonna drive her to The Clinic at ten thirty!

JACKIE: Says who?

DICKIE: Burton Latimer.

JACKIE: Shit! I've only got Alexis left.

TINA: *(Standing.)* Jackie, Naomi Campbell is in Patisserie Valerie! Burton.

JACKIE: I've run out of photographers!

TINA: But she's meeting her mother!

WALLACE: Fight! Fight! Fight! Fight!

JACKIE: Fuck it! I'll go myself!

(JACKIE picks up her coat and camera and leaves. GARTH arrives with golf clubs. LARRY switches to Sky News.)

SCREENS: (On location in a lay-by beyond which is a hedge and trailer park.)

NEWSHOUND: .... 'or to use the English term, permanent caravan, is located. **Mr Pringle noticed a white, transit-style van parked in this lay-by adjacent to the caravan park where the Mills trailer is located.**'

SCREENS: 24-hour BBC news and Kassam is giving an interview to camera outside the Yard. We see the iconic shot of the twins in their Bro merchandising yellow puffa jackets.

KASSAM: Good Morning... *(He adjusts his mic.)*

GARTH: *(To LARRY.)* Has he found them?

LARRY: Kassam couldn't find his own arse with both hands.

KASSAM: I can't solve this crime on my own. I need help. So, I'm making an appeal today – did you kidnap the Mills twins? If so, please ring me on 0800 563 6767.

(Enter WILSON, and PASCHAL O'LEARY from the stairs. O'LEARY is a man of sixty-five, suit but no tie.)

LARRY: Mr O'Leary.

WILSON: Larry's retiring. He's gonna set up a B&B in Wiltshire.

LARRY: Kennels.

WILSON: I wouldn't let my dog stay there! *(All laugh.)*

PAIGE: *(Aside.)* This is our proprietor Paschal O'Leary. I need him to like me, which he will. I'm gonna touch his arm, look him in the eye, say something nice about Ireland. I'll start a dream in his head, the idea that one night after too many tequila slammers I might find his thinning hair, halitosis and liver spots attractive enough to voluntarily fuck his brains out.

(She touches his arm before she is introduced, and looks into his eyes.)

WILSON: You remember Paige Britain our News Editor, she's –

PAIGE: – The most beautiful beach in the world is Dogs Bay Connemara. I was there alone on a Tuesday afternoon.

O'LEARY: – The very best single fucking moment of my entire fucking life happened on that beach. Do you shoot?

PAIGE: I was brought up on a farm. I was born with a shotgun in my hand, which I used to suck.

O'LEARY: Next weekend, on my yacht, Bermuda. It's business, I'm meeting with this Tory fellah, whatshisname.

WILSON: Jonathan Whey.

PAIGE: Shooting on a yacht. It's the best offer I've ever had.

(WILSON rings the bell.)

WILSON: During the election campaign, Paschal is gonna move his base temporarily from County Offaly to the mainland.

HOWARD: Wilson. He's an Irishman. 'The mainland'.

WILSON: Kaw! You Paddies you're so touchy!

O'LEARY: What makes a good editor is not a matter of education or paper qualifications.

WILSON: One O-Level. Fucking woodwork.

O'LEARY: I've flown over here today, from the mainland –

(Laughter.)

'cause I wanted you guys to be the first to hear me plans. Are them doors closed?

GARTH: Staffers only Marcus!

ALL: Fuck off, etc

(MARCUS exits.)

O'LEARY: I'm making a bid to buy up ITV.

ALL: Cheers / Wooh! / yeah!, etc.

O'LEARY: Yep. I'm gonna develop a digitial terrestrial platform with a news channel, a sports channel, a kids channel and seventeen channels of subscription porn.

(Applause.)

WALLACE: Bring it on!

O'LEARY: I'll be sweet-talking this Tory fellah –

WILSON: – Jonathan Whey.

O'LEARY: – as I'll not buy ITV unless the BBC gets stripped of its licence.

ALL: *(Cheers.)*

(GARTH passes the bell to WILSON who rings it. O'LEARY exits.)

WILSON: Right, we haven't had a decent scum story recently. Who are the scum!? The scum are Scousers, obviously – gyppos; the unemployed; druggies; MEPs; feminists; northerners; criminals; prisoners; teenage mums; asylum-seekers; illegal immigrants; legal immigrants; squatters; kiddie- fiddlers; cyclists; trade unionists; the IRA; and career women who rely on childcare. *(Beat.)* Any one of those is a scum story, any two of those is a double-scum story and a guaranteed hard-on. Howard, give me an example of double-scum.

HOWARD: An IRA cyclist.

WILSON: An example of a multiple-scum story please!?

PAIGE: An illegal immigrant Islamist terrorist drug dealing kiddie-fiddler and social security scrounger drives a stolen and uninsured MOT failure into a bus queue of Falklands war heroes.

WILSON: I need to change my pants! OK. No pressure! What have you got?

GEMMA: I've got something. Polar bear numbers are declining.

WILSON: Good! Great! Fuck 'em! 200 words and a picture. Next!

MADDY: Some worrying ovarian cancer statistics linked to –

WILSON: – This is a newspaper, not a well woman clinic! What else!?

TINA: For the election, we asked famous people, like Henry VIII, who they would vote for.

WILSON: Tina darling, Henry VIII's dead. *(Pause.)* Isn't he?

TINA: We used a medium to get in touch with them.

WILSON: Oh! It's a bollocks piece. Fucking hell girl, I thought you'd lost it.

TINA: Shakespeare and Jack the Ripper said they would vote Tory; Trotsky went for Labour; and Vlad the Impaler was a don't know.

WILSON: It's funny, it's in. Larry, what's new on the twins?

LARRY: Pensioner, Eddie Pringle saw a transit van in a lay-by on his way home after a meat bingo.

WILSON: Fucking brilliant! Let's have a meat bingo! Confess to killing the twins! Win a leg of lamb! Tell us where the bodies are – win two pork chops!

WALLACE: That's not bingo man, that's like Crimewatch with meat prizes.

WILSON: Howard?

HOWARD: No.

WILSON: It's funny.

HOWARD: No.

WILSON: *(Worried.)* Is it sick?

HOWARD: Very. Terry and Tracy have young children.

(WILSON looks at TERRY and TRACY.)

WILSON: So you've got fucking fuck-all on the biggest crime story there is?! You're fired.

LARRY: I'm having dinner with the Met Commissioner this evening.

WILSON: No you're not, Paige is. Go on, fuck off and open that hotel in Wiltshire.

LARRY: Kennels!

WILSON: I wouldn't let my dog stay there! Howard, we need a thousand words on how we're getting shafted in Europe. Gemma, find a boffin who can prove that eating Brussels sprouts gives you AIDS. There's no football, we're off stone at half eight. Fantastic!

(WILSON exits to his office. PAIGE makes a call from her landline.)

PAIGE: *(On the phone.)* Could you give me the number for a firing range or a shooting club that does beginner's courses please? Thank you.

(She writes down a number.)

(Aside.) Do I look like I was brought up on a farm?

End of Scene.

SCENE SEVEN

(PASCHAL in direct address.)

O'LEARY: The businessman I most admire is Eddie Stobart. He started with nothing but a ten-ton lorry and a stutter. One day, a fellah ring him up and says – 'I got forty ton of sugar beet I gotta get to Doncaster, can you do it?' And Eddie says 'Nnnnn... Nnnnnn... Nnnnn... oh alright then.'

Eddie's Stobart's stutter is me inspiration.

Now, a lot of shite has been written about me and most of it's true. They say I was a sniper in the IRA. They say I shot a young Brit soldier. They say the bullet went in through his left eye and come out his right side dragging his kidney with it. But I forget. The Army Council got me the hell out of Ireland to Boston and they give me a whole heap o' money to buy a paper 'cause Danny Morrison wanted to 'control the message in America'.

I filled two pages of that Boston paper with me own telephone sex lines, and I made a million dollars, for meself, before Christmas '74. Or was it '75? I think I've got about six sons. They get a country each, and me other son Brendan runs the porn satellites.

Me da knew he'd passed on the terrible fucking memory gene, and because he didn't want me to forget how the Brits had raped Ireland he christened me Paschal 'cause it means Easter, and he wanted me to remember the Easter rising of 19…ah, fuck, it's gone.

SCENE EIGHT

SCREENS: VOICEMAIL INTERCEPTION

BRYN WONG: – 'it's me Bryn, saw you on TV, you looked luscious all in shiny buttons. I want you so bad, come round tonight.' *(Beep.)*

SULLY: – 'Bryn, I'm sorry, this has to end. I'd appreciate it if you could put my Norwich City pyjama bottoms in the post.'

(The Ivy. MACMANAMAN and DOYLE DAVIDSON at a table set for four. Waiters scurry. Enter KASSAM, in full uniform, with hat on.)

KASSAM: I don't like this restaurant.

MACM: It's The Ivy. What's not to like?

KASSAM: Somebody in the toilets asked me if I worked here.

MACM: We got a break on Leroy Baptiste.

DOYLE D: Something we can give Larry.

MACM: Last year he ran a confirmation class which was attended by a drug dealer, and dog fight organiser, called –

DOYLE D: – Marvin Clement.

MACM: SHOT VICAR RAN GANGSTA SCHOOL.

KASSAM: Does that retrospectively justify us blowing his brains out in Lidl?

MACM: Yes. A bit.

DOYLE D: And a bit is all the public need.

KASSAM: I'm against the death penalty on principle. Unless it's for something really serious.

(Enter PAIGE.)

PAIGE: Hi! Paige Britain. I'm the new Larry Arthur. Wilson sacked Larry for not having anything on the twins

MACM: You're better looking than the old Larry Arthur.

DOYLE D: Donald Doyle Davidson. Assistant Commissioner.

PAIGE: That's a lot of Ds. You're Mac MacManaman, which is a lot of M's. You're the best. No one polishes turds like you do.

MACM: Every turd has a silver lining.

FERNANDO: Can I get you a drink Miss Britain?

PAIGE: A large skittlebomb please.

KASSAM: We'd invited Larry because we want a close relationship with The Free Press, get you on the inside, inside our inside, oops upside our head.

PAIGE: You need stories in my paper which big you up.

MACM: I have those stories.

DOYLE D: The communities feel over-policed and under-protected.

PAIGE: Just stop shooting innocent black men then! Sorry! It just came out!

KASSAM: I intend introducing tasers. The electricity bill will go up, but it'll be worth it.

PAIGE: I'd like your stories but I've already got my scoop. You and Bryn Wong.

KASSAM: Bryn who?

FERNANDO: Are you ready to order?

MACM: *(To FERNANDO.)* Fuck off.

Why have you decided to commit career suicide at such a young age? We're the Met.

PAIGE: I'm meeting Bryn tomorrow. Prêt à Manger. He's prêt à parler.

MACM: He doesn't know anyone called Bryn.

KASSAM: My 'civil partnership' with Maurice is very strong

(KASSAM's phone rings. He answers it, looking at the screen first.)

(On the phone.) BRYN! I can't talk now. *(Off the phone.)* Shit!

MACM: We can offer you a better story.

DOYLE D: – No!

MACM: The biggest story there is, at the moment.

DOYLE D: No, no.

PAIGE: The twins?

MACM: Access, to the father –

PAIGE: – Kieron Mills, and an exclusive.

DOYLE D: Can we talk about this!

PAIGE: If I don't touch Bryn.

MACM: Yup.

PAIGE: Cool.

MACM: *(Grabbing KASSAM.)* You're coming with me.

(KASSAM and MACMANAMAN stand. DOYLE D stops them leaving.)

DOYLE D: We are jeapordising Cram's investigation if we give her Mills!

MACM: Yeah. I'm trading Mills for Sully. That's my job, to protect him at all costs. Give her Mills.

KASSAM: DD – that's an order.

(KASSAM and MACM leave and DOYLE D sits. PAIGE moves places to be nearer to him.)

PAIGE: DD? I think I'll call you Ding Dong.

DOYLE D: You can call me what you like.

PAIGE: Why did you become a policeman?

DOYLE D: The Met needed someone who could order in French.

PAIGE: *(Aside.)* A good-looking, funny policeman, who speaks French? It's a parallel reality. There must be a catch.

(To DD.) Are you married?

DOYLE D: I am not married.

PAIGE: *(Aside.)* Cashback! My guess is that we'll casually start talking about sex, and then see what happens.

(To DD.) Like…where's the weirdest place you've ever had sex?

DOYLE D: An industrial walk-in fridge. What about you?

PAIGE: Middlesborough.

DOYLE D: You're funny.

PAIGE: How long can Kassam last?

DOYLE D: Until he shoots the next black guy.

PAIGE: Not long then. I want you to be Commissioner. Are you next in line?

DOYLE D: I'd be a candidate.

PAIGE: So do you guys think Kieron Mills killed his own kids?

DOYLE D: It is usually the dad. But we can't prove it.

PAIGE: If I said I was a superhero with special powers would you let me help? Give me Kieron Mills's mobile number.

DOYLE D: I'm going to give you access to Kieron Mills, you can ask him for his phone number yourself.

(PAIGE leans over and snogs him. FERNANDO comes over.)

PAIGE: That was my impression of…?

FERNANDO: Nancy Dell'Olio?

PAIGE: Yeah.

End of Scene.

SCENE NINE

SCREENS: A short biography of Jonathan Whey in tabloid headlines and scoops.

THE REAR VIEW = MAN ON TOP
Jonathan Whey leads election polls. And photo of Whey alongside Jasmine Wood.

THE GUARDENER = JONATHAN WHEY LEADS ELECTION POLLS

THE DEPENDENT = WHEY WAS MY ETON FAG SAYS BISHOP. And a photograph of Justin Welby.

THE DAILY WAIL = IMMIGRANTS NEVER HEARD OF BOBBY MOORE

(PASCHAL O'LEARY's luxury catamaran on the open sea off Bermuda. WILSON, WHEY, his press officer ST. JOHN FLOWERS, HOWARD, crew. A bikini-clad waitress is serving Pimms from a jug. PASCHAL is firing the Armalite at sharks in the water.)

O'LEARY: It's me favourite fucking thing ever, shooting up fucking sharks off me own fucking yacht!

(Gunfire is heard off, from the bows. The others look to WHEY, it's his turn but he's ogling the waitress.)

ST. JOHN: Jonathan's favourite fucking thing ever is time spent with his wife and family.

(Gunfire is heard off the bows again.)

O'LEARY: You've given up your favourite fucking thing ever to be here, you must want something pretty bad.

WHEY: Your paper's support delivered John Major to Number 10 in '92, and you gave us Blair in '97.

WILSON/HOWARD: I GOT A PONY ON TONY!

WHEY: You're the kingmaker.

(Enter PAIGE in shorts and a bikini top, looking great. She's carrying a rifle.)

PAIGE: I love these rifles.

O'LEARY: I used to smuggle them in on the QEII. The fucking QEII! Now what's the word for that?

WILSON: Smuggling.

(HOWARD stands and goes below. Enter VIRGINIA WHITE. She has very long, curly hair. Alternatively, an afro, whatever, there's some hair statement going on.)

VIRGINIA: Hi!

ALL: Hi / hello / hiya.

VIRGINIA: Cool.

PAIGE: *(Aside.)* This is Virginia White. O'Leary holds a candle for this woman but she's married to a soapstar, one of *Emmerdale*'s shaven-headed Arkwright brothers.

(To VIRGINIA.) How do you and Ronnie Arkwright maintain a marriage given that he's filming in Yorkshire and you're in New York, editing *New York, New York* in New York?

VIRGINIA: Paige, this may come as a shock to you, but I'm not married to 'Ronnie Arkwright'. That's the name of the character he plays in *Emmerdale.*

PAIGE: What!? *Emmerdale*'s not a documentary?!

O'LEARY: Don't let her tease you Virginia, she's as sharp as a razor is Paige, and I need you two to work together.

WILSON: They're gonna be working together are they?

O'LEARY: Aye. What's your favourite fucking thing ever Virginia?

VIRGINIA: Horses. They never let you down.

PAIGE: Unless you're air traffic control and you're trying to coach one of them to land a jumbo jet.

(VIRGINIA looks daggers at PAIGE who stares her out.)

O'LEARY: I just fucking knew you two would get on.

WHEY: I love horses. The smell. The way they can take a shit and keep on walking.

VIRGINIA: You must come and ride one weekend.

WHEY: Do you have a horse big enough?

VIRGINIA: We could always lash two together

O'LEARY: OK, business, Britain is sclerotic, punitive, taxed to fuck. The media is overfuckingregulated.

ST. JOHN: Ah, we have radical media proposals. Universal access to free broadband.

O'LEARY: Free?! People love buying stuff! The only way anyone knows who the fuck they are is by taking a look at the fucking crap they've bought!

WHEY: If you back us, if you get us elected we can ease through your acquisition of ITV.

ST.JOHN: There'll be a fit and proper person challenge from the Commons.

O'LEARY: How am I not a fucking fit and proper person to run a TV station?!

WHEY: You were in the IRA.

O'LEARY: So was Martin McGuinness and he's running a fucking country.

ST. JOHN: Diane Bendall will use the Media Select Committee to challenge you.

WHEY: She's worried that you'll use ITV to flood Britain with porn.

PAIGE: Choice.

WILSON: You used to have to walk a couple of miles to find a newsagent who didn't know your mum.

PAIGE: Wilson. What are you talking about?

WILSON: Buying porn.

PAIGE: Paschal won't buy ITV whilst an unaccountable BBC is allowed to continue to corrupt the market with five billion pounds mugged off the British people.

VIRGINIA: *(To O'LEARY.)* She's good isn't she?

PAIGE: We'll put you in Downing Street if you unpack the Beeb.

WHEY: We can do everything we can do, but we can't promise, because this is a democracy, this isn't Italy.

PAIGE: In Italy you'd also get a cheque.

O'LEARY: How about two million?

ST. JOHN: Yes, please.

O'LEARY: But I'm not spending without buying.

WHEY: But first, I'd like an apology from Wilson for the lies that he has printed about me in the past.

WILSON: They were not lies when I printed them. They were well-researched stories which later turned out not to be true.

WHEY: I can give you the support of the Tory party through the democratic, law-making committee process. But I can't give you guarantees.

O'LEARY: Paige. Tell the fucker what you've got.

PAIGE: We know about Miss Lydia Lovebutton.

ST. JOHN: Who's Lydia Lovebutton?

(Silence.)

Jon? Is she one of our researchers?

WHEY: The licence fee is dependent on an agreement between the Secretary of State for Culture and the BBC which runs out in November. If we get elected, I'll not sign another.

End of Scene.

SCREENS: YOUTUBE. A SULLY KASSAM MASH-UP RAP DEVELOPED FROM ONE OF HIS MANY CRETINOUS PRESS CONFS.

'On my watch there have been disproportionately more Afro-Caribbean men shot and killed by armed officers. I'd like to be able to say that just as many white men had been shot, but unfortunately I can't. We will be putting that right (we will be putting that right.), we will be putting that right (we will be putting that right.), we will be putting that right (we will be putting that right), we will be putting that right (we will be putting that right).'

SCENE TEN

(The News Room. Busy. WENDY, JASPER, GARTH and LEGEND are in a huddle, it looks like they don't have a meeting, have just dropped in. GEMMA is standing before the screens switching channels. WENDY gives a document in an envelope to GARTH.)

SCREENS:

BBC ANCHOR: It's now over a fortnight since Pippa and Paula Mills were snatched from their parents caravan in Kingston, and despite repeated appeals to the public for information, the Met appear to be making no progress in this enquiry. The Commissioner, Sully Kassam, had this to say today.

KASSAM: A clue is the one thing I've not got.

(GEMMA mutes the TV.)

GARTH: So this is…?

WENDY: It's a civil claim for defamation.

GARTH: Where did you find this solicitor Jasper, Yellow Pages?

JASPER: Er…yeah.

WENDY: Your untrue story resulted in the break-up of my client's long-term relationship.

PAIGE: 63% of marriages end in divorce. We did you a favour.

WENDY: Crunk is an unusual word.

PAIGE: Are you saying your client is not crunk?

WENDY: Its occurence in your headline and in the voicemail message on Jasper's phone is a coincidence then?

GARTH: I'll make you a Part 36 offer for ten grand.

JASPER: What's that mean?

WENDY: *(To GARTH.)* Shall I explain?

GARTH: I'm not a lawyer.

WENDY: If we refuse to settle out of court, and we go to court and lose, we would be liable for their costs.

GARTH: Two hundred thousand.

JASPER: I'm made up with 10K.

WENDY: You might be Jasper, but I'm not happy.

GARTH: Which one are you then? Sneezy?

WENDY: I'm small because I have a genetically inherited condition. You're a complete arsehole because?

PAIGE: Garth? She asked you a question.

WENDY: We're going. If we can find the way out.

GARTH: The stairs are to the left.

(WENDY and JASPER leave. WILSON enters wielding a stuffed ferret and starts ringing his bell.)

WILSON: It's Friday! It's ferret-up-the-arse day! Who's got a home for a lonely ferret!?

PAIGE: We do. The Queen herself. Legend?

LEGEND: In 1937, Princess Elizabeth, whilst visiting her German cousins, in Baden Baden, played drums in the Hitler Youth Orchestra.

ALL: *(Laughter / No! / Brilliant / nuts! / incredible! / crap!)*

WILSON: Fabulous! Maddy, why don't you know about this?!

MADDY: Because it's not true.

GARTH: It's bollocks. I'm gonna ring the Palace.

HOWARD: What's the source?

PAIGE: Burton Latimer.

WILSON: Who is this Burton Latimer?

PAIGE: He's the new Clarissa Kingston-Mills.

WILSON: Kosher?

PAIGE: Totally.

WILSON: Good. Gemma! Mock-up a picture of the Queen, playing the drums doing a Nazi salute with a Hitler moustache!

LEGEND: No need. The story is supported by this photograph.

(LEGEND produces a grainy photo in a plastic sleeve.)

WILSON: Fucking hell! There she is the cheeky little Nazi! *(Re. the photo.)* Gemma. Is this halal?

GEMMA: The photoshop boys have cleared it.

PAIGE: QUEEN BANGS DRUM FOR HITLER.

DICKIE: HEIL MA'AM!

GARTH: The palace deny it. It's crap.

WILSON: Fuck! Reverse ferret!

DICKIE: What's it matter? The palace never sue.

GARTH: It matters if it's bollocks.

WILSON: Dickie's right. If it's true, it's brilliant. If it's bollocks, it's brilliant! It's the front page! Legend, don't fuck it up. We go off stone at ten!

(End of meeting, they disperse. Enter MARCUS dressed as an Arab.)

WALLACE: Marcus man! Fucking hell!

MARCUS: *(Disappointed.)* You recognised me?

WALLACE: 'Course. What's this one?

MARCUS: The Counterfeiti Kuwaiti.

GARTH: Counterfeiti?

MARCUS: Kuwaiti.

GARTH: If you've come in here for expenses forget it.

MARCUS: I'm reasonable with money.

GARTH: Seven nights at the Savoy?

MARCUS: I have to get into character.

(GARTH and MARCUS disappear into GARTH's office. PAIGE turns back to the News Room. JIMMY approaches.)

JIMMY: Excuse me, you wanted a bin?

PAIGE: Diane Bendall, Chair of the Commons media committee. *(LEGEND takes a call and hands phone to PAIGE.)*

(PAIGE dials a preset on her mobile. LEGEND is watching. PAIGE nods to him.)

PAIGE: *(On the phone.)* Ding Dong? … The van in the lay-by was a Eurocar rental in the name of Mehmet Aziz, a friend of Kieron Mills… I told you, I have superhero powers. Laters!

(She rings off. And high fives with LEGEND.) Yes! Yes! Yes!

LEGEND: Newspaper of the Year.

End of Scene.

SCREENS: THE FREE PRESS front page HEIL MA'AM and a photo of the Queen as a girl playing drums in the Hitler Youth. Possibly a bubble magnified.

TV news chatting around the papers.

ANCHOR: The Free Press lead with this story HEIL MA'AM. A photograph has been discovered of the Queen playing the drums with the Hitler Youth. The question is, would the Queen have to resign?

JOURNO: If it's true, yes.

JOURNO 2: – not for playing the drums as a child but for the deception as an adult.

SCENE ELEVEN

(The News Room at night. The odd night sub, and runner wandering about. WALLACE uses the remote to switch channels until he finds the British Newspaper Awards at the Savoy in the ballroom. On screen in italics.)

SCREENS:

MC: To present the British Press Awards Newspaper of the Year category, the leader of the Conservative party, Jonathan Whey!

(Boos, it's a rowdy night.)

SCREENS:

WHEY: My great grandfather was mayor of Evesham, my grandfather a trade unionist, and my father was Chancellor. Which makes me the fourth Whey in politics –

(Boos and groans.)

WALLACE: Away and boil yer heed yer cunting posh twat.

(Some laughs.)

WHEY: Right, the Newspaper of the Year. *(Opens envelope. Now reading.)* This paper has produced scoops and front page splashes that have left the other dailies trailing in its wake. *The Free Press!*

(Boos, cheers.)

(JIMMY enters with bin bags.)

JIMMY: Diane Bendall, Labour MP.

WALLACE: For Paige?

JIMMY: Yeah.

WALLACE: Alright, I'll do 'em.

(JIMMY leaves them with WALLACE.)

End of Scene.

SCENE TWELVE

(Her bedroom. Morning. PAIGE and WHEY post-coital.)

WHEY: As John Major said to me 'if you're going to shag, shag upwards.'

PAIGE: I'm upwards?

WHEY: You're the media, you run the world.

(She watches as WHEY sprays his hands with anti-bacterial spray.)

PAIGE: What's that lover?

WHEY: Boots anti-bacterial gel.

PAIGE: Go home!

WHEY: I can't afford to catch a cold during the election campaign. Will you be voting Conservative?

PAIGE: Oh, so this is a focus group. Fuck me, I thought we were having sex. I've never got what I wanted by voting.

WHEY: And what do you want?

PAIGE: More.

WHEY: More power?

PAIGE: I want to be invited to the party. And I want you to get rid of St. John. You look like a bunch of posh boys who've never had a job.

WHEY: That's a bit unfair.

PAIGE: Have you ever had a job?

WHEY: Yes. I was president of the student union.

PAIGE: Imagine St. John running a lobby briefing.

WHEY: That's why I need you, Paige. We don't know how to speak to the lower class. You do.

(His mobile phone rings.)

(On the phone.) Yeah?… I know the schedule, King's Cross for seven. See you there. Oh, and bring the Harris tweed.

(He rings off.)

PAIGE: Scotland?

WHEY: Yeah. You know, there are more pandas in Scotland than Conservative MPs. We have to change that. Any ideas?

PAIGE: Kill the pandas.

End of Scene.

SCREENS: THE FREE PRESS = WE'RE WITH WHEY

THE DEPENDENT = TORY LANDSLIDE

THE REAR VIEW = HO WHEY THE LADS! *(Picture of WHEY and ST JOHN together.)*

THE FREE PRESS = IT WOS THE FREE PRESS WOT WON IT

THE GUARDENER = LABOUR BLAME O'LEARY MEDIA FUNDING FOR TORY LANDSLIDE

THE DEPENDENT = WHEY SUPPORTS KASSAM ZERO TOLERANCE

THE FREE PRESS = STELLA BACKS BLUE BOOB TAX

THE DAILY WAIL = IMMIGRANT VOTED SIXTEEN TIMES

SCENE THIRTEEN
(THE NEWSROOM. MORNING.)

HOWARD: *(On the phone.)* I assume you mean Jonathan Whey, our new Prime Minister?... And can I ask how you know him?... Prep school or Eton?... Eton, that's good... He used to wank into your soup?...was it because he was bullying you or because he liked you? Is this Boris Johnson?...That's OK Boris, you can be anonymous...

PAIGE: *(PAIGE enters.)* Morning.

WALLACE: I done Diane Bendall's bins for you.

PAIGE: Why d'yer do that? You're the TV column.

WALLACE: Chillax, I got my own reasons.

PAIGE: Chillax?

WALLACE: Soz. Texting and like the internet's, like, destroyed my ability to english.

PAIGE: You'll never go through my bins Wallace.

WALLACE: I found something on her.

PAIGE: Go on.

WALLACE: Diane Bendall has a flat in Belgravia, and the Commons pays the mortgage, yeah, but she rents it to a Mr. Lexi Goremykin who pays her two grand a month.

PAIGE: And I thought you were a moron.

WALLACE: Harsh man!

PAIGE: Take the Commons expenses clerks out, buy them lunch, weird sex, a time share in Croatia, anything, but firm this up.

WALLACE: Cool. I got two tickets to Wembley Arena to see Busted, you know, the boy band.

PAIGE: Busted? Wallace, you're asking the wrong girl, I had my first period eighteen years ago.

WALLACE: Yeah but backstage passes, the green room, the party. *(He sniffs/snorts.)*

PAIGE: OK.

(Aside.) That's my weakness. Not the cocaine. The invitation to the party.

(GARTH enters ringing the bell. WILSON, PASCHAL and VIRGINIA WHITE follow.)

O'LEARY: For a long time now I've been desperate to sack Wilson.

WILSON: Fuck off!

O'LEARY: You're like a smelly fucking horse that's been dead a while. I'm promoting him to an R and D role on the telly side. So if any of yous got an idea for a show talk to Wilson and I'll make you a millionaire with the format fees. That's it.

ALL: *(Cheers! Whoops! Yo! Etc.)*

O'LEARY: The new Editor will be this brilliant woman here.

PAIGE: Jesus!

O'LEARY: I never had a daughter, but the feelings I have for this woman can best be described as fatherly. Virginia White, Editor of *New York, New York,* is gonna bring a bit of the same stardust to *The Free Press.* It's all yours kid. *(O'LEARY leaves.)*

VIRGINIA: OK, gather round team. As Editor of *New York, New York* I was –

HOWARD: – this is a newspaper.

VIRGINIA: Sorry?

MADDY: What are you?

VIRGINIA: I think of myself as a campaigner. I want to make the world a better place, for children, animals, and horses.

DICKIE: You're up for some stories that have got animals in?

VIRGINIA: Especially horses.

HOWARD: This is a tabloid newspaper, it is not the RSPCA!

VIRGINIA: Howard, I know it must be difficult for you, I guess you had a dream –

HOWARD: – a dream?!

VIRGINIA: – to one day be Editor yourself –

HOWARD: – don't fucking patronise me lady. I'm going. I'm a journalist! *(HOWARD leaves.)* Slug and Ferret anyone?

WALLACE: We'll be there man!

ALL: Aye / OK / later / c u

VIRGINIA: OK.

GARTH: Gather!

VIRGINIA: My first campaign will be a call to bring back the death penalty for paedophiles who kill. We'll call it, Paula and Pippa's Law.

MADDY: Oh dear. That's a bit of a mouthful!

VIRGINIA: Is it?

PAIGE: How about Kieron's Law?

VIRGINIA: Name the campaign after the twins' father?

PAIGE: It's only fair. He'd be the first to be hanged.

VIRGINIA: Really?

PAIGE: It's honest. Tough. Our readers will love it.

VIRGINIA: OK. Kieron's Law it is

GEMMA: Are you scrapping Page 7?

VIRGINIA: No. I'm a feminist obviously, but I'm not a prude. Now, this is a change I imagine, I will not be running a morning news conference.

ALL: Groans / what? / ohhhh / weird.

VIRGINIA: No. I'm not interested in inputs, I want outputs. Paige as my news editor can run a conference if she wants. Also, I have an office one floor up, in the executive suite, next to Paschal. I'm big picture, Paige is detail. I look forward to working with you all.

(VIRGINIA exits. The journalists gossip, go back to their desks.)

LEGEND: It's a travesty! That was your job my girl!

PAIGE: It's still my job and I'm gonna behave as if it were my job until O'Leary realises his mistake.

GEMMA: Paige.

(Enter DOYLE DAVIDSON, in full uniform. She greets him and kisses him. WALLACE watches.)

PAIGE: Ding Dong! So this Mehmet guy, he makes porn films?

DOYLE D: He owns an industrial amount of porn.

PAIGE: Ah. What word would you use to describe Mehmet's extensive collection?

DOYLE D: Anal.

PAIGE: He's into anal?!

DOYLE D: No, it's in alphabetical order.

PAIGE: Garth! I want you in this! This is big! *(GARTH joins. Enter VIRGINIA WHITE carrying an invoice.)*

VIRGINIA: Sorry. Paige, this contract for Spy Spy, in Leyton?

PAIGE: Private Investigators.

VIRGINIA: Two hundred thousand pounds a year? That's a lot of money, that's more than I'm paid. What's it for?

PAIGE: They're trying to find the twins.

VIRGINIA: Oh. That's alright then. Carry on. *(VIRGINIA exits.)*

LEGEND: Have you found them?

PAIGE: Staffers only.

GARTH: Marcus!

DOYLE D: I will be arresting Kieron Mills and his accomplice, Mehmet Aziz on Saturday morning.

PAIGE: And we will be the only paper there.

MADDY: But it's Thursday!

TINA: The girls might be alive.

DOYLE D: There is no ticking clock.

PAIGE: In what kind of world are those girls still alive Tina?

GEMMA: I don't understand what's happening here.

PAIGE: It wos the dad wot dun it.

DOYLE D: A tip off from Paige's source –

TINA: – Burton Latimer?

PAIGE: Correct.

DOYLE D: – lead us to Mehmet Aziz, and in his van we found fibres from the twins' puffa jackets.

PAIGE: We have two days to make the most of this story. Tomorrow it's my interview with Kieron Mills discussing his lifelong struggle with Asperger's. Dickie I want 500 words on Asperger's. The usual.

DICKIE: What are the symptoms? Can you catch it off toilet seats?

PAIGE: Perfect. Saturday I want photographers at both arrests and I want a clear pic of Mehmet's porn collection. I want our readers to be able to read every title from A to Z. From arseholes to zebras. Now, procedurally, the Assistant Commissioner will talk you through the detail.

DOYLE D: Kieron Mills will get a four o'clock knock Saturday morning, just in time for your six o'clock edition.

PAIGE: We'll be publishing Mills's arrest and naming him at the very moment he is arrested.

LEGEND: What about contempt of court?

DOYLE D: Reporting restrictions are active from arrest, but they're really really active from charge, and we charge them both mid morning.

PAIGE: This way we totally wipe the floor with the other dailys.

GARTH: The others will get a Met press release on Saturday afternoon, so it'll be Monday before they can publish, and then they'll be constrained by contempt of court.

PAIGE: Not only did we solve the case, but we're breaking the story!

TINA: Excuse me, are the Met OK with all this?

DOYLE D: We need this.

PAIGE: This is team work.

DOYLE D: Effective PR is as much a part of policing London as –

MADDY: – shooting black vicars.

PAIGE: Harsh.

DOYLE D: But true.

SCREENS: Kieron Mills six o'clock knock is shown in a linear storytelling series of print media stills. This ends with the curtain screen of *The Free Press* front page photo of Kieron Mills clearly shown staring terrified at the camera –

IT WAS THE DAD WOT DONE IT

End of Act One.

INTERVAL

Act Two

SCENE ONE

(The Monday morning after the Saturday of Kieron Mills' arrest.)

SCREENS: THE GUARDENER = TWENTY-NINE-YEAR-OLD MAN ARRESTED IN TWINS CASE

THE DEPENDENT = SUSPECT CHARGED WITH MILLS TWINS MURDERS

THE REAR VIEW = LOCAL MAN CHARGED WITH TWINS NAP

THE DAILY WAIL = IMMIGRANTS LOWER NATIONAL IQ.

TINA: Jimmy! Can you do me Ronnie Barker's bin please?

JIMMY: Ronnie Barker? He died this week din't he.

TINA: Yes. And can you do Ronnie Corbett's bins an'all.

JIMMY: Has he died?

TINA: No, but Ronnie Corbett was at Ronnie Barker's bedside when he died.

JIMMY: I see. So you're hoping that Ronnie Barker, on his death bed, might have given Ronnie Corbett something which, he later on, put in the bin.

TINA: Exactly.

(VIRGINIA walks in and approaches PAIGE. She is holding a photo.)

VIRGINIA: Paige? This Stella Stone story, it's tragic, painful, I cried when I read it.

PAIGE: Great!

VIRGINIA: What's the source?

PAIGE: Burton Latimer.

VIRGINIA: Is that someone who knows Stella?

PAIGE: No, it's a small market town in Northamptonshire.

VIRGINIA: You don't have to reveal your sources.

PAIGE: No.

VIRGINIA: Oh. You journalists! Ha!

(VIRGINIA exits leaving the picture and story in PAIGE's hands.)

PAIGE: Gemma!?

(GEMMA approaches.)

Is Stella Stone anorexic? I've seen more fat on a butcher's pencil.

GEMMA: I don't know.

PAIGE: You don't know?! Gemma, we have superhero powers. Do her phone! *(Enter GARTH. Journos gather.)*

GARTH: Gather, gather, circulation figures. Circulation figures! Saturday circulation figures.

WALLACE: IT WAS THE DAD WOT DONE IT! *(Cheer.)*

LEGEND: Up forty thousand!? *(Nah.)*

TINA: Higher!

WALLACE: Sixty thousand!?

GARTH: Higher!

ALL: Yeah/come on!/tease!

GARTH: Up ninety thousand!

ALL: Woo! / cheers / no way!

GARTH: Well done everyone. And, carry on. *(Enter CLARISSA KINGSTON-MILLS.)*

CLARISSA: Good morning darlings.

GARTH: How did you get in here?

CLARISSA: Morning Legend.

LEGEND: Is this in the diary Clarissa?

CLARISSA: Impromptu.

PAIGE: If you're not flogging a kiss and tell what are you doing here?

CLARISSA: *(Loud.)* Is it just The Legend or do you all do it?

WALLACE: Do what man?

CLARISSA: The Royal Protection Squad at Buckingham Palace were told by Vodafone that the Royals' mobiles were being called twenty, thirty times a day, from two numbers. A private eye in Leytonstone, and a phone number traced to this office. The Queen, herself, called me –

GARTH: – bollocks.

CLARISSA: – and asked me to help set up a sting. My niece left a message on the Queen's voicemail claiming to have a photograph of Her Majesty playing the drums in the Hitler Youth Orchestra.

LEGEND: Your niece?

CLARISSA: Hers was the voicemail message you intercepted. She's in her final year at RADA. She was also the maid from whom you bought the photo. I've sold the story, and my niece has paid off her student loan. So thank you for that.

GARTH: What do you want?

CLARISSA: This newspaper businsess is a competitive sport, and you, *The Free Press,* are drugs cheats.

PAIGE: *(To CLARISSA.)* New territory for you Clarissa – the moral high ground. I hope you wiped the blood off your feet on the way in.

CLARISSA: I like it up here, the air's clean.

GARTH: You were killing this industry.

CLARISSA: I invented it!

PAIGE: You did. The sale for profit of private information.

CLARISSA: Within the law.

GARTH: What do you want?

CLARISSA: I've got what I want.

GARTH: Revenge.

CLARISSA: Buy the *Guardian* tomorrow. *(CLARISSA leaves.)*

PAIGE: Dickie, get her.

End of Scene.

SCREENS: THE GUARDENER = O'LEARY JOURNALIST HACKED QUEEN'S PHONE.

THE REAR VIEW = HITLER YOOF SPOOF THE DEPENDENT = ROYAL PHONES HACKED

THE FREE PRESS = CLARISSA PIMPED HER MOTHER

(Picture of old woman in tacky lingerie.)

PAIGE: *(On the phone.)* Stevie, Bodger. It's me. Change your phone. Phones. Wipe everything. Burn everything else. You don't know me. I don't know you. Delete this message.

(Phone off.)

(Direct address.) It looks shitball for me I know, but I have a *meeting* with the Crown Prosecution Service, and the Met. Yes, instead of arresting me, they've invited me to discuss the situation. Ha! If this is corruption – by which I mean the acquisition of money, power, or assets in a way that escapes the public view, and is usually illegal, and which binds different interest groups into a relationship of mutual dependence – then all I can say is – Booya! Twenty people, talk to twenty people, who talk to twenty people. Democracy? Gimme a break. Hand on your wallet, what would you rather have? Efficiency or accountability? Do you think democracy and accountability could deliver seventeen channels of porn into your bedsit ten minutes after

you've paid for it! Accountability is gridlock. Democracy is downtime. Yes, of course it's important to retain what I call the nice to haves – Parliament, the judiciary, elections, but there is only one way to run a country and that's the twenty twenty twenty way. That's my way.

SCREENS: 24-hour News Anchor 'The Queen herself has not commented on the hacking, she's visiting a mobile needle exchange in Bracknell…sorry, we interrupt this item to bring you some breaking news…it seems that there has been a terrorist incident at Liverpool Street Station, the station is closed, this is just coming in now, the situation's confused, there are reports of three dead in a terrorist incident at Liverpool Street Station……'

SCENE TWO

(CRAM, DOYLE D, MACMANAMAN, KASSAM, NATALIE, a CPS lawyer.)

MACM: No. Nein, Non, Nyeht! Bu!

CRAM: Boo?

MACM: 'No' in Chinese. You can't lock these guys up, they work for me.

CRAM: The Queen's phone has been hacked, I need a collar.

(Enter PAIGE.)

PAIGE: Sorry, Liverpool Street closed down, a terrorist incident, three dead, you know, like dead, as in not breathing any more, never seeing their kids again, no chance of lying in grassy meadow watching a skylark ever again. That kind of dead. All as a result of a proper crime aka terrorism.

(She notices NICOLA.)

Oh, what are the chances of that?! Another girl!

DOYLE D: Nicola heads up the Crown Prosecution Service.

PAIGE: A successful woman!? You must have been on *Woman's Hour*?

NICOLA: I don't have an hour.

DOYLE D: The reason I insisted on Paige being here –

PAIGE: – stop before I burst into flames! Who didn't want me at this meeting?

NICOLA: It's unusual to have a suspect attend their own case conference.

KASSAM: Effective policing involves a lot of people sharing a one-man tent.

NICOLA: A symbiotic relationship?

KASSAM: No, but we are dependent on each other in a mutually beneficial way.

DOYLE D: Our job is to build legitimacy and consent in the communities we serve. *(NICOLA picks up a mission statement pamphlet from the table.)*

NICOLA: 'Working together, today, to make tomorrow a bit better than yesterday.'

KASSAM: Mission statements always sound ridiculous but an organisation without a mission statement hasn't got a mission statement.

NICOLA: This is persistent, on-going, law-breaking as a business.

KASSAM: I can't arrest people just because they've broken the law! There are three types of criminals. Criminals we know about, and we know what they've done; criminals we know about, and we don't know what they've done; and criminals we don't know about, and we don't know what they've done. If we arrest all the criminals we know about, the only criminals out there will be the ones we don't know about, and trust me lady, you don't wanna live in that town.

CRAM: Royal Protection Officers came to us –

PAIGE: Who's he?

DOYLE D: DCI Cram. He's our best detective.

PAIGE: As the cleaners at Liverpool Street wash the blood from the tiles the Met's top detective buries his head in a phone hacking enquiry.

MACM: Quite! Invasions of privacy are odious, but they don't kill you.

CRAM: They're illegal.

PAIGE: *The Free Press* has a public interest defence. The public have a right to know if the Queen played drums for the Hitler Youth Orchestra.

CRAM: She didn't. You were stung by Clarissa Kingston-Mills.

KASSAM: But what about the photograph? That was definitely the Queen on drums.

NICOLA: Over a hundred other victims have been identified and we –

MACM: – did you hear that loud crack? That was my heart breaking for these underpaid celebrity victims.

PAIGE: Yes sister, the alpha male cut you up.

NICOLA: We have an obligation to inform people if they've been hacked.

MACM: Why can't we keep the poor suffering fuckers in the dark?

DOYLE D: This technology helped us to convict Kieron Mills.

NICOLA: Irrelevant. The law is 100% clear that the interception of voicemail is a criminal offence.

CRAM: I need an arrest. The Queen –

KASSAM: – oh the Queen! Again! I mean, who does she think she is?!

PAIGE: OK, what if this was a rogue reporter, and an unhappy and exceptional event in the two-hundred-year history of *The Free Press.*

CRAM: Because it's an industrial-scale operation!

PAIGE: Charge The Legend, buy him a new front door, and he'll plead guilty.

CRAM: *(To PAIGE.)* Can I at least arrest the Private Is?

PAIGE: I don't know them, I've never met them.

NICOLA: You ask me if you can arrest them, not her.

CRAM: Can I arrest them?

NICOLA: Yes, go ahead.

CRAM: OK. They'll get a six o'clock knock tomorrow morning.

KASSAM: At what time?

CRAM: Six o'clock.

KASSAM: Good! I'd be there if I could be, but I can't be, because I'll still be in bed. Thank you everybody.

(All leave. DOYLE D waits for PAIGE, but she's on the phone.)

PAIGE: *(On phone.)* Legend!?…listen, you plead guilty, it was an isolated incident. O'Leary will pay your court costs, and he'll continue your salary to 65…you're 68?…alright, we'll re-employ you as a freelance when you come out… Ford Open probably, which is like a Premier Inn but not as noisy.

SCENE THREE

(A small dark room. A pile of boxes, and files, white boards, and archive boxes. DOYLE D and CRAM, now a Commander.)

CRAM: This Bodger character's a godsend. He's written everything down. There's 20,000 pages here.

DOYLE D: Is every page like this?

CRAM: Yeah. The name in the corner is the journalist. Thirty-three names are regulars, all journos at *The Free Press.* Dickie, The Legend, Tina, Jackie, Wallace –

DOYLE D: – You're moving quickly.

CRAM: Sorry sir, I'll slow down.

DOYLE D: I meant your career.

CRAM: Accelerated Promotion Scheme sir.

DOYLE D: 'What's the most difficult decision you've had to make in your career so far?'

CRAM: I said I had to make a decision whether to challenge you over the arrest of Kieron Mills. I was SIO on the twins. We never found the bodies.

DOYLE D: What's your moral assessment of this Cram? In light of the Liverpool Street terrorist killings.

CRAM: That's the job. You arrest a terrorist one minute, half an hour later you're nicking someone for riding a bike without lights.

DOYLE D: When did you last arrest someone for riding a bike without lights?

CRAM: All the time in Dorset.

DOYLE D: I want you out there catching terrorists.

CRAM: Promotion? I –

DOYLE D: You're wasted on this.

CRAM: Yes sir.

DOYLE D: Congratulations, Superintendent. *(CRAM leaves. The phone on the desk rings.)*

DOYLE D: Send her down…give her a badge.

(DOYLE D in direct address.) Coppers are like bananas, they grow on trees. With good basic pay, fabulous overtime, and incredible pensions, there's never a shortage.

I was a weird kid, I had a laser eye for justice. I used to say things like – 'I think it's wrong to smash the windows of that empty house'. Weird. 'It's not right to beat up the Jewish boys on our bus'. Weird. 'In what sense is this bus our bus?' Really weird. In the police canteen I tried to fit in. I stopped using words like expedient, serendipity, and exegesis and limited my vocabulary to fuck, shit, bastard and muppet.

But I was an outsider, and I was glad to escape to Bramshill on the Accelerated Promotion Scheme. 'What is the most difficult decision you've had to make in your career so far?' I answered, 'Turning down an invitation from a Commander to join his Masonic Lodge.' I was proudly nailing my anti-corruption colours to the mast. The feedback said 'Doyle Davidson was completely honest in his interview, which was a serious mistake on his part.'

(Enter PAIGE.)

PAIGE: Is this it?

DOYLE D: Ya. I've looked at it and because there is nothing here to justify the diversion of manpower away from the real and present danger of making London safe from terrorist attack, I've promoted Cram out of trouble.

PAIGE: You're learning!

DOYLE D: And I've taken over the investigation.

PAIGE: Into me! Can we burn it then!?

DOYLE D: Traditionally, the Met has three types of information. Sensitive information, which we don't share with the public; classified information, which we don't share with each other; and damaging information which we shred.

PAIGE: I love shredding!

DOYLE D: I'm going to dead file it, for now, and hope it –

PAIGE: – dies.

(She kisses him.)

I want to interview Kieron Mills in prison.

DOYLE D: He's in Broadmoor.

PAIGE: You can make that happen, you're a powerful man.

DOYLE D: Can I see you tonight?

PAIGE: Not tonight. I'm seeing Busted at Wembley.

DOYLE D: Who with?

PAIGE: You're jealous. Don't be jealous. I'm yours. Kieron Mills, please.

(She kisses him forcefully, pushing him on to the boxes of evidence.)

End of Scene.

SCENE FOUR

SCREENS:

THE FREE PRESS = STELLA QUITS CLINIC

THE FREE PRESS = 4 STONE STELLA

THE FREE PRESS = FORCE FEED STELLA

THE FREE PRESS = STELLA STARVING

(In a hospital room.)

DAD: What's all this about Babs?

BABS: I'm guessing it's the papers.

STELLA: How much did they pay you?

MUM: Don't talk to me like that, I'm your fucking mother.

STELLA: How much did they pay you dad?

DAD: Now Babe, I'm your dad. I'm not gonna sell stories to the papers am I.

STELLA: The only three people who know about it.

BABS: Your doctor knows.

STELLA: My doctor lives on millionaire's row, he's got a sauna and a swimming pool. I can't see the motivation.

MUM: We're family, and Babs is your best friend.

STELLA: I can measure out my life in best friends who've ripped me off.

BABS: This is paranoia Stell.

STELLA: It ain't paranoia, it's maffs. There's four people in the world what knows I can't eat. My doctor, but he don't need the money, so that leaves you three.

MUM: I love you. You're my baby. Why would I damage what we got?

STELLA: Money.

MUM: Money?

STELLA: It's someone in this room. A Judas.

(Silence.)

BABS: It wasn't me Stell. But I can't prove it.

STELLA: I can't eat, and I shared that with you, the last people on this earth I can trust and one of you sells it. I'm fucking dying!

(Her mum starts crying quietly.)

DAD: It weren't me babe. I don't need the money. I mean, not that I would do that even if I needed the money.

STELLA: You…are…in…this…room.

End of Scene.

SCENE FIVE

SCREENS: BBC 24-HOUR. STATE OPENING OF PARLIAMENT

(The newsroom. On the screens is the state opening of Parliament. WILSON is hanging around aimlessly. PAIGE, O'LEARY, and GARTH are with a Civil Servant type in the interview room. We can see them but not hear them. JACKIE and DICKIE are laughing at the water cooler, DICKIE doing Jimmy Savile impressions. WALLACE approaches WILSON.)

WILSON: Who's the bloke on the sofa?

WALLACE: My Civil Servant. MP's expenses innit. Yeah.

WILSON: I miss it. This TV programme development, it's not me.

WALLACE: I got an idea man. You'll fucking love it, but it's my format fee alright?

WILSON: Course. Go on then. Give me an erection.

WALLACE: It's called 'Shag'.

WILSON: Shag.

WALLACE: Shag. One word titles are rad. Like *Emmerdale*, *Traffic*, or *The Bill*.

WILSON: I like it so far.

WALLACE: You parachute a celebrity into a remote location, and then you see how long it takes them to get a shag.

WILSON: *(Beat.)* So, you drop Salman Rushdie onto the Isle of Skye –

WALLACE: – the clock's ticking, cameraman running behind, he legs it to the nearest crofter's cottage, knocks on the door, and asks for a shag.

WILSON: It's a fucking Bafta!

(In the interview room.)

PAIGE: We don't need to know your name. So chillax.

GARTH: How much do you want?

CIVIL SERVANT: Three hundred thousand pounds.

O'LEARY: Me auld da used to say never buy a horse until you seen its teeth.

PAIGE: I've seen the teeth. He has a hard drive with all the details of every expenses claim made by every MP in the last eight years, including Diane Bendall.

GARTH: Have you stolen this disk?

CIVIL SERVANT: Hard drive. No I'm a whistle blower.

O'LEARY: So you're a fucking *Guardian* reading principled do-gooder whistle blower who wants 300 fucking grand.

PAIGE: It could keep this paper going for years.

GARTH: Have you signed the Act?

CIVIL SERVANT: Course.

GARTH: So I'd be corrupting a public official. A criminal offence.

PAIGE: Paschal, buy this hard drive, please. There's something on everyone in there.

CIVIL SERVANT: Details of 650 MP's expense claims for the last eight years. You get some criminality, some tragedy, and an awful lot of comedy.

(O'LEARY nods to GARTH. GARTH gives the CIVIL SERVANT a business card.)

GARTH: Ring that number. Orla Gilhooley. Tell her your real name, and she'll wire the money to Western Union St. James, take some ID.

CIVIL SERVANT: Who's Orla Gilhooley?

GARTH: She's your grannie.

CIVIL SERVANT: No, my grannie's dead.

GARTH: A lot of people have difficulty with this system, but just try it, see if it works.

MADDY: Queen's speech!

(MADDY turns the volume up on the screens. They all gather, including VIRGINIA WHITE.)

THE QUEEN: 'My Lords and Members of the House of Commons, this year my Husband and I look forward to our visits to Bermuda, Barbados, and Pitcairn's Island. My Government will introduce legislation to remove the royal charter from the BBC and discontinue the licence fee.'

O'LEARY: – this is a great day for freedom, for the little man. Privilege, and entitlement which is the stinking, rotten heart of England is being challenged today by me and the Queen!

PAIGE: Alright…

(They disperse. VIRGINIA approaches PAIGE.)

VIRGINIA: Paige. The paediatrician in Portsmouth getting beaten up and burned out of her flat by a mob.

PAIGE: Really, really funny story. Paediatrician / paedophile. It's hilarious!

VIRGINIA: No. It reflects badly on my Keiron's Law campaign. Take it out please. *(Enter MARCUS dressed as the Sham Imam complete with a hook for his right hand.)*

PAIGE: OK, conference…Marcus!?

MARCUS: You recognised me?

WALLACE: What's this one man?

MARCUS: The Sham Imam.

WALLACE: What's that?

THIERY: Assonance.

WALLACE: No, I meant his right arm.

MARCUS: A hook.

(MARCUS wanders out with WALLACE and THIERY. VIRGINIA turns on her heels and is gone. They gather for conference.)

PAIGE: Alright! What do we have today, who's gonna blow my doors off!?

DICKIE: Jimmy Savile.

ALL: *(Groans.)* This is a vendetta / what is it with you and Savile? / oh come on Dickie / leave him alone / you'll never get / you're obsessed / three years.

PAIGE: Have you got anything on him yet?

GARTH: What's your source?

DICKIE: Two girls in Broadmoor.

PAIGE: Two teenage headbangers? Have you been to Burton Latimer?

DICKIE: Burton couldn't get anything, Savile set his own PIN.

PAIGE: How did he know to do that?

DICKIE: I'm telling you, he's a serial paedo. He has to be clever.

PAIGE: Dickie, how much do you give to charity?

DICKIE: I don't.

PAIGE: Shut up then, Savile is the only reason the NHS isn't bankrupt. Now spike it!

DICKIE: Spike it?! Mark my words Paige, you're missing a scoop. Wilson would've nailed him.

MADDY: There is another story here, The elevation to national treasure of a talentless, narcissistic bore.

IAN H: What's Esther Rantzen got to do with this?

PAIGE: Next! Stella Stone. Where are we?

TINA: She's in hospital, and she's not expected to make a recovery.

PAIGE: Great! Her career started with a Page 7. So we own her, she's ours. Garth, offer her an exclusive contract to cover her death. Right, we're off stone at ten, there's football.

(PAIGE leaves.)

End of Scene.

SCREENS: TV COMMERCIAL

(Girl in School uniform.) This week, your fun-packed Free Press features Page 7 stunner, greengrocer's daughter Melanie Took!

(Bikini / censored.) – the bad news is, she's only fifteen – ooooohhhhh

(Censored topless.) – the good news?! She's sixteen on Friday! Hurrahhhhh!

Buy *The Free Press* every day this week – including Friday – and claim two free booze cruise tickets to France, so don't be a plonker, get the plonk in, don't dilly dally, sail to Calais.

The Free Press, less than a finger of fudge at 20p!

PAIGE: *(Aside.)* I know what you're thinking – how can a paper that is campaigning to bring back the death penalty for paedophiles also publish topless photos of sixteen-year-old girls. The answer is because – 'although we abhor paedophilia, there's nothing more British than wanking into a hanky'.

SCENE SIX

(Video wall, Broadmoor Hospital Prison. Interview room at Broadmoor. A PRISON GUARD, PAIGE and KIERON MILLS.)

PAIGE: Hello Kieron. Thank you for seeing me. It's a lovely day out there.

MILLS: I didn't want to see you, they told me I had to or they'd take my meds away. And I can't handle it without my meds. They think I'll kill myself.

PAIGE: Will you?

MILLS: Yeah. I lived for my girls. They were my life. The whole of my life.

PAIGE: You killed them.

GUARD: Miss! Please. No provocation.

MILLS: No provocation. I'm on suicide watch. They're bricking it about me.

PAIGE: Thanks for doing the interview the day before you were arrested.

MILLS: You stitched me up.

PAIGE: If you didn't kill them Mehmet did.

GUARD: Miss, please! I need you to stay off the subject.

PAIGE: What other subject is there?

GUARD: Miss please.

PAIGE: *(Beat.)* What's it like in here?

MILLS: It's like a high security psychiatric hospital.

PAIGE: I'm not mad, or criminal, so wouldn't know.

MILLS: I used to take the girls, when they were younger, to the Wacky Warehouse. Like a big soft play shed. Couldn't hurt yourself.

(MILLS puts his head in his hands.)

The noise! Screaming. Crying. It's like that in here, only with injections. You're calling this law of yours Kieron's Law…

GUARD: Woah

MILLS: … That's sick.

PAIGE: I'm not sick. You're sick…

GUARD: Hey miss.

PAIGE: … Where are the girls Kieron?

MILLS: They're alive, and someone should be looking for them.

GUARD: Easy.

PAIGE: You sold them to Mehmet…

GUARD: Miss please.

PAIGE: …who took them to Turkey where they were filmed, and then killed.

GUARD: Back up! That's it. You're done Miss. Thank you.

MILLS: It's a stitch up. You got your story, why don't you let it lie.

PAIGE: I want the bodies. Where are they?

MILLS: I did not! I did not! I did not!

(The GUARD grabs him, and presses the buzzer. Another guards storm in and restrains him.)

End of Scene.

SCENE SEVEN

(The News Room during the day. The screens are tuned to the Parliamentary Committee preparing for hearing. Dialogue in italics is the committee.)

(WALLACE takes a mobile and turns the volume up. The Parliamentary Media Committee plays.)

TORY MP: Diane Bendall.

BENDALL: Mr. O'Leary –

O'LEARY: – Can I just say that this is the hungriest day of my life. I been here since seven this morning and not so much as a biscuit.

TORY MP: I saw some custard creams earlier. In the back.

O'LEARY: Or a Cornish pasty. But not from fucking Cornwall!

BENDALL: Mr. O'Leary, are you continuing to pay Billy Cain's salary, and legal fees?

O'LEARY: I never heard of the fellah.

BENDALL: Billy, The Legend, you invited him to your daughter's wedding in March.

O'LEARY: *(Beat.)* Feck! Have I got a daughter!?

PAIGE: Mr O'Leary suffers from Early Onset Familial Alzheimer's.

BENDALL: Can I put it to you, Paige Britain, that you were happy to pay Spy Spy two hundred thousand a year because they extended the portfolio of Fleet Street's dark arts?

PAIGE: You must be confident that your life can withstand tabloid examination?

BENDALL: Are you threatening me? Before committee, in the House?!

PAIGE: You rent your flat in Belgravia to Mr. Lexi Goremykin and charge him two thousand a month rent, even though the mortgage for the property is claimed through your House of Commons expenses.

BENDALL: That arrangement is perfectly above board. *(From now on PAIGE and BENDALL are talking over each other.)*

PAIGE: No, it's a clear breach of Commons rules and also criminal fraud. *(Uproar in Committee, and the public galleries, and cheers in the News Room.)*

BENDALL: This committee is set up to consider whether Mr O'Leary is a fit and proper person to –

O'LEARY: *(Standing.)* Or a curly fucking wurly!

PAIGE: *(Shouted over.)* How can you justify to tax payers the £187.50 you claimed for a Brazilian wax with heart-shaped landing strip?!

(Uproar, laughter.)

End of Scene.

SCREENS: A *Free Press* front page = WAX ON TAX (and a picture of Diane Bendall with the strap line BRAZILIAN ON THE HOUSE.)

SCENE EIGHT

SCREENS: (Image of the small-time law practice KHAKWANI, KLINKARD & UL HAQ in Eccles. Their services are listed as WILLS, LANDLORDS, CRIMINAL, IMMIGRATION, NO WIN NO FEE, DIVORCE, CONVEYANCING, ASYLUM.)

(WENDY's offices in Lancashire. GARTH is there, just arrived, looking out the window.)

GARTH: It'll be alright there will it? Outside Greggs.

WENDY: I wouldn't park there myself.

GARTH: What I meant was, can I park there? Is it within a controlled zone?

WENDY: Park where you like in Lancashire.

GARTH: *(He remains standing.)* So, I'm here. What do you want?

WENDY: The Legend has admitted the criminal charge of intercepting the Queen's voicemail. Shortly before that he penned a defamatory piece about my client Jasper Donald, which included the word 'crunk'. Bexy Ann Blane described my client as 'crunk' in a voicemail message left on Jasper's phone. *The Free Press* front page was instrumental in the collapse of my client's engagement to Matilda Bees. Whom he loves, and had dreams of lifelong happiness with.

GARTH: Our lawyers made you a Part 36 offer for ten grand.

WENDY: This is criminal invasion of privacy.

GARTH: The highest payout for invasion of privacy was Catherine Zeta-Jones and that sex addict.

WENDY: Michael Douglas.

GARTH: They got fourteen K from *Heat* magazine.

WENDY: *Hello* magazine. And it was fourteen thousand six hundred.

GARTH: OK. Twenty thousand. As a Part 36.

WENDY: No. I'm in a strong position. O'Leary has yet to demonstrate to the Media Committee that he is a fit and proper person, not a gangster. He'll want to settle out of court.

GARTH: I'm not leaving until you pick up the fucking phone and offer Jasper 20K!

WENDY: My client would like to be vindicated in court, or, failing that, made obscenely wealthy.

GARTH: This is personal isn't it. OK, I'm sorry about the short jokes. Is that it? Well fuck you lady. This is a free country, just, it's not yet compulsory to watch the paralympics, which is why no one does.

WENDY: I'll be applying for a Norwich Pharmacal Order.

GARTH: A what? I'm not Rumpole, I'm not a lawyer.

WENDY: Norwich Pharmacal versus Customs and Excise is a precedent, which forces a third party to disclose any evidence they're holding.

GARTH: Who's our third party?

WENDY: The Met. I hear they have twenty thousand pages of evidence.

GARTH: OK. How much?

WENDY: How far have you driven?

GARTH: Two hundred miles.

WENDY: Two hundred thousand.

GARTH: This is crazy.

WENDY: Wait a minute! You have to drive back! Four hundred thousand!

GARTH: I'll ask.

WENDY: You know what your big mistake was?

GARTH: Parking outside Greggs.

WENDY: Leaving London. You never leave London.

End of Scene.

SCENE NINE

SCREENS: TV Advert – 'Every day this week in your funtastic *Free Press* we're giving away a pull out MP's expenses special. How much has your MP trousered? We publish the definitive league table. Champeeeeonns! It's flipping flabbergasting! Every day this week in your funky *Free Press*! You can't afford 30p?! Put it on expenses!'

THE DAILY WAIL = IMMIGRANT EMPLOYED ON MP'S EXPENSES.

24-HOUR NEWS. A talking head is speculating on the MP'S expenses story.

ANCHOR: 'Speculation is that a Civil Servant has been paid a substantial amount of money to pass on a data disk. Technically this is corruption of a public official and outside the PCC code of conduct, as well as being illegal.' *(WALLACE mutes the TV.)*

(The newsroom. DICKIE's phone rings.)

DICKIE: News? …yeah you can talk to me…who am I talking to please? *(DICKIE starts making notes.)*

(In the Editor's office.)

GARTH: So, she's thrown us a fuck off price.

O'LEARY: How much?

GARTH: Four hundred thousand pounds.

O'LEARY: Fuck off!

GARTH: A court case would mean she gets disclosure. That is access to all our documentation and emails on phone hacking.

PAIGE: We can delete all that. In preparation for the new IT system.

GARTH: It's not our documents I'm worried about. She's employing an obscure legal manoeuvre to give her access to any evidence the Met have.

O'LEARY: She's pissing all over you man!

GARTH: Paige, Bodger's notes, will they sink the rogue reporter defence?

PAIGE: There's over a hundred named targets and journalists other than Legend mentioned, so to answer your question, too fucking right it will.

GARTH: Your reputation will not survive a court case, and four hundred thousand for a terrestrial TV network is a bargain.

PAIGE: I can sort the Met.

GARTH: You can sort the Met?!

PAIGE: Yes. And we can sort this Lancashire solicitor too. *(They exit to the newsroom. DICKIE is on the phone still.)*

Jimmy! Jimmy. Couple of days in Lancashire. Can you do?

JIMMY: If it's gonna be worth it.

GARTH: It'll be worth it little man. That's her office address.

JIMMY: Celeb?

PAIGE: No, but give her the celeb treatment. The bins, tail her, I want her followed, and filmed. She suffers from dwarfism.

GARTH: I don't think you can say she suffers from dwarfism.

PAIGE: She enjoys dwarfism. And she's disabled, in a wheelchair.

JIMMY: Should I get a wheelchair? You know, to blend in. No.

PAIGE: I want her to know that you're watching her. I want her to know the limits of what I can do within the law.

(VIRGINIA enters.)

VIRGINIA: Paige! You lied to me. I thought Burton Latimer was a legitimate source. I just can't believe you were listening to people's private messages. Whatever were you thinking?

PAIGE: I was thinking, 'fucking brilliant!' actually. *(DICKIE puts down the phone and crosses to PAIGE, GARTH and VIRGINIA.)*

GARTH: What is it Dickie?

DICKIE: Kieron Mills. He was jumped last night by six inmates. Stabbed with a meat skewer, through the eye. He died half an hour ago.

VIRGINIA: Why are you looking at me?

DICKIE: Kieron's Law. You got what you wanted.

VIRGINIA: Oh no!

PAIGE: This is the price we have to pay for power without responsibility.

End of Scene.

SCREENS: THE GUARDENER = DID THE FREE PRESS KILL MILLS?

THE DEPENDENT = VIGILANTE KILLING BLAMED ON KIERON'S LAW

THE REAR VIEW = KIERON'S LAW / KIERON'S DEATH

THE DAILY WAIL = IMMIGRANTS EAT SWANS

VIDEO FOOTAGE OF NEWS JOURNO REPORTING DEATH OF KEIRON MILLS

'Kieron Mills, an early and some might say easy suspect, for the abduction and killing of his own daughters was found murdered yesterday early evening in the kitchen block by what the Broadmoor authorities are describing as a conspiracy of six inmates. He was viciously stabbed eighteen times although the fatal blow appears to have been a skewer through the eye. Speculation and criticism of *The Free Press* and its Kieron's Law campaign has already begun with Labour MPs criticising the tabloid for licensing vigilante killing.'

SCENE TEN

(DOYLE D's grace and favour flat overlooking the Thames.)

DOYLE D: I can't destroy evidence. I'm a fucking policeman!

PAIGE: You're a beautiful fucking policeman, and a world class shag, with a cock like a Cornetto.

DOYLE D: Why don't you just get O'Leary to pay this solicitor off?! *(DOYLE D sits, stressed, with his head in his hands.)*

PAIGE: Hey, come on lover, we're cool aren't we?

DOYLE D: That solicitor has filed a court order, an obligation on the Met Commissioner to disclose whatever evidence he's got.

PAIGE: Disclosure. So that solicitor can sit and read all Bodger's notes.

DOYLE D: Yeah.

PAIGE: And read all the names, in the documents. Surely that's some kind of invasion of privacy isn't it. You know, a stranger, reading transcripts of your phone messages.

DOYLE D: Yeah. Actually. Yes! We can redact the names.

PAIGE: Redact?

DOYLE D: Black them out. Protect the identities of those people who were being hacked.

PAIGE: And the journalists who requested the hacks.

DOYLE D: Yes, it's Article 8 of the Human Rights Act. The right to a private and family life.

PAIGE: Excuse me I'm the genius! I'm going to buy you a huge black felt tip pen you gorgeous fucker.

(She kisses him. The doorbell rings. DOYLE D exits to the door. She goes to the balcony and lights a cigarette. Re-enter DOYLE D with a uniformed Inspector, a woman.)

DOYLE D: This is Inspector DaCosta.

PAIGE: Hi. Are you any relation to Tony DaCosta at the *Mirror*?

DACOSTA: He's my husband.

PAIGE: Handy. What do you want?

DACOSTA: Sir?

DOYLE D: Police business.

(PAIGE goes out on to the balcony and closes the doors.)

DACOSTA: A vagrant, Wale Malumba Okwonko aged fifty-six, was tasered tonight in Kensal Rise and died in the Central Middlesex ten minutes ago.

(She gives him a piece of paper.)

DOYLE D: *(Reading.)* Wale Malumba Okwonko. Is he black?

DACOSTA: Yes sir. He's that shiny blue black you often get with them Africans.

DOYLE D: Have you done the 'embracing diversity course'?

DACOSTA: No sir, I pulled a sickie that day. Had a hangover.

DOYLE D: It's an excellent programme. Don't delay. I'll deal with this. *(DOYLE D shows her out. PAIGE comes back in.)*

DOYLE D: A vagrant's been tasered to death. A black guy.

PAIGE: Fantastic! This should be the coup de grâce for Kassam. But we have to make sure. How can we make it worse?

DOYLE D: A man's died!

PAIGE: Make Kassam culpable. Involved.

DOYLE D: He's in New York! Back Thursday.

PAIGE: Kassam comes back, and he doesn't know about the death.

DOYLE D: How could he possibly not know about a death?!

PAIGE: You don't tell him. The guy's a vagrant, no family. The hospital will sell the story to me, I'll buy it and sit on it. You arrange a press conference to launch the use of tasers. Kassam agrees to demonstrate they're safe by being tasered himself, live on TV.

DOYLE D: *(Giggling.)* That's too funny. He's a coward. He'll never agree to that.

PAIGE: He reports to the Home Secretary, who reports to the Prime Minister, –

DOYLE D: – Who reports to you?!

PAIGE: How did that happen? A little girl from Bristol.

(They kiss.)

End of Scene.

SCREENS: 2ND SULLY KASSAM MASH-UP RAP

'I need help, I need help. I can't solve this crime. I need help. I need help. I need help. I can't solve this crime. I need help'

SCENE ELEVEN

(A press conference at the Yard. KASSAM, DOYLE D and MACMANAMAN, and SERGEANT OJO. A gym mat before the table. Other journos and DICKIE for The Free Press.*)*

KASSAM: Transgender, ladies and gentlemen. Welcome to New Mary Seacole Yard. As Commissioner, there is a joyful obligation on me to serve the eight million citizens of London blind, as it were, to their race, religion, gender, disability, sexual orientation, and size. And in this context I am thrilled to introduce the taser. Yes, there have been over a hundred and fifty taser deaths in the United States but the victims all had pre-existing medical conditions or were already ill. One obese wheelchair-bound woman in Jacksonville died when she was tasered ten times in four minutes, which highlights the importance of counting. They say 'show don't tell', so I will this morning allow myself to be tasered, under controlled conditions, by Sergeant Ojo here.

(SERGEANT OJO steps forward with a taser. MACMANAMAN is giggling. DOYLE D is trying not to. KASSAM puts on safety helmet, glasses and picks up a kid's knife and plastic beer glass.)

So I'm a very drunk, let's say, Sunderland fan. Nothing against Sunderland fans, or northerners in general, just for illustration. *(Singing.)* Sunderland til I die, I'm Sunderland til I die! I know I am, I'm sure I am, I'm Sunderland til I die. Oi! Pig! Vindaloo, vindaloo, vindaloo!

SERGEANT OJO: Taser! Taser! Taser!

(SERGEANT OJO tasers him. His reaction to the tasering is normal. His muscles paralyse, and he collapses backwards on to the safety mat, but then he convulses and starts screaming like a stuck pig. MACMANAMAN is helpless and DOYLE D is covering up his own laughter.)

KASSAM: Aaarghh! Fuck! Turn it off you daft African twat!

(OJO turns the electricity off.)

Oh, argh, oh. OK. Any questions?

DICKIE: Hunter Dickson, *The Free Press.* Can the Commissioner give us any information about the death by tasering three days ago of a Mr. Wale Malumba Okwonko, an immigrant from Zaire.

KASSAM: What?

DICKIE: Was tasering a contributing factor in Mr Okwonko's death?

KASSAM: Mac?

MACM: Don, one for you? *(DOYLE D stands.)*

DOYLE D: There is an internal inquiry. At the present time tasering is continuing, and is considered safe. The Commissioner has staked his career on this policy, and the Met senior team are fully behind him. Thank you.

End of Scene.

SCREENS: THE FREE PRESS = GAY TERMINATOR 3 – BLACKS 0 (and a picture of the dead guy in a police cell.)

THE GUARDENER = KASSAM ON THE ROCKS

THE REAR VIEW = TASERED (and picture of Kassam screaming like a stuck pig in the taser demo)

SAMPLE OF KASSAM FROM PRESS CONFERENCE – A VIDEO THAT HAS GONE VIRAL **'Sunderland til I die'**

SCENE TWELVE

(The News Room. Late afternoon, less hectic. PAIGE is in her Editor's office alone. Enter JONATHAN WHEY rather surreptitiously.)

WHEY: Could I see Paige Britain please?

TINA: Do you have an appointment?

WHEY: No. Sorry.

TINA: I know your face. Are you the Prime Minister?

WHEY: Yes.

TINA: I'll see what I can do. Do you want to sit here?

WHEY: Thank you.

(TINA enters PAIGE's office. PAIGE is re-arranging the furniture, placing a small, basic chair in front of her desk and pumping up her chair to make it higher.)

PAIGE: – I've seen him.

TINA: Shall I show him in?

PAIGE: No. I'll get him when I'm ready. *(We see PAIGE doing nothing, just making him sweat.)*

WALLACE: Woah!? It's the main man! Alright big chap! Wallace Gee. 'How Big's Your Telly?!'

WHEY: Hi.

WALLACE: Man, I gotta have a pic! This is fucking dynamite! Cheers mate! *(WALLACE does a selfie with his phone and the PM. PAIGE comes out.)*

PAIGE: Come in.

WHEY: Thanks.

WALLACE: Laters!

(PAIGE stands in the doorway and lets WHEY in.)

PAIGE: What do you want, I'm busy. *(WHEY sits on the sofa.)*

WHEY: You haven't answered my calls.

PAIGE: I rang on Wednesday.

WHEY: To tell me to tell Kassam to get tasered. My diary column, that you write, has to end. There has to be distance between me and phone hacking.

PAIGE: Your problem is your press officer.

WHEY: St. John got me elected.

PAIGE: No, he didn't, I did. His lobby briefings are terrible. Your voters, your back benchers will be looking to UKIP, and I've got someone for you, who could out-UKIP UKIP.

WHEY: Wilson?

PAIGE: Yup.

WHEY: Wilson's insane!

PAIGE: The British people are insane. When Wilson talks to them, he's talking to himself. That is his genius.

(Enter WILSON who spins around and leaves straight away.)

WILSON: Oh fuck, sorry. Keep forgetting this isn't my office.

PAIGE: *(To WHEY.)* We're done. You can go.

WHEY: When can I see you again?

PAIGE: Next Tuesday. What do you want to do?

WHEY: I want to…I want to make love to you so slowly and for so long that in years to come it'll look like a gap in your CV.

End of Scene.

SCENE THIRTEEN

(New Mary Seacole Yard. The evidence room. It's gloomy, dark. DOYLE D is redacting Bodger's notes. Enter MACMANAMAN.)

MACM: What's this then?

DOYLE D: Operation Estragon. The redacted files.

MACM: He jumped.

DOYLE D: What?

MACM: Kassam. He jumped.

DOYLE D: Off the building?

MACM: He jumped, as in, 'was he pushed or did he jump?'.

DOYLE D: Oh Jesus! Jesus. I thought he'd killed himself.

MACM: Are you alright DD?

DOYLE D: I'm fine. Who's doing the presser?

MACM: That's up to you sir. You're in charge now. Let me know what you want. You know where I am. Congratulations.

(MACMANAMAN leaves.)

SCREENS: THE GUARDENER = KASSAM RESIGNS

THE FREE PRESS = TERMINATOR TERMINATES

THE DAILY WAIL= IMMIGRANT STEALS RAILWAY

End of Scene.

SCENE FOURTEEN

(Number 10. The lobby briefing. About ten journalists and a lecturn. WILSON enters.)

WILSON: Welcome to my very first lobby briefing as Prime Minister's Official Spokesperson. I shoulda started yesterday but I had a check-up with my urologist. I have a small irritating stone lodged in my urinary tract. Now I know what Jerry Hall had to put up with. Ha, ha, alright, fuck 'em, let's get started! Henry?!

HENRY: Will the Prime Minister sign the EU Accession Treaty today?

WILSON: The Prime Minister believes that decent, hard working British people won't tolerate thousands of Romanians coming over here picking our pockets and nicking our barbecues. So no, he won't sign it. Next! You love?! Who are you?

CLAUDIA: Claudia Clarkson, the *Guardian.*

WILSON: Or as I prefer to call it, *Auto Trader*!

CLAUDIA: Will the Prime Minister sign the covenant against the importation of Amazonian hardwoods given that loggers destroy a rainforest the size of Belgium each year?

WILSON: Yeah he will. We're all agreed if you're gonna destroy somewhere the size of Belgium, why not Belgium! Dez!?

DEZ: I understand the Prime Minister has booked a holiday in the Maldives?

WILSON: He has. What about it?

DEZ: Does he share the concerns of Greenpeace that sea level rise will, by the end of this century, consume the Maldives?

WILSON: He is worried about that yes, which is why he's going this summer. Thank you! I'm in the Rose and Crown if anyone wants to buy me a lunch!

End of Scene.

SCREENS: THE FREE PRESS front page = F*** U-EU (And a picture of a two fingered salute to Jose Manuel Barrossa with the strap line that Jonathan Whey refuses to sign the accession treaty allowing in Bulgarian and Romanian workers from the EU.)

THE DAILY EXPECTORANT = GO BACK DRAC! Whey says NO to vampire invasion from Romania! (Picture of Whey weilding a cross and garlic.)

THE REAR VIEW = NO WHEY JOSE! (With a picture of triumphant Jonathan Whey waving from a train window.)

THE DAILY WAIL = IMMIGRANT DOLE CHEAT'S CAT ATE SALMON

SCENE FIFTEEN

(The Ivy. O'LEARY, PAIGE, GARTH, WAITERS as required. They haven't yet ordered.)

O'LEARY: Where's Virginia?

PAIGE: Sharm el Sheikh.

O'LEARY: She's no fucking use to me in Sharm el Sheikh!

PAIGE: She's setting up a sanctuary for underage Egyptian police horses that have been abused.

O'LEARY: What is it with her and –

PAIGE: – Horses?

O'LEARY: No, abuse.

(WENDY arrives, walking, not in her wheelchair.)

WENDY: Hi.

PAIGE: Fuck, you can walk!?

WENDY: Yes, but I'm lazy.

O'LEARY: How are you's then –

GARTH: – Wendy.

WENDY: Recovering. I was burgled last week.

GARTH: That's terrible.

O'LEARY: Did we take much?

WENDY: A couple of bin liners.

O'LEARY: Sentimental value?

WENDY: They'd been in the family for a week.

PAIGE: Chillax, there was nothing in them. Would you like a drink?

WENDY: Champagne please.

PAIGE: Appropriate since we have good news.

GARTH: We're going to pay.

O'LEARY: I'm buying silence, alright? I give you four hundred thousand pounds and you give me a stuffed dog.

WENDY: The price for the stuffed dog, has changed. My client says he wants a million. And I want two hundred thousand costs.

O'LEARY: *(Standing.)* One million two hundred fucking thousand?! Fuck you lady! *(The front of house manager comes over.)*

FERNANDO: Excuse me sir! *(FERNANDO moves off.)*

GARTH: What's changed?

WENDY: I've seen the disclosure documents from the Met. There's 20,000 pages and over a hundred other names have been redacted. Victims.

O'LEARY: So?

WENDY: So your isolated incident, rogue reporter defence is about as much use as Stevie Wonder's sunglasses.

PAIGE: You just made a disablist joke.

WENDY: Jews can tell Jewish jokes.

O'LEARY: One million two hundred thousand?!

WENDY: Or we can go to court. But if you go to court, it will be interesting to see what the Americans make of it.

O'LEARY: What's this got to do with Afuckingmerica?!

PAIGE: Anyone with a conviction for corruption in another country can be prosecuted under the Foreign Corrupt Practices Act. Siemans AG were recently fined 450 million dollars.

O'LEARY: *(To GARTH.)* Do you know about this?

GARTH: Yup.

O'LEARY: The fuck you do. *(O'LEARY gets his cheque book out.)*

(To WENDY.) Earlier, when I said 'fuck you lady' what I meant was…'who do I pay?'

WENDY: Khakwani Klinkard and Ul Haq ltd.

O'LEARY: Which are you?

WENDY: Klinkard.

(The cheque signed he hands it over.)

WENDY: Thank you. That's the end of that one.

O'LEARY: That one?

WENDY: I've read every splash on Paige's watch and I've written to other potential victims. Including Stella Stone, Clarissa Kingston-Mills, three politicians, two footballers, etcetera. Seventeen in all. Do you have seventeen million?

PAIGE: You don't threaten us, OK.

WENDY: Plus costs.

GARTH: You've gotta pay. She's got us by the short and curlies.

FERNANDO: Are you ready to order now?

WENDY: I'll have the crab bisque, followed by the roast Devonshire chicken and a bottle of Chablis.

FERNANDO: The Devonshire whole roast chicken is for two madam.

WENDY: Yes, I know. What time to do you close?

(PAIGE leaves The Ivy and walks to her next scene.)

PAIGE: *(Aside.)* She doesn't have me by the short and curlies because I don't have any. After Diane Bendall's Brazilian I became interested in the whole field of genital depilation. Can we call it a field? Not any more obviously. I went for 100% hair removal treatment, which is called 'a Hollywood', after the place that invented the concept. If it was named after where I'd had it done, it would be called 'an Isle of Dogs'.

End of Scene.

SCENE SIXTEEN

(DOYLE D's grace and favour flat. PAIGE is there, enter DOYLE D in uniform. PAIGE tries to kiss him, and succeeds but DOYLE D is restrained. PAIGE gives DOYLE D a copy of her report.)

DOYLE D: What's the O'Leary Management and Ethics Committee?

PAIGE: It's er…me. It's an in-house investigation into the criminal sub-culture which developed in a group of journalists which was anathema to the Best Practice Guidelines of O'Leary Media as outlined in appendix seven.

(DOYLE D looks for appendix seven.)

DOYLE D: There is no appendix seven.

PAIGE: I haven't written it yet.

DOYLE D: You want me to arrest your staff?

PAIGE: Why not? Ding Dong, you've been away overnight, you come back and you're not frisky. I'm gonna phone Relate, get an emergency appointment!

DOYLE D: We've found the twins.

PAIGE: Oh no. Together?

DOYLE D: Buried, side by side.

(PAIGE is properly moved by this news and sits and mourns.)

PAIGE: Were they, I dunno, intact?

DOYLE D: The pathologist will confirm if they had been sexually assaulted. *(PAIGE is crying. But DOYLE D is not caring for her.)*

DOYLE D: It's over for you now then isn't it. The twins' gravy train has stopped.

PAIGE: *(Tearful still.)* Every morning I have to give the public what they want. And what do they want? Tits, bingo, and the death penalty for paedophiles.

DOYLE D: We found the bodies in Keswick, the Lake District.

PAIGE: That's a long way.

DOYLE D: Too far for Kieron Mills. He didn't kill them. It was some other nonce. Some nonce, to be fair to Kieron Mills since he wasn't actually a nonce. Some nonce on remand at HMP for child murder who admitted to it, and took us to the graves.

PAIGE: Who is he? Did Mills sell him the twins to make child porn?

DOYLE D: For fuck's sake no – he didn't!

PAIGE: OK, OK. Let's stay rational. Who knows about this DD?

DOYLE D: No! No! No! No! No! Who knows about it!? The six guys who dug them up, the prison guards, the bus driver, me, the cooks, cleaners and caterers of Cumbria Police Authority. You cannot control the truth! That's it! It's over. No! Don't touch me!

PAIGE: DD?

DOYLE D: Kieron Mills was entirely blameless. And I put him away.

PAIGE: He was white trash, trailer park scum.

DOYLE D: I killed him.

End of Scene.

SCREENS: 24-HOUR ROLLING NEWS. LOCATION REPORT. A MOOR.

JOURNO: 'It was here, not two miles from where Wordsworth wandered lonely as a cloud, that the Mills twins' bodies were discovered. Police led to the shallow graves by a fifty-six-year-old inmate of Manchester Strangeways prison. Kieron Mills it seems did not kill his own girls.'

SCENE SEVENTEEN

(New Mary Seacole Yard. The evidence room. DACOSTA is alone, now a Chief Inspector, looking at the redacted evidence. CLARISSA KINGSTON-MILLS arrives accompanied by a PC.)

PC: Ma'am. Clarissa Kingston-Mills.

DACOSTA: Hi. I'm Chief Inspector DaCosta.

(The PC leaves.) I'm in charge of this operation, Operation Estragon.

CLARISSA: 'Nothing to be done' then.

DACOSTA: Let's hope eh.

CLARISSA: I was quoting Estragon, from the Samuel Beckett play, *Waiting for Godot.* 'Nothing to be done'.

DACOSTA: I like musicals. I've found two occasions when I think you were hacked. See, Kingston-Mills. Is that your mobile number?

(Shows her the first sheet.)

CLARISSA: Yes.

(Shows a second sheet.)

DACOSTA: And this one a month later where it looks like you and your sister were hacked on the same day. There's two numbers.

CLARISSA: My sister lives in the Azores.

DACOSTA: No way?! *(Enter DOYLE D.)*

DACOSTA: Sir?

DOYLE D: What are you doing?

DACOSTA: This is Clarissa Kingston-Mills, I believe she had her phone hacked.

DOYLE D: Yes, and what are you doing?!

DACOSTA: She has the right to know if that's the case.

CLARISSA: Yes, I do.

DOYLE D: Fine. Carry on.

DACOSTA: So is that your sister's number? In the Azores.

CLARISSA: No. And that other number's not my number.

DACOSTA: But this sheet is headed Kingston-Mills sisters. Are there any other Kingston-Mills sisters, like, in celebrity circles?

CLARISSA: No. That dash there, could be just that, a dash, linking Kingston, the place, with Mills.

DA COSTA: So Kingston-Mills is not a name?

CLARISSA: Mills is a name. Mills sisters. In Kingston.

DACOSTA: Are there any famous Mills sisters in Kingston?

DOYLE D: Yes. The twins.

CLARISSA: Twins are sisters.

DACOSTA: Those little girls. Did they have phones?

DOYLE D: Twelve year olds have phones.

DACOSTA: My God. They hacked the twins' phones. How could they do that?

CLARISSA: I know them. They could to that.

End of Scene.

SCENE EIGHTEEN

SCREENS: THE DEPENDENT = DEAD TWINS' PHONES HACKED

THE GUARDENER = DID FREE PRESS HINDER POLICE?

THE REAR VIEW = O'LEARY PRESS HACKED TWINS

THE DAILY WAIL = IMMIGRANTS MELT ARCTIC

(Enter GARTH.)

GARTH: Listen everyone! Laptops. Has everyone wiped their laptops?

GEMMA: You want us to destroy evidence?

DICKIE: I own the copyright on my work. It's mine.

GARTH: Wipe the fucking hard drive you fucking pervert!

DICKIE: Fuck you! You created pressure for story, you and Paige. You've turned us all into criminals.

TINA: Celebs is one thing, but them poor girls. Knowhatimean?

GARTH: No, I don't know what you mean.

GEMMA: We don't mind hacking a bunch of coke snorting, bed hopping celebs –

MADDY: – but those girls were raped and murdered.

GARTH: You don't know that. *(PAIGE enters.)*

PAIGE: OK, this is conference. This is an ordinary working day. We have a paper to build. Tina, Garth. Where are we with Stella Stone?

TINA: *(Tears.)* No. I don't think I can do it any more!

PAIGE: Garth?!

GARTH: She's in a private hospital, we're paying. She'll die within the week.

PAIGE: And we have an exclusive, with pictures?

GARTH: Yes.

PAIGE: Now the splash I want Saturday morning is STELLA STONE 1978 to 2005.

MADDY: But she might still be alive!

PAIGE: No. We control when she dies. The other dailies have to wait until Monday.

TINA: No! No! No!

PAIGE: We're paying her a hundred thousand pounds! Garth, go to the hospital with Dickie, explain what we want.

(Enter PASCHAL.)

O'LEARY: Them fannies at Tesco have pulled their advertising. And Aldi, and Lidl. I'm shutting the paper. This is the end of *The Free Press.*

(Uproar.)

All your legal, statutory entitlements will be honoured, unless, unless your dismissal is 'cause of a breach o' company ethics and policy –

WALLACE: A what?

(MARCUS bursts in, followed by VIRGINIA.)

MARCUS: The cops are coming up the stairs! The cops are coming up the stairs!

VIRGINIA: What have we done?!

GARTH: Get the cameras. I want a police raid on a free newspaper recorded. Smash the computers!

(PAIGE retreats to the Editor's office. GARTH starts attacking the lap tops on the desks. Journalists start taking pictures with flash, intimidating the police. The police stream in.)

CRAM: Nobody move! OK. I'm the arresting officer Commander Cram.

GARTH: I want to see your warrant! We're a newspaper, we are protected by Article 10 of the European Convention on Human Rights.

CRAM: My forensic team need to search and confiscate, if necessary, material and data relevant to a conspiracy to intercept communications.

PAIGE: Where's DD?

(A forensic team move in, white suited, they start taking computers away.)

CRAM: I have a warrant for the arrest of the following individuals. Hunter Dickson?

DICKIE: I was just obeying orders. *(He is read his rights.)*

(OFFICER: I am arresting you on suspicion of conspiracy to intercept communications. You do not have to say anything, but it may harm your defence, if you do not mention when questioned, something which you will later rely on in court. Anything you do say may be given in evidence.)

CRAM: Garth Ellerington…

GARTH: Here.

CRAM: … Gemma Charles…

JACKIE: Yes.

CRAM: … Madeleine FitzPatrick….

MADDY: Here.

CRAM: …. Christina Ursal….

TINA: Here.

CRAM: … Wallace Gee.

MARCUS: How Big's Your Telly! I knew sweet FA about the phone stuff!

CRAM: Tell the judge. Virginia White!

VIRGINIA: Me? Phone hacking? There must be some mistake! I'm a campaigner for social justice.

CRAM: Read her her rights. *(OFFICER 2 cuffs VIRGINIA.)*

(OFFICER 2: I am arresting you on suspicion of conspiracy to intercept communications. You do not have to say anything, but it may harm your defence, if you do not mention when questioned, something which you will later rely on in court. Anything you do say may be given in evidence. One by one they step forward and are arrested & have their rights read. PASCHAL approaches PAIGE.)

PAIGE: Paschal?

O'LEARY: Let's talk about the future. I need you Paige. America. What do you think?

PAIGE: California?

O'LEARY: Aye, it's a dreadful place, and the fucking sun never takes a day off. And a house with a pool is awful stressful what with worrying about leaves getting stuck in the filters. Do you want it?

PAIGE: I want it.

O'LEARY: That's my girl! *(PAIGE crosses to CRAM.)*

PAIGE: Paige Britain.

CRAM: Paige Britain. I am arresting you on suspicion of conspiracy to intercept communications.

(During the next, CRAM reads her her rights. The forensic team bag up computers etc.)

PAIGE: *(Direct address.)* It's still a sensational privilege to live in this nation, isn't it? We're still Great Britain. No other country is branded like we are. There's no Fabulous Latvia; Marvellous The Gambia; Not Bad Norway. That's our genius. Oxford and Cambridge, leather on willow, fair play, the common law, Richard Curtis and the Lark Ascending. Goodness and integrity runs though our country as if through a stick of rock. NO. It wasn't true thirty years ago. It's never been true. I paid a House of Commons civil servant a cash bung for a data disk full of MP's ludicrous, and criminal expenses claims. I corrupted a public servant, a crime, but a crime for which I was universally lauded. I listen to a whole heap of celebrities' voicemails, a criminal act many times over, and no one gives a fuck, not even the police, and they knew about it. I listen to the twins' voicemail, and I'm pilloried. Phone hacking? Give me a break, it's riding a bike without lights. None of you give a damn about us hacking a bunch of trouser dropping, publicity seeking celebrities, or Royals. For Christ's sake, isn't that what you pay them for!? The truth is, you know as well as I do, that if that hacking had led to the cops finding the twins alive, I'd be a hero.

SCREENS: THE EXPECTORANT = GOTCHA!

(Picture of PAIGE arrested, under blanket.)

THE GUARDENER = WHEY CONDEMNS TABLOID MORALS *(Photo of WHEY.)*

THE DEPENDENT = O'LEARY USA IN CRISIS *(O'LEARY photo.)*

THE REAR VIEW = COPS KNEW SAYS HACKER *(Photo of BODGER.)*

THE DAILY WAIL = NEWS EDITOR DENIES HACKING KNOWLEDGE *(Artist's impression of her in court.)*

THE GUARDENER = O'LEARY DEMENTIA SINCE SIX YEARS OLD *(Photo of O'LEARY and photo of him at six years old.)*

THE FREE PRESS = SORRY! *(Photo of PAIGE in tears / hanky.)*

THE GUARDENER = NEWS EDITOR GETS TWO YEARS

THE REAR VIEW = WHEY DENIES AFFAIR – FANTASY! *(Photo of WHEY and PAIGE kissing at newspaper awards.)*

THE DEPENDENT = WAS THIS WOMAN RUNNING THE COUNTRY? *(Photos of PAIGE with WHEY and SULLY and the Queen and finally the Lord High Admiral.)*

THE DAILY WAIL = OUT IN 6! Paige Britain the hacking editor is out having served only six months of a two year sentance.

THE GUARDENER = Britain LEAVES FOR NEW O'LEARY JOB IN USA

(The band burst into chat show intro music. Crazy lights. Audience sounds. A voiceover announces –)

VOICEOVER: Our first guest tonight is the mother of Malawi, who's that girl! She's like a virgin, yes, we are desperately seeking Madonna!

(Applause, MADONNA takes a seat on the couch.)

Please welcome, the saint of Saint Petersburg, from Russia with love, he's the most powerful man in the world… Vladimir Putin.

(Applause. PUTIN takes the couch.)

And finally, he's infallible, he's Argentinian, he's the hand of God but he's not Maradonna… Pope Francis!!!

(Applause. The POPE enters and takes a seat. Drum roll.)

Your host tonight…she's said sorry and served her time let the punishment fit the crime she's the lag you love and a fair cop guv.

Ladies and Gentlemen… Paaaaaaaaaaige Britain!

(PAIGE comes down the steps to her theme tune, her song, and takes the applause. The band crash a chord to end the song.)

SNAP TO BLACK.

THE END

THE NAP

Acknowledgements

I'd like to thank my good friend Don Black, a snooker nut, for sparing the time to beat me on the baize and share with me his passion for the game. More technical snooker advice and support was given by Katie Henrick, the snooker professional at the RAC club. John Astley contributed further research notes on the modern world of snooker, and astonished me with his skill. Dennis Taylor was generous with his anecdotes, and liberal in giving out useful phone numbers. I visited the Gambling Commission in Birmingham and Richard Watson explained to me a typical match fixing scenario and thus supplied the plot.

I'd like to thank family and friends for reading the first few drafts and giving notes – Erica Whyman, Chris Campbell, Clive Coleman in particular. Robert Hudson, a fine Sheffield actor, helped me enormously with local colour.

Richard Bean, 2016

Characters

DYLAN SPOKES, 23

STELLA SPOKES, 50

BOBBY SPOKES, 55

DANNY KILLEEN, 60

MOHAMMAD HABIB, 40

ELEANOR SARGENT, 25

WAXY CHUFF, 50

DUNCAN FERRYMAN / DANNY CARR, 30

TONY DANLINO, 30

SETH, 50

Referee, stewards, etc as required

The Nap was first performed on 11 March 2016 at the Crucible Theatre, Sheffield, with the following cast:

BOBBY SPOKES	Mark Addy
DUNCAN FERRYMAN/DANNY CARR	John Astley
REFEREE/SETH/STEWARD	Chris Brailsford
STELLA	Esther Coles
DANNY KILLEEN	Dermot Crowley
WAXY CHUFF	Louise Gold
MOHAMMAD BUTT	Youssef Kerkour
TONY DANLINO/MC/	Ralf Little
DYLAN SPOKES	Jack O'Connell
ELEANOR SARGENT	Rochenda Sandall

Creative team and company

Director	Richard Wilson
Designer	James Cotterill
Lighting Designer	Johanna Town
Composer	Olly Fox
Casting Director	Robert Sterne CDG
Assistant Directors	Charlie Kenber Celine Lowenthal
Assistant Lighting Designer	Kellie Zezulka
Costume Supervisor	Sydney Florence
Production Manager	Dan Franklin
Stage Manager	Sarah Gentle
Deputy Stage Manager	Jen Davey
Assistant Stage Managers	Amy Hawthorne Kim Towler

Act One

SCENE ONE

A British Legion snooker room in Manor Top in Sheffield S12. Morning, but in this windowless basement, it's dark. A clock on the wall shows 1.13 pm. The snooker table is bare, no balls are set, the table lights are not on. Enter DYLAN, *a young man of about 25. He is wearing a baseball hat or youth hat a-la-mode, hoodie, jeans and trainers. He could be a burglar, and not the snooker professional that he is. He turns the main room lights on, and stands by the switch, not entering the room. He takes it in, expressionless. He is carrying nothing but a solid snooker cue case, and the room key which has two keys on it: one for the room, and one for the cupboard. A snooker room, for him, is a church and so all his actions are reverential and ritualistic as if to do something wrong would be to upset the God of Snooker. He does not suffer from OCD but his sport demands a ritual to which he adheres. He chooses to sit at one chair and table, sits and puts his cue case down. He gets the feel of the location, feels it's wrong and so, not dramatically, he moves to the other table, sits, feels that it's right, and only then does he make it his 'office'. He puts his cue down, takes his hoodie off which reveals a Stone Roses T-shirt (I Wanna Be Adored). He takes off first his hat, then a signet ring from one of his fingers, and the St. Christopher medallion chain from around his neck and places them on his side table. It is as if he is purifying himself before touching the cloth. With care and patience, takes out his 3/4 cue and inspects the tip, which, finding it wanting, he files with a piece of sandpaper from his cue case. He then chalks it. Having done that, he finds his talcum powder in his cue case and dresses his cue with it. He puts one 20p piece in the light meter. The table lights come on. He approaches the table, looks at it as if trying to build a relationship with it. He runs his hand in a short stroke from baulk end to spot end and then back from spot end to baulk end. Having felt the nap, and judged the quality, depth and age of the baize he is convinced it needs ironing. He locates the cupboard and opens it with the key. From the cupboard, he takes the table iron and plugs it in. He takes the box of balls, inspects them, and takes one ball and rolls it against the cushions. He sets three or four balls for a trick shot, and plays it. Enter* BOBBY, *a man of about 55, his father. He has a copy of the Sun newspaper and a pack of prawn sandwiches, a yellow past the sell-by-date offer sticker, and a string bag of clementines. They acknowledge each other but don't speak as* DYLAN *plays a shot. After the shot.*

BOBBY: Do you want a prawn sandwich?

DYLAN gives him a look of contempt.

DYLAN: I don't eat owt wi' a brain.

BOBBY: They're prawns, they're not novelists.

DYLAN: Tony's coming round.

BOBBY: I don't like Tony.

DYLAN: Why don't you like Tony?

BOBBY: 'Cause he dun't like me. Why dun't he like me?

DYLAN: 'Cause I told him you don't like him.

BOBBY: I think Tony is a total bastard. But that's no reason for him not to like me.

DYLAN: It's the way the world works, innit. Zen out, man.

BOBBY: What a dump. What a dump! What a dump. What a dump. What a dump. I mean … what … what … what … I mean … what a fucking dump. What a dump?! What kind of … I mean, look at that … if yer gonna … I mean, stands to reason, knowhatimean. I mean … what the fuck is … what a fucking dump. What a dump. Do you like it?

DYLAN: It's perfect.

BOBBY: It's not the Crucible, is it? What's new?

DYLAN: Kittichat Wongsawat has pulled out.

BOBBY: Wahey!

DYLAN: Went home, to Bangkok. Stress.

BOBBY: You done that!

DYLAN: Yeah.

BOBBY: I went to Bangkok once. Kaw! Twenty hairy-arsed telecomms engineers on fifty quid a day spenders. First pub I went in there's a lass sitting on the bar firing ping pong balls out of her fanny. Yeah! They'd be doing that in Worksop if they didn't have television. You beat Wongsawat, eh? Must've felt good, eh?

DYLAN: Self-actualisation.

BOBBY: What's that when it's at home?

DYLAN: It's the highest possible state of human happiness, when your mind and body are come together in, like, a beautiful symphony.

DYLAN plays a shot. BOBBY offers DYLAN an orange.

BOBBY: Do you want an orange? I don't think they got brains. Got a bag full. £1.90 reduced. Was two pound forty, that's a saving of er … £2.40 minus £1.90 is £2, no, er … £1 … fuck it, I saved a lot of money.

DYLAN: No, ta.

BOBBY: Do you know why there's no orange ball in snooker?

DYLAN: You're gonna tell me.

BOBBY: Back in 1875, when them army officers invented the game in India, they didn't have orange. Oranges are the only thing in the natural world what's orange. And they'd never seen one. Orange, the colour, didn't exist.

DYLAN: Everyone's always had orange, the colour.

BOBBY: No.

DYLAN: Bits of parrots.

BOBBY: Bits of parrots?

DYLAN: Yeah, and tigers, and lots of flowers, the inside of mangoes, and goldfish –

BOBBY: – alright! –

DYLAN: – and a whole section of the rainbow, and –

BOBBY: – alright! Someone in a pub told us, I didn't think it through.

DYLAN: Lights.

BOBBY goes to the light meter.

BOBBY: 20p for eighteen minutes?! Do you want me to go and hit him for you?

DYLAN: No.

BOBBY: I was at school with that Gavin. If you threatened to punch him, he'd give you his milk.

DYLAN: I don't want his milk. Close the door.

BOBBY goes to the door.

BOBBY: Ten quid the door doesn't close properly.

DYLAN: I'm not betting on whether a door closes or not.

BOBBY: Bet on anything. Football – first throw in; cricket – broken windows; snooker – who'll turn up with a black eye.

BOBBY closes the door, which doesn't close properly.

You owe me ten quid!

DYLAN: I didn't take the bet.

BOBBY: Alex Higgins turned up once, pissed, two black eyes, and obviously slept in a hedge. He was playing Steve Davis – sober, 20/20 vision, memory foam mattress.
Alex wiped the floor with him, 25 – 4. In his speech, Higgins tore the cheque in half, called the ref a cunt, fell over, cut his head on the trophy, and spent the night in A&E. Yeah, that's what's missing from the modern game, personalities.

DYLAN starts ironing the table, running it from baulk end to spot end in lines with a slight overlap. BOBBY reads his paper.

BOBBY: Brilliant! I love it. Fantastic!

DYLAN: What is it?

BOBBY: Robin Gibb's died.

DYLAN: Who's he?

BOBBY: One of the Bee Gees.

DYLAN: And why is that brilliant/fantastic?

BOBBY: Cheers me up every time a vegetarian dies of cancer.

DYLAN: Why do you find it so ridiculous that someone might choose to live by a set of principles?

BOBBY: Alex Higgins. He had a strict diet.

DYLAN: Vegetarian? The Hurricane? Bollocks!

BOBBY: He'd only eat raspberry jam sandwiches.

DYLAN: Why?

BOBBY: 'Cause they're the only thing that tastes just as good coming up as they do going down.

DYLAN: What did he believe in?

BOBBY: Booze, birds. My mate, Eddie Fredericks, brilliant amateur, he was a believer. Jesus Christ.

DYLAN: He was a Christian?

BOBBY: Christianity, yeah. It was like a fucking religion to him.

BOBBY is reading the paper.

Here, let me do that.

BOBBY takes over the ironing.

To be fair, it's in good nick, for Manor Top. No puke on the baize, no skag needles in the pockets, and no one's had a shit in the bin.

DYLAN: It's not a bad table, as it happens.

BOBBY: Glad to be back home, are you? Your room alright?

DYLAN: Yeah, cool.

BOBBY: I don't let out your room, you know. I could. Could get eighty quid a week if I put another student in there, but I don't.

DYLAN: The toilet was blocked.

BOBBY: Tell me about it. Problem is, see, the house has gorra two-inch pipe system, and that sociology student has gorra three-inch arsehole.

DYLAN: There was no hot water.

BOBBY: That's why I give you a kettle.

DYLAN gives him a look.

DYLAN: I'll get you a new boiler, Dad.

BOBBY: No! Them Wongsawat winnings is yours.

DYLAN: Duncan Ferryman's staying at the Kenwood Hotel.

BOBBY: Oh son, you can't stay in a hotel in Sheffield. This is your home town. Anyway, you won't get a room, they're already three to a bed at the Premier Inn.

DYLAN: Dennis Taylor stayed at the Kenwood when he beat Steve Davis.

BOBBY: I was there you know.

DYLAN: In his hotel room?

BOBBY: The Crucible! The greatest final ever, nineteen summat.

DYLAN: Nineteen eighty-five.

BOBBY: That was the night the modern game was born. Eighteen million people watched on telly. Ten years earlier, 1972 –

DYLAN: – thirteen years earlier.

BOBBY: The World Championship final was played in a poxy Birmingham British Legion, just like this dump, people sitting on beer barrels, smoke, you couldn't breathe, you couldn't see, there was a power cut, miners' strike. I slept in the car. Alex Higgins, a young kid then, your age, beat John Spencer, thirty-seven, thirty-two. Prize money? Four hundred quid. I don't know what they learned you at Q school but that's the true history of this game.

DYLAN plays a shot.

You're not saying you need to stay in a hotel for confidence are you?

DYLAN: Not for confidence, no, for a shower. But, since you mention it, the psychology is interesting. One player stays at the Kenwood, sleeps in Egyptian cotton sheets, room service, big white towels, the other's in a box room down the Eccy Road, in a single bed, under a fifteen-year-old poly cotton Ninja Turtles duvet.

BOBBY: What's your point?

DYLAN: Home is where you wet the bed.

BOBBY: I stayed at the Kenwood once, didn't stop me wetting the bed. You don't need this psychological bollocks. You beat the number seventeen in the world, who's beaten Mark Selby! You can beat Mark Selby!

DYLAN: I'm cool. The philosophy's working for me.

BOBBY: Philosofuckingphy. In Cardiff you was beating Sean Murphy and you threw it away!

DYLAN: I'd touched the pink and –

BOBBY: – the ref hadn't seen it! Murphy hadn't seen it. I didn't see it. Bloody hell, you didn't see it!

DYLAN: I felt it.

BOBBY: You felt it?! That lost you the game! Five thousand quid!

DYLAN: I have to honour the game.

BOBBY: Whose game do you think you're honouring? This game is a way for working-class lads who were shit at school to make some money.

DYLAN: I wasn't shit at school, I was dyslexic.

BOBBY: Alex Higgins, Jimmy White, Ronnie O'Sullivan. This game don't belong to them toff army officers back in the Raj.

DYLAN lines up a shot. BOBBY opens his can of beer at the worst moment.

DYLAN: For fuck's sake!

BOBBY: You shouldn't have heard that! Next week, in the Crucible there's an audience, crisps, mobile phones going off, applause, laughter. You got to stay focused, stay in the zone. Focus. What's stopping you fulfilling your potential?

BOBBY holds open Page 3 of the Sun and holds it in line with the cue line and the shot.

DYLAN: You.

BOBBY: Distractions. You need to find a nice girl, get married. It would do you good, a bit of tedium, bit of misery. You're as horny as a mink on a mink farm.

DYLAN pots the ball. Enter MOHAMMAD HABIB and ELEANOR SARGENT. MOHAMMAD is dressed in a suit and wears an ID badge around his neck. ELEANOR is dressed in jeans, and a leather jacket. She wears no ID.

BOBBY: *(Standing.)* Oi! Fuck off, this is a private room.

MO offers up his ID badge.

MO: Mohammad Butt, Integrity Officer, International Centre for Sport Security and –

ELEANOR: – Eleanor Sargent. Of the NCA.

DYLAN: Police?

ELEANOR: Yeah.

BOBBY: *(Beat.)* And which bit of 'fuck off, this is a private room' don't you understand?

DYLAN: Dad. It's alright. *(To MO.)* You'll want a urine sample, yeah?

MO: Yup.

MO takes out a sample kit, and shows it to DYLAN. DYLAN signs forms.

BOBBY: *(To ELEANOR.)* I wanna see your ID. *(To DYLAN.)* How do they know you're here?

DYLAN: I told them. They have to know where I am. They can demand a sample whenever they want. There's a loo down the hall.

MO and DYLAN leave the room.

ELEANOR: Bobby Spokes?

BOBBY: Maybe. Which nick are you then?

ELEANOR: I'm not Sheffield. I'm NCA, National Crime Agency. They've given me a desk at Snig Hill, for the championships.

ELEANOR holds up her ID card which BOBBY studies slowly, looking at her now and then to check reality against the photo.

Happy?

BOBBY: No, I can't see a thing without my glasses. Might as well be your Primark card.

ELEANOR: You going straight now, Bobby?

BOBBY: I was in the wrong place at the wrong time.

ELEANOR: In a building society with a sawn-off shotgun.

BOBBY: Exactly.

ELEANOR: Not dealing, neither?

BOBBY: If I go down Pitsmoor, they'll kill me. They got more guns than you have. I got bedsits now. Students. And I don't serve it up no more. Do you deal drugs?

ELEANOR: I'm a policewoman. Dealing drugs is frowned upon.

BOBBY: When you've been passed over for promotion six times, and your career's going nowhere, one day you'll bust a kid with a bag of white and a street value of fifteen thousand and you'll be tempted. Then, you'll be no better than me.

ELEANOR: So you're still dealing then?

BOBBY: No better … than the way I used to be … when I did deal drugs, before I didn't. Alright, fucking search me!

He drops his pants, and points his arse at her.

ELEANOR: I don't have any rubber gloves.

Enter MO and DYLAN.

Do you have any rubber gloves Mo?

MO: Yeah, I do.

BOBBY: Fuck off!

Pulling up his pants.

Are you done?

MO: No. What do you know about global, criminal betting?

BOBBY: Do I look like I'm doing well out of organised crime?

ELEANOR: He's got bedsits.

BOBBY: And I coach him.

DYLAN: The dodgy betting's mainly Far East, in't it?

MO: The main problem's the Philippines yes.

ELEANOR: Dylan, do you know Norman Twig?

BOBBY: You don't have to answer son –

DYLAN: – Twiggy? Course I do.

BOBBY: Who is he?

ELEANOR: He's the integrity officer at the WPBSA.

BOBBY: So?

MO: My organisation, the ICSS, are working with Norman and the Gambling Commission.

ELEANOR: And the police.

MO: It is our responsibility to monitor the integrity of the Championships.

BOBBY: Are you saying he's bent?

DYLAN: Shut it, Dad!

BOBBY: Alright, alright.

MO: The Gambling Commission get information from the industry.

BOBBY: Snooker?

ELEANOR: The betting industry. They know how much money would normally be bet on any match.

MO: When there is a spike in liquidity, the Gambling Commission get told, and they tell us.

BOBBY: This boy will never tank a game. He's a vegetarian.

ELEANOR: We know all about Dylan.

BOBBY: Yeah, well, unlike me, he's got principles. He lives his life by a code. I'm very proud of him. You would not believe he was my son.

MO: In Brussels last week, you beat Kittichat Wongsawat. Ten four. And you won the first frame.

DYLAN: I won the first six frames.

MO: There was a spike on the first frame.

ELEANOR: A pile of money went on.

MO: All of it placed on you to lose.

DYLAN: I won.

ELEANOR: So someone lost a lot of money.

BOBBY: Who?

MO: We don't know. Do you know?

DYLAN: No. I don't even bet on myself.

ELEANOR: The investment was smurfed. Do you understand what we mean by smurfing?

DYLAN: Yeah, the punter employs an army of small blue dwarfs to place cash bets across the country.

ELEANOR: Exactly.

BOBBY: Eh? Small blue dwarfs?

DYLAN: Shut up, Dad.

BOBBY: No one asked him to lose.

MO: The money was on Dylan to lose the first frame.

DYLAN: I beat him hard man!

MO: The liquidity statistics, are cold, unemotional, they don't lie.

ELEANOR: It was set up to be a bent frame.

BOBBY: He fucking won it!

ELEANOR: Yeah, he won it, and let someone down.

DYLAN: No, no, no. I would never tank a game.

MO: Match fixing doesn't take place at the top of the rankings. You're ranked 107 with prize money so far this year of next to nothing.

BOBBY: Two thousand euros.

MO: Which is less than my wife's annual budget for taramasalata.

BOBBY: You're a comedian an'all are you? Do you know the snooker world?

MO: I admit snooker's not my passion. Cricket and rugby.

BOBBY: Rugby Union?

MO: What else is there?

BOBBY: Rugby League. You're beginning to sound like English Public School?

MO: Charterhouse. My parents were Moroccan diplomatic corps.

BOBBY: Bloody hell. I went to Twickenham once. Did my head in. A hundred thousand hedge fund managers singing negro spirituals.

MO: Let me describe to you a very typical scenario.

DYLAN: I'm not typical.

BOBBY: He's not typical.

MO: A talented young man goes to Q school, qualifies for the tour, gets a two year card. He is befriended by a wealthy man –

ELEANOR: – or woman, let's be fair.

MO: Let's use the term sponsor – his sponsor buys him drinks, pays his hotel bills, flights. The agreement is that the sponsor gets 10% of winnings.

ELEANOR: Which never come. He's ranked 107.

MO: And the debt builds up. One day he gets drawn to play Ronnie O'Sullivan in the first round of a championship, a game he's not expected to win. The sponsor will ask him to lose a specific frame.

ELEANOR: A frame he's likely to lose anyway.

MO: Could you beat Ronnie O'Sullivan?

BOBBY: He's already beaten Ronnie.

ELEANOR: Has he?

BOBBY: Not at snooker but –

DYLAN: – shut up, Dad.

MO: He agrees to lose the frame.

DYLAN: No.

MO: The sponsor stakes his money, the rookie tanks the frame, no one's suspicious because he was going to lose anyway.

ELEANOR: The debt is wiped.

MO: It goes on.

BOBBY: Of course it goes on, it's as old as Lulu.

DYLAN: I'm saying this for the second time now, I will never tank a game.

MO: How did you pay your hotel bill last week in Brussels?

DYLAN: I paid it myself out of my winnings.

ELEANOR: Do you have a sponsor?

DYLAN: No.

MO: OK. This visit is educational.

BOBBY: My lad's got more GCSEs than Jimmy White and Alex Higgins put together.

ELEANOR: One, then?

BOBBY: Yeah.

MO: My job is to secure snooker as a clean sport for this and future generations. The soul of the game is precious.

BOBBY: You don't need to tell him that.

MO: Dylan. What is snooker?

DYLAN: It's a game, a bit like golf but you can't lose the ball.

MO: It's an exercise in integrity. Trust. If the public lose faith, the game is finished.

DYLAN: I know that.

ELEANOR: It might look like easy money Dylan, but it could be your last money.

MO: In the first ten years of my marriage –

BOBBY: – Fucking hell, marriage guidance an'all!

MO: – I had an affair, and I felt bad about it. But I forgave myself. But at school, during a cricket match, I was caught by the keeper off a faint nick which the umpire didn't hear. To my shame, I didn't walk. I have sleepless nights about that maybe six or seven times a year. On my death bed, it will be my greatest regret.

BOBBY: Has your wife forgiven you?

MO: I didn't tell her. She loves cricket.

BOBBY: I meant the affair.

MO: Oh yeah, she's cool on that.

DYLAN: I been doing a lot of listening. It's nice. But can I tell you guys something?

ELEANOR: Sure.

DYLAN: Without snooker, what am I? I'm running a skunk farm, signing on, getting me legs blown off in Afghan. When my mates was drinking cider and supergglueing tortoises to the railway line, I was in a shed –

BOBBY: – dedicated snooker room, with double glazing.

DYLAN: – practising. But practice in't my edge. My advantage is psychology. I am a fish and snooker is my sea.

BOBBY: He's the Eric Cantona of the billiard room.

MO: Fish defecate in the sea.

BOBBY: I'm getting confused now.

ELEANOR: We're on your side, Dylan, but our profiling has identified you as vulnerable.

ELEANOR gives the document to MO, and steps forward.

DYLAN: I am not vulnerable. I honour my game. I know the history of the game. Snooker is the result of a century of human negotiation. A celebration of cooperation and civilisation. It doesn't exist other than in the hearts of players and fans. It is a set of rules, abstractions. It is a fiction.

ELEANOR: Fiction's not real.

DYLAN: What colour are zebras?

MO: Black and white.

DYLAN: Wrong. Zebras are brown and white. We think they're black and white 'cause zebra crossings are black and white. It's an agreed fiction, like snooker.

BOBBY: Don't look at me.

DYLAN: You know what Ted Lowe said on TV – 'for those of you watching in black and white, the pink is next to the green'.

ELEANOR: I've heard that one, yeah.

DYLAN: It made perfect sense to me.

He picks up the green ball.

Green is not a colour in snooker. Green is a place, there, and three points. Being green is the least important thing about the green ball. We could play this game with twenty-two white balls, if our memories were good enough.

He replaces the black with the yellow.

If we made the yellow worth seven points and swapped it for the black, it wun't change the game one bit. But if we made the yellow worth seven points and kept it up the baulk end of the table, the game would change out of sight. Everyone would be trying to gerr up that end of the table. There'd be no 147s, ever. It'd be too hard.

ELEANOR: What's your point?

DYLAN: That snooker is one hundred percent created by man, there is nothing natural about this game. There is nowhere on earth that is as flat as a snooker table. There is nothing in nature as perfectly round as a snooker ball. The earth itself is not round. I was lucky to be born when I was, 'cause I coulda been born a caveman. Imagine, a fucking caveman with a talent for snooker.

ELEANOR: But no snooker table?

DYLAN: Exactly. It is only through snooker that I understand the world and my place in it. This game is my life. I have nothing else. Are you seriously suggesting I'd be stupid enough to fuck up my own life?

ELEANOR: Money, corrupts.

DYLAN: Not me. Come here. Take that ring off. Run your hand along the baize from baulk end – that's the baulk end, to spot end, that's the spot end.

ELEANOR strokes the baize.

How is it?

ELEANOR: It's smooth.

DYLAN: Now run your hand the other way.

ELEANOR: Ooh! Yeah! It bristles!

DYLAN: That's called the nap. Playing with the nap, the ball will run straight with the natural line. Playing against the nap, the ball can deviate and drift off line. I play straight. I honour the God of Snooker and he or, let's be fair, she looks after me.

ELEANOR: That's good of her.

DYLAN: I could not tank a frame, mentally, physically, whatever else there is. Impossible. So please, thank you for the visit, thank you for the warnings, you have your urine, but you can go now.

MO puts a DVD on the baize.

BOBBY: The baize!

BOBBY takes the DVD off the baize.

MO: A short film by the cricketer, Mervyn Westfield. He describes how taking money from a betting syndicate to bowl an over which would cost twelve runs, ruined his whole life. Watch it. I cried.

DYLAN: After all I've said, do you still think I'm vulnerable?

ELEANOR: The syndicates may tempt you with something other than money.

A beat or two.

MO: A woman.

DYLAN: I knew what she meant.

ELEANOR: You're not married. You're not in a steady relationship.

MO: And you're not gay.

BOBBY: Where d'you find all this stuff out?

ELEANOR: His blog. His diary.

BOBBY: His diary? That's private innit!?

DYLAN: It's on the Internet!

MO: You're the third player we've seen today.

ELEANOR: If you want to talk, here's my card.

ELEANOR gives DYLAN a business card. MO gives BOBBY a business card.

MO: It's an offence not to report an approach.

They turn to go.

ELEANOR: You know, I don't really like snooker, OK, but I had to watch your Wongsawat match, you know, for this, for work, and you were brilliant. I mean, like, really woo! … Anyway, yeah. I didn't know snooker could be … well whatever. Good luck against Ferryman. I hope you win.

DYLAN: Ta.

They're gone. BOBBY closes the door properly.

BOBBY: Fucking hell! If you could put her on a chocolate bar you'd make a fortune. 'Sexy.'

DYLAN: What?

BOBBY: The word she didn't say. 'I never knew snooker could be … sexy.'

DYLAN: I never knew coppers could be sexy.

Holding up Mo's business card.

BOBBY: Swap you. The fat Arab, for the gorgeous copper.

DYLAN takes the card but doesn't give BOBBY Mo's.

BOBBY: Eh? Who did pay your hotel in Brussels?

DYLAN: Waxy.

BOBBY: Has Waxy ever asked you to tank a game?

DYLAN: Dad?! No. We're cool. She gets ten percent of winnings.

BOBBY: What's ten percent of two thousand euros?

DYLAN: *(Beat.)* You were a telecomms engineer and a drug dealer and you can't do ten percent of two grand?

BOBBY: Age, innit? Tempus fucksit. I picked up a banana yesterday, held it in my hand, and I couldn't for the life of me remember what it was called. Had to look it up on the Ocado website. In me favourites. So if Waxy gets ten percent what does Tony get?

DYLAN: Dunno.

BOBBY: Haven't you got owt written down?

DYLAN: He said we'd talk about that when I won summat.

BOBBY: Did you know them two was gonna turn up?

DYLAN plays a shot. DYLAN's phone bleeps a text.

DYLAN: They'd written to me, yeah.

(Re: text.) Mum's coming round. How does she know where we are?

BOBBY: I don't talk to her. Nowadays, we communicate via rumour.

DYLAN: Liar. You're on her Facebook page.

BOBBY: She sent me a friend request, which I accepted. I felt I had to.

DYLAN: Why?

BOBBY: I dunno. She's my wife?

DYLAN plugs the iron back in to heat up again.

Don't give her any money.

DYLAN: Do you need any money, Dad?

BOBBY: All I want is a bit of recognition.

DYLAN: You taught me all you know.

BOBBY: No! I was a good amateur. If I'd taught you all I know, you'd be a good amateur. You're good because I left you alone.

DYLAN: And built me a snooker shed.

BOBBY: Snooker 'centre'. Sheds don't have double glazing, and a full-sized snooker table.

DYLAN: Nicked from the Catholic Club in Birkenhead.

BOBBY: *(Beat.)* Yes! And how many dads would do that?

DYLAN: You're legend. Except in Birkenhead. The sighting ball helped me.

BOBBY takes out the sighting ball. It is a white ball but on it, in permanent board marker pen, he has drawn a series of dots in different colours so that the ball is basically totally polka dotted but any given spot is a different colour from the other spots adjacent to it. He rolls it onto the baize, and against a cushion. DYLAN picks it up.

DYLAN: You should do a whatsit on it, you know, copyright, patent.

BOBBY: *(Negatively, fatalistically.)* Yeah, yeah.

DYLAN: Your problem is you got a negative tape looping round your head.

BOBBY: Either that or my life is shit.

Enter TONY. He is a youngish man about thirty, mobile phone in hand.

TONY: *(On the phone.)* You're breaking up, you sound like you're in a toilet. You are in a toilet? That's a tad disrespectful … no … I can hear you … can you hear me?… hello … hello … walk about a bit then! Wanker … sorry! I didn't think you could hear me … I can't hear you either. Fuck it.

(Off the phone.) Vodafone eh. Hundred quid a month eh for what? A load of fucking grief. Dylzo, my man! Who beat Wongsawat?!

DYLAN: Believe!

TONY: Boom town!

TONY hugs him even though DYLAN doesn't really want to be hugged.

You alright man?

DYLAN: Cool. You know Dad, don't you?

TONY: Alright, Dadzo?! He's lush, in't he?! Gonna be a star, your lad.

BOBBY: With the right management he will be, yeah.

TONY offers BOBBY his business card.

I've got one.

TONY: We're all gonna make a shedload of fucking money! How's it feel Dylz? How's it feel to be on the foothills of Shangri-fucking-la?! Eh? Eh?

He hugs him again.

I'd like to chop you into little bits and fucking snort you up, you talented bastard! You beat Wongsawat?! How did that feel Dylzo?!

BOBBY: If you'd been there you'd know.

TONY: Dadz. I tried. But I couldn't get to Amsterdam.

BOBBY: Brussels.

TONY: Brussels? My bad. Alright, my bad.

TONY leaves.

BOBBY: Where's he gone?

DYLAN: He does this.

Enter TONY.

TONY: How did it feel beating Wongsawat? I bet you felt like the King of Holland. Belgium. Where's Uncle Tony's chocolates, Dylzo?!

DYLAN: Sorry.

TONY: I don't need chocolates Dylz, I got you. Wongsawat! Eh, eh. Sixteenth on the planet.

BOBBY: Seventeenth.

TONY: Sixteenth, seventeenth, what's the difference?

BOBBY: One. *(Beat.)* We've been doing maths all morning.

TONY offers BOBBY a business card.

BOBBY: I said, I've got one.

TONY: Rough innit, round here.

BOBBY: And Manchester, isn't? What's wrong wi' Yorkshire?

TONY: Nothing. We're the same. Boddingtons/Tetley's? They both end up as piss.

BOBBY: Boddingtons starts as piss.

TONY: Let it lie, Dadz.

(To DYLAN.) Who have you drawn in the first round?

BOBBY: Duncan Ferryman.

TONY: He's weak.

BOBBY: Ferryman's earned four hundred thousand pounds so far this year. How weak is that?

TONY: Any man who chooses to visit Bovington tank museum on his honeymoon is a weak.

BOBBY: Maybe he likes tanks.

TONY: We're gonna get you on a honeymoon with some fucking lingerie model in the Maldives before they fucking sink!

DYLAN: Boom town!

TONY: You beat Wongsawat! Bang! Logo deal! Ha! You've kicked the fucking doors open, kid! I'm gonna have you covered in patches, and every one of 'em a five figure deal. Exhibition matches. Singapore, Malaysia, China, Wales. Fuck Wales, I will never make you go to Wales. Product endorsement.

DYLAN: Like cues and that?

TONY: I can't get you John Parris cues, Ronnie's got that tied up. But yeah, some other, you know, crap cue maker, deffo.

DYLAN: Would I have to use a crap cue?

TONY: *(Laughs. To BOBBY.)* This kid. This kid is so pure. Do you think Gary Lineker eats Walkers Crisps?

DYLAN: What?

TONY: He will only eat crisps from Marks and Spencer's. They put the M and S crisps in a Walkers bag for him.

BOBBY: What's your percentage?

TONY: On prize money, twenty percent.

BOBBY: Twenty!?

TONY: Plus VAT.

DYLAN: That's normal, Dad.

BOBBY: How much is twenty percent of two thousand?

DYLAN: Four hundred.

TONY: Plus VAT.

BOBBY: It's normal that he gets four hundred quid –

TONY: – plus VAT –

DYLAN: – four hundred and eighty.

TONY: VAT on professional services.

BOBBY: That's near enough five hundred quid for being in Canada with his other clients?

TONY: The game's changed since your day, Dadz. Dylan tells me you played a bit.

BOBBY: I was a good amateur.

TONY: Highest break?

BOBBY: 21.

TONY: Is that all?

BOBBY: Seven yellows.

DYLAN gets a cheque book out.

DYLAN: Is a cheque alright?

TONY: For now. Yeah. I'll get my office to set up all future payments to me and you don't have to worry about anything.

BOBBY: Wait a minute, any prize money in future is paid to you?

TONY: Electronically.

DYLAN: That's normal, Dad. So, er … four hundred and eighty. Who do I pay?

TONY: It's alright, leave that blank.

TONY notices the sighting ball.

What's this?

DYLAN: That's Dad's sighting ball. He invented it. You imagine a ball with a straight line pot, and you see what colour spot you have to hit. And you aim for that.

TONY: What about the cue ball though?

DYLAN: There's only one bit of the cue ball that can hit that spot. So the spot on the sighting ball tells you all you need to know.

TONY: Gizza go.

DYLAN places the sighting ball at an easy angle to a pocket, and places the cue ball about two foot from the sighting ball. TONY imagines a ball in line.

DYLAN: Which spot is it?

TONY: The red one. (Or whatever one it is)

DYLAN: Hit the red spot. (Or whatever one it is)

TONY pots the ball.

TONY: Dadz. Have you got a suit?

BOBBY: Why?

TONY: We're going on Dragon's Den. I'll do the talking. Boom town!

Enter STELLA and DANNY. Both looking rough.

What the fuck is this, the kid's tryna practise?! Who the fuck are you?!

DYLAN: This is my mum.

TONY: Mumzo! Hello! Alright. Soz. My bad.

STELLA: My little baby! I heard you won! I cried!

BOBBY: Don't give her any money!

DYLAN and STELLA hug.

STELLA: You can fuck off, Bobby Spokes!

(To DYLAN.) This is Danny. He smells but he's alright.

DYLAN: Hello.

DANNY: Aye, now young fellah, this is an honour, I want to shake your hand now son.

They shake hands.

I been watching you, you know your cueing arm is not vertical –

BOBBY: – Oi! Shut up! Don't listen to him.

DANNY: You're not in line with yerself, son. The Lord made us symmetrical, with two of everything, on opposite sides –

BOBBY: – I don't have two of everything on opposite sides.

DANNY: – and all perfectly in line, but you're all to cock, if you don't mind me saying son, and I say that out of a love for your mother.

BOBBY: Who is this bloke?

DANNY: I'm an outrider on the carousel of life.

BOBBY: Nice. What's the attraction with this one Stella?

STELLA: He can get red diesel.

BOBBY: *(To DANNY.)* Oh. You must be a hit with the ladies?

DANNY: Aye, I do alright if they're elderly, short of cash, and drive a diesel.

DYLAN: Tony here's my manager.

TONY gives STELLA a card.

TONY: My card. Don't phone after midnight.

(To DANNY.) Do you need one?

DANNY: Oh yes please!

STELLA: *(To DYLAN.)* Dylan, son –

BOBBY: – no money!

STELLA: I got a blue badge here for you Bobby, d'yer want it? Twenty quid.

BOBBY: Is it a fake?

STELLA: You're not disabled, and I'm not the council, so what do you think?

Producing a forged blue badge for parking. BOBBY looks at it.

DYLAN: *(To TONY.)* I'm sorry about this.

TONY: No, I want to get to know your family.

BOBBY: Whose is it copied off?

STELLA: Mine.

BOBBY: What the fuck have they given you a blue badge for?

STELLA: My depression.

BOBBY: I'm depressed but I can still park a fucking car!

STELLA: D'yer wannit or not?

BOBBY: No.

STELLA: Tony?

TONY: I'm cool.

STELLA: I can see that, but do you want to park like fucking anywhere in Sheffield? You don't have to fake a limp, you can say you're a carer. You need a passport photo on there. No smiling. Try and look a bit bipolar. That's it.

TONY: Mumz, I come to Sheffield once a year.

STELLA: *(Producing steaks.)* Alright. Steaks?

BOBBY: Where d'yer pick these up?

STELLA: Waitrose.

BOBBY: Waitrose?! You can't pay their prices.

STELLA: I don't pay their prices do I. Son –

DYLAN: – Mum! I been vegetarian ten years. What do you want, Mum?

BOBBY: Money.

STELLA: No! I come to see my little boy. You done well beating that Chinese bloke.

DYLAN: Thai.

BOBBY: Don't give her any money!

STELLA: I'm in trouble.

BOBBY: She drinks, she smokes, she's got Sky Sports. Oh yeah. She's got a thing for Gary Neville.

STELLA: Don't be ridiculous.

TONY: How could anyone possibly have a thing for Gary Neville?

DYLAN: What d'yer want, Mum?

STELLA: Waxy. She's coming here.

BOBBY: He has to practise! Who told Waxy where we are?

TONY: Who's Waxy ?

BOBBY: She's a woman, who used to be a man.

TONY: What is she to you?

DYLAN: A friend.

TONY: Friends are dangerous, Dylzo. Look what happened to Jesus.

STELLA: And Gazza.

TONY: Concur.

BOBBY: Shut up will you! What does Waxy want? Why's she coming here?

DANNY: Spit it out, woman! That's what you come here for. She wanted to go to Cleethorpes, bury her head in the sand, but I made her come here.

STELLA: Since you got your whatsaname.

DANNY: Tour card, aye.

STELLA: Waxy's been ringing me up.

TONY: Who is this Waxy?

BOBBY: Mickey Chuff.

TONY: She's a man?

BOBBY: Used to be a man. When he was Mickey, if he didn't like you, he'd shake hands, and palm you a ten pence piece. Then he'd look you in the eye and say 'ring an ambulance, you're gonna need it'.

TONY: He's a gangster then?

STELLA: No, she's lovely.

TONY: Has he become a woman or a man?!

STELLA: He's become a lovely woman.

TONY: Why's she called Waxy?

BOBBY: Ten year back when he was Mickey, he bought a chain of beauty parlours, and nail bars –

TONY: – he's a gangster! –

BOBBY: – that did bikini waxes, and of course with his second name being Chuff, people were desperate to call him Waxy. Waxy Chuff.

TONY: Waxy Chuff? That's his name?

BOBBY: Her name.

STELLA: The name stuck.

BOBBY: Her and him had a thing, didn't you? It was like that film.

TONY: Which film?

STELLA: Danny's good on film.

DANNY: Pub quiz. Aye.

BOBBY: That film. Summat to do with the moon.

DANNY: Apollo 13.

BOBBY: No. The lead has dark hair, big nose –

DANNY: – Dustin Hoffman.

BOBBY: No, she's a woman –

DANNY: Tootsie.

BOBBY: No! She's a singer, curly hair, was in that double act with a bloke who died in a skiing accident.

STELLA: Peters and Lee?

BOBBY: No! In the film she's from that island, the football bit to Italy.

TONY: Sicily.

BOBBY: She plays a Sicilian in the film.

DANNY: The Godfather.

BOBBY: No! She was one of the witches of somewhere with him what was in that film where a big Indian chucks a sink out of a window.

DANNY: Rear Window?

TONY: Jack Nicholson. One Flew Over the Cuckoo's Nest.

DYLAN: The Witches of Eastwick.

DANNY: Ah! Michelle Pfeiffer. Susan Sarandon. Cher.

BOBBY: Cher! So in this film I can't remember the title of, Cher falls in love with this baker with a wooden arm.

DANNY: Pinocchio!

BOBBY: Will you just fuck off?

DYLAN: What's this got to do with Waxy, Dad?

BOBBY: I'm trying to explain Waxy's relationship with your mother. It was the same as in this film.

STELLA: What film?

BOBBY: THE FILM I CAN'T FUCKING REMEMBER!

TONY: What happens in the film?

BOBBY: Cher falls in love with this baker played by that actor who's drunk in that other film about leaving that town where all those films are set where they're always in a team of eleven or twelve.

DANNY: Twelve Angry Men.

TONY: Ocean's Eleven!

DANNY: Leaving Las Vegas.

TONY: Nicholas Cage!

BOBBY: Yes.

TONY high fives all round.

BOBBY: So Cher and Nicholas Cage. It's a love story, and the film's got the word 'moon' in it.

DANNY: Moonraker. Moonlighting. Moonlight Sonata. Moonstruck.

BOBBY: That's it!

Cheers.

STELLA: *(Re: DANNY.)* I told you he was good.

TONY: What about Moonstruck?

BOBBY: HIS FUCKING MOTHER THERE AND WAXY WAS LIKE THE PLOT OF MOONSTRUCK!

TONY: Maybe, but Tony Danlino's not seen it.

STELLA: I can't afford to go to the pictures.

DANNY: Sorry, no.

DYLAN: Me neither.

BOBBY: Fuck. Nicholas Cage was gonna marry someone he didn't love, but subconsciously he trapped his arm in a baking machine and lost it.

STELLA: Waxy lost his arm in a car crash.

BOBBY: Your life's not gonna be exactly like the fucking film is it, or you'd be getting royalties. Waxy was engaged to someone he didn't love, lost his arm, wedding cancelled, and then he fell in love with you!

TONY: This all happened before you two were married?

BOBBY: No, whilst we were married.

TONY: When Waxy was a man?

BOBBY: When Waxy was Mickey Chuff.

TONY: OK. Cool. I think I understand.

(To STELLA.) So back to you, Mumzo. What's the problem with Waxy?

DYLAN: Yeah, what's happened, Mum?

STELLA: I sold Waxy some inside information.

DYLAN: Some what?

She kneels before him, hanging on to his leg.

STELLA: I told Waxy that you'd agreed to lose the first frame against that Chinese fellah, Whatshisname.

DYLAN: Wongsawat. Thai. What information?

STELLA: I had me rent coming up son, and the council have cut me social 'cause of the bedroom tax! I'm sorry!

She hangs on to him.

DANNY: Yer told him now, that's good. I done my job.

DANNY sits.

TONY: So you sold to Waxy the so-called inside information that Dylan was gonna tank the first frame?

DYLAN: I was never gonna tank it.

BOBBY: He won the first six frames.

STELLA: Don't I bloody know it!

TONY: How much did Waxy pay you? For the information?

STELLA: Two hundred quid.

BOBBY: You money-grabbing crab! How'dyer expect to get away with that?

STELLA: 'Cause you told me he'd fucking lose!

All look at BOBBY.

DYLAN: Did you tell her I was gonna lose?

BOBBY: Son. Everyone thought you'd lose. I had ten quid on you losing.

STELLA: The lekky were gonna cut me off.

BOBBY: You're on a key.

TONY: How much did Waxy stake?

STELLA: Dunno.

TONY: Is Waxy a risk taker, a gambler?

BOBBY: She's had a sex change operation!

DANNY: Waxy sent me to Rotherham with six hundred, cash. I did twenty-six shops in a day, with nothing but a fish dinner to keep me going.

BOBBY: She smurfed it. What about you?

STELLA: Chesterfield. A thousand pounds.

DANNY: And there was seven others that I know of. Colleagues of mine.

BOBBY: Winos?

DANNY: I don't know what you mean sir.

BOBBY: Do your colleagues drink alcohol before breakfast?

DANNY: Aye, they do.

BOBBY: You don't have to say 'aye' all the time, we're not fucking pirates.

Enter WAXY. A woman of about fifty-five, well dressed, heavy make-up, and a wooden left arm with a silk glove on it.

WAXY: Dylan. Come here!

WAXY hugs him, pushing his head into her bosom. WAXY looks over DYLAN at STELLA, quite hard and unemotional. STELLA looks at the floor.

WAXY: You beat Wongsawong, I knew you could. This is the beginning of the Beguine.

The hug continues with a sense that DYLAN is a little uncomfortable.

In the future, this day will be the past, the day you flowered, because that's what you've done Dylan, you've flowered, like a caterpillar.

She lets him go and looks at him.

How's the terminal colon cancer coming along Bobby?

BOBBY: Eh? I don't have terminal colon cancer.

WAXY looks at STELLA. She looks at the floor.

WAXY: Stella told me you had terminal colon cancer and three months to live.

BOBBY: I wondered why you sent me a get well card.

WAXY: What did you do with the card?

BOBBY: I put it in the bin.

WAXY: That's not very nice.

BOBBY: What did you want me to –?

WAXY: – all that matters is that you're better.

BOBBY: I were never fucking ill!

WAXY: Good, 'cause terminal colon cancer can be very nasty.

He moves on to TONY. Who offers his hand to shake.

TONY: Tony Danlino.

They shake hands but WAXY keeps hold of his hand, not shaking but holding.

WAXY: Felicity Chuff.

TONY: Felicity? Right. Hi.

WAXY: Everyone calls me Waxy. Waxy Chuff. They think it's funny.

TONY: You don't seem to mind.

WAXY: If God gives you only lemons, make some marmalade. There have been some famous Chuffs. We've had a Chuff on the moon. And the oldest man to cycle round the world was a Chuff.

TONY: A sore chuff.

WAXY: Funny man. Visa visa Dylan you are …?

TONY: I'm his manager.

TONY gives WAXY his card.

My card. Don't ring in the afternoons. You're …?

WAXY: – His good and generous friend. Aren't we all lucky to have this child effigy in our midst?

DYLAN: I owe you two hundred quid Waxy. Ten percent of my winnings. Will a cheque do?

WAXY: Do you like money Tony?

TONY: Makes the world go round dunnit.

WAXY: Who says the world goes round?

TONY: I read it somewhere. School.

WAXY: And you believe everything you read?

TONY: No.

WAXY: *(To DYLAN.)* Have you signed a written contract with Tony?

DYLAN: Er … dunno. Don't think so.

WAXY: Tony might have a contract in his pocket today.

TONY: We had a deal. As soon as he was in the winnings we'd do the paperwork.

TONY produces two copies of a contract which he gives to DYLAN.

Sign both. Keep one.

(To WAXY.) Do you want to read it?

WAXY: I don't like reading. It's in one eye, and out the other.

DYLAN: *(To WAXY.)* Is a cheque alright? For the two hundred?

WAXY: Unlike Tony, I won't cash it. I'll frame it. Because it's going to be the first of many. And it would be a shame to fritter it away, on … I don't know, fritters.

DYLAN is writing a cheque out. WAXY finds the sighting ball in a pocket.

What's this? Billiards?

TONY: That's Bobby's invention, he's patented it. Haven't you, Bobby?

BOBBY: Yeah.

WAXY: How's it work?

BOBBY: It trains you to sight the point of contact on the object ball. D'yer want a go?

BOBBY sets up the ball.

WAXY: I invented a home kebab system once. Thought it'd make me rich. Small doner kebab on an electric revolve, vertical grill panel. I sold seven. Got a garage full of them. Do you want one, Bobby?

BOBBY: Yes please.

WAXY: *(To TONY.)* Do you want one?

TONY: Yes, please.

WAXY takes the glove off her hand, goes in her handbag, and screws in a snooker bridge into her wooden hand. She is given a cue by DYLAN.

WAXY: I been in love with the game ever since I got a colour telly. Before that, I found the game pointless and confusing.

BOBBY: Still got your full-size table?

WAXY: It is the only reason I live in Hathersage, in a barn.

WAXY, having fitted the bridge, bends low to play a shot, but pulls up.

Look at that baize. Like Wembley, with holes.

BOBBY: Line up an imaginary ball for a straight pot and decide which colour spot it's hitting.

WAXY: Red cross. (Or whatever)

BOBBY: Hit the red cross then.

WAXY pots the ball.

TONY: Me and Bobby are going on Dragon's Den. It's patented.

WAXY: And you're on ten percent?

TONY: Plus VAT.

WAXY: *(To TONY.)* Bobby couldn't patent his own shoes. If Bobby was a Red Indian – you can't say Red Indian no more, can you? If Bobby was a member of a tribe of ingenious peoples, after forty-five years of trying he still wouldn't have a single fucking feather.

BOBBY: What do you want, Waxy?

WAXY takes out a small accounts ledger from his handbag.

WAXY: I've paid Dylan's bills for three years.

(To TONY.) Take a look.

TONY opens the ledger.

What's the first entry?

TONY: Registration at Q school. Six hundred pounds.

WAXY: His father didn't have six hundred pounds. Stella, his mother, come to me 'cause she knows I got six hundred pounds and that I loved her once. Our story, me and Stella, it's like that film –

ALL: – Moonstruck!

WAXY: Yeah. Keep going, Tony. You're the big reader.

TONY: *(Reading.)* March 2011 Cardiff. Return train fare. Holiday Inn. Three hundred and sixteen pounds ninety-two pence.

WAXY: His father didn't have three hundred and sixteen pounds ninety-two pence. Stella, his mother, come to me etc etc. Can you spot a pattern revolving?

TONY flicks to the middle of the ledger.

TONY: September 2014. Hong Kong. Singapore Airlines. Two thousand seven hundred and fifteen pounds.

WAXY: Club class.

TONY: Harbour Lights Hotel. Six thousand and seven.

WAXY: Hong Kong dollars.

BOBBY: Alright, alright, we get it.

WAXY: Read the total.

TONY turns to the final page.

TONY: Forty-eight thousand, six hundred and fifteen pound, ten pence.

WAXY: Let's call it fifty, shall we? That is the accumulated aggregate of my commitment to this boy. To this family, this fuck up family.

TONY: I've heard you been betting on him.

WAXY: I have. Stella works for me in the beauty parlours.

STELLA: Don't tell anyone, for security reasons. Social security reasons.

WAXY: She tells me whether Bobby thinks he's gonna win or lose. All perfectly illegitimate. Last week, was different, she told me –

STELLA: – I'm sorry son, I'm sorry –

WAXY: – she said you was going to deliberately lose the first frame –

STELLA: – I was down to the bones of my bum!

WAXY: – against that Chinese fella Wongsawit.

BOBBY: Wongsawat.

DYLAN: Thai.

WAXY: What do gamblers like more than anything Tony?

TONY: Dunno. Winning?

WAXY: Knowing the result before it happens. The odds were short, three to one on, 'cause everyone expected Wattsawong to win. So, to clear that fifty grand I had to stake 120.

TONY: Jesus!

WAXY: He can't help. So now I'm down one hundred and seventy thousand pounds. I'm not rich, I'm a self-employed business woman. Beauty parlours, nails, bikini waxing. It hurts.

TONY: I've heard.

WAXY: Losing money hurts.

BOBBY: I'll say it again. What do you want?

WAXY: You can go Stella. What's that smell?

DANNY: That's me.

DANNY offers his hand.

I smurfed some of the bets for you last week.

WAXY: Get out!

DANNY: I'm gone.

STELLA: I'm staying, Waxy, he's my son.

WAXY: Anything that is now said in this room, was not said, and has already been forgotten. Cheltenham House rules, then. How many frames are you gonna take off Duncan Ferryman on Tuesday?

DYLAN: I can beat him.

WAXY: Dylan. I've nurtured you this far. Nothing would give me more pleasure than to see you beat Ferryman, and go through to the next round, but don't win frame four.

DYLAN: Don't ask me to do that, Waxy!

WAXY: Beat him if you can, wet wipe the floor with him. But give him frame four.

DYLAN drops to his knees.

DYLAN: No, no, no!

TONY: He's my boy, no gangster's gonna threaten him.

WAXY: Gangster? Someone been making allegations? Bobby, are you one the allegators?

BOBBY: I gave him a history lesson.

WAXY: This will not affect his career. No one outside of this room will know.

BOBBY: He can't play to lose! It'd kill him!

WAXY: Or … there is an 'or'. Pay me one hundred and seventy thousand pounds. Bring it to me in Hathersage by seven o'clock tomorrow. Stella's got my address. Dylan, let me give you some advice. All living things need a backbone, except invertebrates, but what are invertebrates? They're worms, and a bit shit, so fuck 'em. Life, for us vertebrates, is a series of disappointments and appointments. Forget your disappointments and don't forget your appointments. Remember that and you won't be disappointed. Hathersage, tomorrow, at seven.

End of scene.

SCENE TWO

1875, The officers' mess, of 11th Devonshire Regiment, Jubbulapore, India. MO enters in Indian wallah costume and sets the table for Pyramids. Enter two officers, in uniform, post dinner. LIEUTENANT NEVILLE CHAMBERLAIN (BOBBY), and CAPTAIN LORD PERCY TATTON-SHANKS (DANNY). They are carrying drinks. NEVILLE, somewhat conspiratorially, closes the door.

PERCY: What an absolutely splendid curry that was!

NEVILLE: Goat.

PERCY: I've been in India three years now and I still don't honestly know why eating a curry like that doesn't kill one from the inside.

NEVILLE: Percy, the Gatling Gun is not why we're the dominant imperial power. What gives us the edge is the flameproof British arsehole.

PERCY: Concur! I'd like to see the French eat a curry like that and all still be ready to ride out at dawn.

NEVILLE: No chance. They'd all be pants down on a bridge somewhere, crying for their mothers, squitting into a river.

PERCY: Or calming their rings with fermented milk.

NEVILLE: And in this modern warfare there's no easier target than a naked Frenchman sitting on a bucket full of yoghurt.

NEVILLE takes a look at the table, which is set for Pyramids.

What's this, Percy?

PERCY: I had Mo set the table for Pyramids.

NEVILLE: That's no good. We, that is, you and I, need to be able to conspire.

PERCY: Against Georgie?

NEVILLE: Against Georgie.

PERCY: Do you believe the posting at Kundham is certain death?

NEVILLE: The last two batteries have been massacred. Not a horse, not a man surviving. Only Benjie limped free with a broken leg.

PERCY: Benjie?! The regimental goat? What did we do with her? Provide her with the very best veterinary care in India?

NEVILLE: No, I shot her.

PERCY: You had to put her out of her misery?

NEVILLE: That, yes, and we had nothing for the curry.

PERCY: *(Re: the curry he's just eaten.)* Benjie?!

NEVILLE: I have to say the old girl makes a damn good vindaloo, eh?

PERCY: Bloody war!

NEVILLE: I love war. Never happier.

NEVILLE clears the reds from the table.

How many of us are there?

PERCY: Me, you, and Georgie.

NEVILLE: And that new Snooker, what's his name?

PERCY: Dylan.

NEVILLE rolls on to the table, not in any order the white ball, a red, yellow, and a green.

Not pyramids then but Life Pool?

NEVILLE: Appropriate, isn't it? If we're playing for our lives. We'll make sure Georgie chooses the white.

PERCY: How can we do that?

NEVILLE taps the side of his nose as if to say, 'I know how'. He then finds three more white balls and puts all four whites in the one bag.

NEVILLE: He's choosing a ball from a bag that only has whites in.

PERCY: Nev, that's a bit Spanish.

NEVILLE: Yes, it is. You don't think I'm doing this because I'm a coward?

PERCY: Not a bit of it Nev.

NEVILLE: It has to be done for the good of the regiment, and the Queen. I'll be red.

NEVILLE puts the red ball in his pocket and gives the yellow to PERCY.

You can be yellow. That way we follow each other so the one can set up the other to have a crack at Georgie's white.

PERCY: What about the new Snooker?

NEVILLE: I'll slip Dylan the green.

PERCY: So we work together to set up Georgie's white for a pot.

NEVILLE: We pot Georgie's white three times and he takes the posting at Kundham.

PERCY: He dies, and we live.

NEVILLE puts ten rupees in the pool pot.

Why, if we're playing for our lives, did you put ten rupees in the pool?

NEVILLE: I thought, for those of us who come out of it alive, it'd be a jolly thing to make a bit of dosh.

PERCY: You're a devil Neville!

PERCY puts in ten rupees. Enter CAPTAIN GEORGE DE LACY, drinking.

GEORGIE: I don't know why the Major's so upset! All I said was – I've had your wife!

NEVILLE: What did he say, Georgie?

GEORGIE: Nothing. But his horse collapsed and died of a heart attack.

NEVILLE: I don't believe that old war horse of the Major's would drop dead on hearing about a bit of marital infidelity.

GEORGIE: It was with me!

PERCY: Your reputation is well known Georgie, even amongst the horses.

NEVILLE: Our horses are not sensitive to social conventions. Most of them eat and shit at the same time.

GEORGIE slams his cue down on the baize.

GEORGIE: Are you calling me a liar?!

NEVILLE: You lied to the new Snooker at dinner.

GEORGIE: I did not!

PERCY: *(Shouting into the dining room.)* Snooker! One second please!

Enter DYLAN naked.

GEORGIE: Foccacia bread and olives, he's naked!

PERCY: Cover your todger, man!

NEVILLE: Snooker, how did this officer introduce himself to you at dinner?

DYLAN: He said – 'Good evening, I'm the king of Belgium'.

GEORGIE: I am the damned King of Belgium!

PERCY: So what are you doing in India with the 11th Devonshire foot?

GEORGIE: Learning about ruddy chocolate!

PERCY offers him the bag of white balls.

NEVILLE: Pick a ball.

GEORGIE: What are we playing?

PERCY: Life Pool.

GEORGIE: What's the stake?

NEVILLE: As agreed at dinner, whoever loses takes the posting at Kundham.

GEORGIE: We're playing for our lives then?

NEVILLE: Pick a ball.

GEORGIE picks out a white ball.

GEORGIE: Bloody white! Have to go last!

GEORGIE turns his back and places the white on the table. NEVILLE offers the same bag to PERCY who has his yellow ball in his hand. GEORGIE is not interested, he's choosing a cue.

NEVILLE: Percy, pick a ball.

PERCY puts his hand in, holding the yellow and takes it out showing GEORGIE the yellow.

PERCY: Yellow.

NEVILLE pulls out the red.

NEVILLE: Red. That means you're green, Dylan.

NEVILLE gives DYLAN the green ball.

DYLAN: I don't know the rules of Life Pool.

NEVILLE: Simple, we each have our own ball, and three lives –

DYLAN: – Life Pool.

NEVILLE: Indeed. Every time your ball is potted, you lose a life.

PERCY: Get potted three times and you've lost.

NEVILLE: *(Shaking the pool pot.)* The pool's light?!

NEVILLE/PERCY: Georgie!?

GEORGIE chucks ten rupees into the pot.

DYLAN: I don't have any money.

NEVILLE: I shall sub you, young man.

PERCY: If you're potted, you pay the base stake into the pool.

DYLAN: That's the Pool bit of Life Pool?

GEORGIE: He's a clever one, this one! Games! Games! Where would we be without games?! God, I need distraction. I hate India. The rain! It's like Leeds. With snakes!

PERCY: The order of play is red on white then yellow, and green.

Immediately, NEVILLE puts his red in the baulk D and targets GEORGIE's white ball, trying to set it up for PERCY to pot.

Cricket is a jolly way to waste your life, if it's distraction you need.

GEORGIE: Can't play cricket, I'm dyslexic.

DYLAN: Old MacDonald was dyslexic, E-I-O-I-E.

Amazed silence.

NEVILLE: Put some damn clothes on, Snooker.

DYLAN: Sorry, sir.

PERCY puts his yellow ball in the baulk D and targets and hopefully pots NEVILLE's ball.

GEORGIE: Why did you go for my ball? Are you trying to set me up?

PERCY: Have you tried living like a woman?

NEVILLE: I was a woman on Tuesday, all day.

GEORGIE: Did you pee sitting down?

NEVILLE: Five times.

GEORGIE: What's it like?!

NEVILLE: Thrilling. It all happens kind of underneath you, so there's nothing to look at. It's like listening to a radio play.

PERCY: If one sits down, both hands are free. So one can get on with stuff.

NEVILLE: I read the paper.

GEORGIE: I don't want to read when I pee! I want to aim at stuff! I want to hose something down. I want to chase something along a gulley! And get the damned better of it with the sheer force of my flow!

NEVILLE: Your go, Dylan. Put your ball in the D.

DYLAN puts his green ball in the D and targets the white ball.

GEORGIE: All three of you have gone for my white!

GEORGIE plays his shot.

PERCY: Dylan? What kind of a ruddy stupid name is that?

DYLAN: My dad likes Bob Dylan.

GEORGIE: Bob Dylan. Sounds Jewish.

They all look at each other confused. NEVILLE targets GEORGIE's white ball.

GEORGIE: You're targeting me! It's a conspiracy!

DYLAN: If we're playing for our lives, I don't think Life Pool is appropriate. Two players can conspire.

NEVILLE: What rank are you?

DYLAN: A hundred and seventh, sir. I beat Wongsawat last week.

GEORGIE: You're a damned Snooker.

DYLAN: People have been calling me Snooker all night.

PERCY: It's not an insult, Dylan.

NEVILLE: It's what the Devonshires call a first year from the Woolwich Military Academy.

PERCY: We three were all Snookers once.

PERCY targets GEORGIE's ball.

GEORGIE: Shih-tzu puppies for sale! There are other balls on the table!

NEVILLE: Your go, Dylan.

He doesn't play.

DYLAN: What does it mean? Snooker.

NEVILLE: A Snooker is someone who's damned useless.

GEORGIE: We were all damned useless once.

PERCY: The music hall act? Hooker and Snooker?

NEVILLE: Snooker was the idiot.

GEORGIE: My wife went to the West Indies last year.

PERCY: Jamaica?

GEORGIE: No, she went of her own accord. She's going to Italy for the summer.

PERCY: Genoa?

GEORGIE: Course I know her, she's my wife. She wants to go to Anchorage next year, wherever that is.

PERCY: Alaska.

GEORGIE: No, I'll ask her myself, I'm seeing her this evening. She was born in France.

PERCY: Toulouse?

GEORGIE: It's not enough toilets for a nation of forty million, is it? She's currently in Singapore.

PERCY: Jakarta?

GEORGIE: No, she travelled first class, British Airways!

NEVILLE applauds.

GEORGIE: I saw them once. They were awful. Fortunately, I had a bag of oranges and a girl with me, so it wasn't an entirely wasted evening.

PERCY: Did you throw the oranges at them?

GEORGIE: And waste the oranges? No. I ate the oranges, and threw the girl.

PERCY: It's awful fuggy in here.

ALL: Mo! Mo! Mo! Mo!

MO appears in Indian dress carrying a big fan.

PERCY: Mo! A little fanning, s'il vous plait?

DYLAN: Look, OK, what we need is a game where there's only one cue ball and the field is the same for everyone.

PERCY: Pyramids is too difficult.

DYLAN: Difficulty is what we need.

MO: How about every time a player pots a ball they have to give a urine sample?

GEORGIE: But if you pot four balls, that's four urine samples.

MO: I thought you asked for difficulty?

DYLAN takes the white and puts it in the baulk D. And, during the next, he sets the reds in the triangle.

DYLAN: Why don't we combine Pyramids and Life Pool? We have fifteen reds –

GEORGIE: – like in Pyramids.

DYLAN: Just one cue ball.

PERCY: We all use the same cue ball?!

NEVILLE: That's a bit filthy!

DYLAN: After potting a red, you can build a break by potting a colour.

PERCY: There are no colours in Pyramids.

DYLAN: We have the colours from Pool.

PERCY: This is a whole new game, man!

DYLAN: Yes, a difficult game, but a fair game.

DYLAN places the colours on the table as they are for snooker.

GEORGIE: How many points for a black?

DYLAN: Dunno. How many coloured balls on the table?

GEORGIE: Six.

DYLAN: Six points, then.

NEVILLE: No. Reds are one point, so the lowest colour must be two points.

DYLAN: Yes! So if black is ranked highest it's worth seven. Pink six, Blue five, yellow four, green –

ALL: – No!

NEVILLE: No. Yellow's an awful, insipid colour.

PERCY: The colour of custard.

GEORGIE: Piss!

NEVILLE: Puke!

GEORGIE: Piss!

DYLAN: OK. Yellow is the lowest. Two points.

GEORGIE: Actually, my piss isn't yellow. It's blue. Is that normal?

NEVILLE: You're an officer, aren't you?

DYLAN: Done!

The balls are set for snooker as we know it.

NEVILLE: It looks … symmetrical.

PERCY: Natural.

GEORGIE: Balanced.

DYLAN: Beautiful.

NEVILLE: What do we call it?

PERCY: The Snooker invented it. It should be named after him.

NEVILLE: Dylan?

GEORGIE: I'm not playing any ruddy game called Dylan!

NEVILLE: It's got a certain ring. Dylan. Let's have a game of Dylan.

DYLAN plays the white ball, breaking the reds.

GEORGIE: It's me now, then?

PERCY: With the same cue ball.

STELLA enters accompanied by ELEANOR. Dressed in officer's uniform.

GEORGIE: Everybody! Stand to attention! Women in the mess!

STELLA: Stand easy! This is Lieutenant Sargent who has joined us from Nagpur.

PERCY: Where are you posted Lieutenant?

ELEANOR: Kundham.

DYLAN: Kundham?

GEORGIE: They say it's certain death. Kundham.

ELEANOR: Which of you will be my commanding officer?

PERCY: We're playing a game for it.

ELEANOR: What game are you playing?

GEORGIE: *(Re: DYLAN.)* Dylan. It's a game of Snooker's.

ELEANOR approaches DYLAN.

ELEANOR: You're the Snooker? It's your game is it?

DYLAN: Yeah.

NEVILLE: He invented it.

ELEANOR kisses him passionately. It's a long kiss. And DYLAN gets into the kiss.

GEORGIE: Foccacia me!

ELEANOR then leaves.

STELLA: Snooker? Is that what this game's called?

NEVILLE: Now that is pretty spiffo!

PERCY: Snooker! It's a damned sight better than 'Dylan'.

GEORGIE: I like it.

DYLAN: Er … sorry, a minute ago, I think I touched the ball.

NEVILLE: What?

DYLAN: I touched the ball. A foul.

PERCY: I didn't see it.

NEVILLE: Nor I.

GEORGIE: I wasn't looking.

DYLAN: I touched it. I know it. A life to each of you.

GEORGIE: Come on, man!

NEVILLE: No one saw it, Dylan!

PERCY: You're playing for your life, man!

GEORGIE: You don't want to go to Kundham, you can't be giving a life away!

PERCY: For God's sake man, Georgie's the one we want killed!

DYLAN: I'll take the posting at Kundham, and if I die, I'll die in her arms.

End of scene.

The snooker table drops to the understage and leaves DYLAN *alone with* ELEANOR *in his hotel room. He's in pyjamas.*

SCENE THREE

ELEANOR and DYLAN in his hotel room. He has on only his pyjamas.

DYLAN: Couldn't sleep.

ELEANOR: I'm shocked you're in bed. Young man like you, in Sheffield, snooker star. Thought you'd be out there, you know, like operating.

DYLAN: I need sleep. I had a dream about you.

ELEANOR: OK.

DYLAN: Not that kind of dream.

ELEANOR: Dreaming takes place in REM sleep, not the band, rapid eye movement. They taught us that at Hendon.

DYLAN: I've not been sleeping well at me dad's.

ELEANOR: Is this work?

DYLAN: Totally.

ELEANOR: Jim-jams. I'm surprised.

DYLAN: Sorry.

ELEANOR: I'm cool.

DYLAN: They were a present.

ELEANOR: Has any young man ever bought his own pyjamas?

DYLAN: I wasn't expecting you to turn up, you know, straight away. At one in the morning. It's happened.

ELEANOR: Your balls have dropped?

DYLAN: You what?

ELEANOR: Soz. I've been watching boxsets of Mrs Brown's Boys.

DYLAN: Someone's asked me to tank a game.

ELEANOR: Who?

DYLAN: Waxy Chuff.

ELEANOR: Who's she?

DYLAN: You know her?

ELEANOR: No.

DYLAN: She's my sponsor. Felicity Chuff, used to be Mickey Chuff.

ELEANOR: She's transgender?

DYLAN: Yeah. And Sheffield's biggest nutter. That's how I know her, through Dad, with his drug-dealing and Mum with her, you know, skaggy life.

ELEANOR: Lush! You've got a mini bar!

DYLAN: Yeah. It's a fantastic hotel, this. This is the very room where Dennis Taylor stayed in 1985 when he beat Steve Davis on the black.

ELEANOR: Steve Interesting Davis?

DYLAN: Yeah.

ELEANOR: Was he interesting? Sexy?

DYLAN: No, Taylor beat him on the last ball of the last frame. It's the greatest, most historic moment in snooker history.

ELEANOR: Before you were born.

DYLAN: Before you were born.

ELEANOR: I'll have a Bloody Mary.

DYLAN: What kind of cop drinks Bloody Marys on a case?

ELEANOR: A cop who likes Bloody Marys.

DYLAN opens the mini bar and mixes her a Bloody Mary.

DYLAN: This hotel used to be the St. George and when they had the refurb, they kept this room exactly the same as it was on that night.

ELEANOR: Have they changed the sheets?

DYLAN: You don't care do you?

ELEANOR: Whatchamean?

DYLAN: Flirting.

ELEANOR: Wash your mouth out! You think I'm flirting?

DYLAN: Yeah, you're a right come-on.

ELEANOR: OK. I'll stop being me. And just do my job. You wanted to talk to me Mister Spokes?

DYLAN: I'm cool with the flirting.

ELEANOR: No man! You blew it! That's gone!

DYLAN: You don't know when you're flirting.

ELEANOR: OK, gorgeous, what exactly has Felicity Chuff asked you to do?

DYLAN: Tank frame four against Duncan Ferryman on Tuesday.

ELEANOR: And you said –?

DYLAN: I didn't say owt. She's saying I've got to go see her tomorrow, in Hathersage.

ELEANOR: Cool. I want you to go.

DYLAN: Why can't you arrest her now?

ELEANOR: For what?

DYLAN: It's illegal, innit?

ELEANOR: The CPS won't act on this little evidence.

DYLAN: So, what do you want me to do?

ELEANOR: Mo wants information. Names. Phone numbers. Emails. Go to Hathersage, talk some more, and agree to tank the game.

DYLAN: I can't fucking tank a game! What is it with you people, don't you listen?! What do I have to do to – ?

ELEANOR: – Dylan! Stop going into one.

DYLAN: *(Going into one.)* I am not going into one!

ELEANOR: No one's ever gonna ask you to tank the game. Lie to Waxy. What Mo needs to see, what I need to see, is the money going on, the phone transcripts, the emails.

DYLAN: I'm working for you then. The Filth.

ELEANOR: Man, that's not very nice.

DYLAN: I've lived under the heat of the law all me life.

ELEANOR: Your dad. Can I say something? Dealing drugs is illegal.

DYLAN: Dad was a junkie. And he had me. To feed. To raise.

ELEANOR: A martyr. Mum not around?

DYLAN: Alcohol. Fuck knows what else. It's a gateway drug, innit, alcohol?

ELEANOR: Gateway. Aldi. Lidl.

DYLAN: You're funny.

ELEANOR: You're flirting.

DYLAN: That's not flirting. I just said you're funny.

ELEANOR: What are you protecting? Your cherry?

DYLAN: Fucking hell man, what kind of copper are you?

ELEANOR: I'm a fucking good copper who likes Bloody Marys. Do you think I'd make National Crime Agency at my age if I was a muppet?

DYLAN: You want me to string Waxy along, then?

ELEANOR: Yeah. The money goes on twenty minutes before the frame.

DYLAN: That late?

ELEANOR: Yeah. If we can follow the money trail, we can make a collar.

DYLAN: I lie to Waxy, but I can play to win?

ELEANOR: Yeah. Can you beat Ferryman?

DYLAN: I can beat anyone.

ELEANOR: But he's the favourite and no one would be surprised if you lost that frame. Clever. That's how everyone gets away with it.

DYLAN: But what happens if I do win? Waxy's a gangster. When she was Mickey Chuff, she killed a guy with a spade.

ELEANOR: She's a woman now.

DYLAN: Women can be violent. Joan of Arc. Boadicea. Naomi Campbell.

ELEANOR: Waxy'll be inside by then.

DYLAN: She's got good lawyers. She didn't go down for the murder with the spade.

ELEANOR: Did anyone?

DYLAN: Yeah, the gardener. *(Shrug of shoulders.)* What about when Waxy comes out?

ELEANOR: Dylan? Are you questioning the ability of the prison system to reform hardened criminals?

DYLAN: Yeah.

ELEANOR: Do you want me to come with you? To Hathersage.

DYLAN: Fuck off. Take a copper to Waxy's? Are you mad?

ELEANOR: You could say I was your girlfriend.

DYLAN: Me mum knows I don't have a girlfriend.

ELEANOR: Your new girlfriend.

DYLAN: No. No way. You're disappointed.

ELEANOR: I'm cool. What's your mum got to do with this?

DYLAN: Mum sees Waxy every day. She works for her.

ELEANOR: Don't tell Waxy you'll tank the game without a bit of a struggle. She won't believe it.

DYLAN: OK. Understood.

ELEANOR: There, we've finished work then, have we?

DYLAN: You're terrible!

ELEANOR: What?

DYLAN: Flirting!

ELEANOR: I'm not flirting!

DYLAN: Stay over there.

Gives her a Bloody Mary.

ELEANOR: No celery?

DYLAN: It's a mini bar, not Morrisons.

ELEANOR: Relax, Dylan, I'll keep my distance!

DYLAN: That's cool.

ELEANOR: Do you feel safe?

DYLAN: No! I can't see your hands.

ELEANOR: I'll sit on the bed. Not an invitation. I'm just taking the weight off my feet.

DYLAN: What's your story then?

ELEANOR: Have we finished work?

DYLAN: Yeah.

ELEANOR: I wanted to be an actor. Went to drama school. Three years.

DYLAN: It didn't happen.

ELEANOR: Did a lot of waitressing.

DYLAN: I bet you got some tips.

ELEANOR: Big tips. But I couldn't live on tips. I started dancing.

DYLAN: Dancing?

ELEANOR: Yeah, not Strictly neither.

DYLAN: Pole dancing.

ELEANOR: You guessed.

DYLAN: Something about you.

ELEANOR: I liked it. Learned a lot about myself. And a lot about –

DYLAN: – poles. Different kinds of poles. Or maybe poles are all the same.

ELEANOR: You think I'm funny. You're funny.

DYLAN: What did you learn about men?

ELEANOR: What I knew already. That they want me. They want to have me.

DYLAN: Sex.

ELEANOR: They only take me seriously when they find out I'm a cop.

DYLAN: Is that why you like being a cop?

ELEANOR: It's fun and you don't have to take your clothes off. Unless you want to.

DYLAN: You're doing it again! Fucking flirting!

ELEANOR: No way.

DYLAN: Have you got a boyfriend?

ELEANOR: Not as such.

DYLAN: What does that mean?

ELEANOR: There's a guy, but I'm not settled.

DYLAN: I don't understand that. You've either got a boyfriend or you haven't.

ELEANOR: You don't understand girls like me do you.

DYLAN: I do. Girls like you always have someone. Have we stopped work. Have you stopped work?

ELEANOR: Yeah. I'm not at work.

DYLAN: Shall we kiss?

ELEANOR: Kiss what? Each other?

DYLAN: What else is there to kiss?

ELEANOR: The ghost of Dennis Taylor.

DYLAN: Knowing Dennis, he'll be watching with them big specs of his.

He kisses her. It's his move.

End of scene. Interval.

Act Two

SCENE ONE

Hathersage. WAXY has her table set for a game of snooker. She has her bridge hand screwed in.

WAXY: Shakespeare said 'either a lender or a borrower be'.

She plays a safety shot to bring the cue ball back up to the baulk end.

DYLAN: I'm here aren't I. We can talk about the debt.

DYLAN plays a shot.

WAXY: Don't be a nail, Dylan.

DYLAN: A nail?

WAXY: If you live your life like a nail, everyone's a hammer.

WAXY picks up the target ball and replaces it with a white ball covered in spots.

I done that. With them permanent marker pens.

DYLAN: Is it working for you?

WAXY: Yeah. It's brilliant.

WAXY plays her shot. From now on every time WAXY plays a shot she replaces the target ball with the spotted ball.

WAXY: I don't want you to miss an easy pot. I want you to pot the easy pot, but play too much bottom, leave yourself two inches out of position. I don't want you missing, missing, missing. Bloody hell, it's on telly, someone will say hang on, wait a minute, this in't halal. This is haram. This should be KFC, but it in't. It looks to me like the chicken died in pain with only the blessing of Allah sending it into the deep fat fryer.

DYLAN: It's easy enough. I'll do it. I'll tank frame four for you.

WAXY: Easy?

DYLAN: Yeah.

WAXY: Don't lie to me Dylan. This isn't easy for you. You're different.

DYLAN: I'm not lying.

A shot is played.

WAXY: This game saved your fucking life.

DYLAN: I'm dyslexic. That's all. Like you.

WAXY: Nothing wrong with me. Although I do have a peanut analogy.

DYLAN: I didn't mean there's anything wrong with you, just that we have stuff in common.

WAXY: You think? What's your sexual preference?

DYLAN: Really?

WAXY: You can tell me.

DYLAN: From behind.

WAXY: I meant men or women.

DYLAN: Oh. Sorry. Girls.

WAXY: Have you been in love? Do you understand its power?

DYLAN: Words confused me, as a kid. Love seemed to mean hate, and home was fucking hell. They were trying to kill each other every night. He poured a kettle of boiling water over her in the bath. Next day she nailed him to the floor by his ball sack.

WAXY: No she didn't. I did. How's your mum gonna nail a grown man's ball sack to the floorboards unless she's got some moral support?

She plays a shot.

I loved your mother. Drunk or sober. Me drunk, her sober; she drunk, me sober; both drunk; or both sober. I loved her. She's the reason I wanted to be a woman.

DYLAN: Anyone who puts themselves through what you've put yourself through deserves to be happy.

WAXY: I wanted to be an attractive young woman, not this. But I became a woman just in time for a hysterectomy.

DYLAN: I guess now that I've got a tour card this is your opportunity to make a few bob. Make hay while the sun shines.

WAXY: I have no intention of making hay, Dylan. That's a job for a farmer.

A shot is played.

DYLAN: Do you like living in the country?

WAXY: I love it. The lousy internet connection, the smell of shit, the wind turbans.

DYLAN: I'll tank frame four. No one's expecting me to win anyway.

WAXY: I was able to get a good price for the information that your mother sold me about you throwing the Wingawotsit game. It's a global world now, Dylan.

DYLAN: It's always been a global world.

WAXY: The Filipinos lost fifteen million. They're not happy with me. They sent someone over to threaten me. He's a huge Bronson fan.

DYLAN: Charles Bronson? Death Wish?

WAXY: Emily Bronson. Wuthering Heights. He's visiting Haworth today.

DYLAN: So I'd be tanking the frame for them, not you?

WAXY: You'll never tank a frame, unless you have to.

WAXY opens a door and shouts through.

(To SETH.) Bring 'em in.

SETH enters with DANNY and STELLA both tied up with sacks over their heads.

WAXY: Your mother Red Diesel.

WAXY pulls the sack off STELLA's head. She has duct tape over her mouth. WAXY gets out a gun and screws the silencer on. SETH leaves and comes back with a plastic sheet which he spreads on the carpet.

DYLAN: Fuck, man. What's happening?

WAXY: If you don't tank frame four on Tuesday, I'll kill your mother.

STELLA groans behind the duct tape.

DYLAN: You're insane.

WAXY: The Filipino Bronson fella is gonna kill me!

DYLAN: You wouldn't kill my mum.

WAXY: How do I get you to believe that I would kill your mother?

DANNY starts struggling and moaning.

What's his name?

SETH: Danny.

SETH steps in and replaces the sack and gets DANNY to kneel on the plastic.

DYLAN: Why don't you just threaten to kill me?

WAXY: You'd do a runner.

DYLAN: Oh Jesus! Waxy. For fuck's sake man! I'll tank the frame, I will!

WAXY shoots DANNY in the back of the head. DANNY slumps forward. We see copious amounts of blood.

SETH rolls the body of DANNY up in the plastic and drags him out.

Have we got a contract?

DYLAN: *(Sobbing, is nodding.)*

WAXY: Words, I want words!

DYLAN: I'll do it!

WAXY: Frame four?

DYLAN: Frame four!

WAXY: Good lad.

WAXY: I'll give you a lift home.

End of scene and the snooker table drops to the understage and he is back in his hotel room.

SCENE TWO

DYLAN is in his hotel room talking to ELEANOR, and MO.

DYLAN: She fucking executed him! Shot him in the head.

MO: Sergeant?

ELEANOR: Yeah, yeah. OK.

DYLAN: Don't you believe me?!

ELEANOR: Chill.

DYLAN: Chill?! Fucking chill?!

ELEANOR: Yes, man. Chill.

Knocking on the door.

DYLAN: That'll be Dad.

DYLAN opens the door. It's BOBBY.

BOBBY: You alright, son?

DYLAN: No. No, I'm not alright. How could I be alright?

BOBBY: Chill.

DYLAN: I have no intention of fucking chilling!

BOBBY: Don't chill then. But calm down, will yer?

DYLAN: I will not calm fucking down! Alright?

BOBBY: Not like you to swear.

DYLAN: Well, I'm fucking swearing now.

BOBBY: Are you going to arrest Waxy?

ELEANOR: We sent a couple of cars up there.

DYLAN: And you didn't arrest her?!

ELEANOR: We spoke to Waxy. She denied everything, and –

DYLAN: – I saw her shoot Danny!

ELEANOR: OK, look everyone …

DYLAN: Chill?

ELEANOR: South Yorkshire. Murder Investigation Team. They went up there, there's no evidence of anything –

DYLAN: – fuck man!

ELEANOR: We've done a search on this Irish Danny, but we don't have a second name.

(To BOBBY.) Do you have a second name?

BOBBY: Desmond.

ELEANOR: Danny Desmond?

BOBBY: No, Desmond is my middle name.

ELEANOR: Do you have a second name for this Danny?

BOBBY: Your lot should know him, he's in the red diesel game.

ELEANOR: Cool. Now we're working.

ELEANOR presses a preset on her mobile.

(On the phone.) Guv?… Yeah, we've got a lead on Irish Danny. He touts red diesel … see if that smokes out someone.

BOBBY: Was Mum there?

DYLAN: Yes.

BOBBY: Oh fuck! Why didn't you tell me?

DYLAN: 'Cause I knew you'd go mad.

BOBBY starts ringing a predial on his phone.

BOBBY: She's not answering.

BOBBY turns his phone off.

BOBBY: Voicemail.

Knocking on the door. DYLAN opens it. Enter TONY, talking on the phone.

TONY: *(On the phone.)* Latvia, I think, or was it Lithuania? Fuck it, they're both the same.

(To the room.) Riga. Anyone?

MO: Latvia.

TONY: *(On the phone.)* Latvia, like I said. Er … hang on.

(To MO.) Where is Latvia?

MO: The Baltic.

TONY: *(On the phone.)* Near Russia … their Wifi's slow. I dunno. Hang on.

(To MO.) Do they speak English?

MO: They speak Latvian.

TONY: *(On the phone.)* No, they speak their own shit, yeah, you're fucked … Ciao!

(Off the phone.) Wanker! Dylzo! This is well heavy man!

He gives DYLAN another unwanted hug.

Tony Danlino. I'm this genius's manager.

He gives MO his card.

Big fella, my card. Don't ring in the mornings.

He gives ELEANOR his card.

Who are you darling?

ELEANOR: Police.

Gives a card.

TONY: Respect. Ring anytime you like.

(To DYLAN.) Dylz, have they found your mum?

DYLAN: Not yet.

BOBBY: *(To ELEANOR.)* Can you get a whatsaname?

ELEANOR: Maybe?

BOBBY: A summat cell summat it's called.

TONY: Sickle cell anaemia?

ELEANOR: What?!

TONY: Sorry, I'm not helping, am I? I'll go and come back in.

TONY leaves.

MO: What's he doing?

DYLAN: He does this.

Knocking. DYLAN lets in TONY.

TONY: Hi. Cell site analysis.

BOBBY: That's it! You can pinpoint where someone is.

ELEANOR: We're on that. Any activity on her phone and we've found her.

TONY: So this is the room is it, Dylz?

ELEANOR: *(Explaining to MO.)* Dennis Taylor stayed here when he beat Steve Davis on the black.

TONY: You been here before then, eh, love? Eh? Eh? Dylzo?

MO: Who's Dennis Taylor?

TONY: *(Beat.)* Boomtown! You've got a mini bar!

TONY opens the mini bar.

DYLAN: Waxy wants me to tank a frame. And I'm gonna fucking have to.

TONY: No way man!

DYLAN: Or he'll kill my mum.

TONY: Oh, I see. Alright, then. *(To MO and ELEANOR.)* Is that alright?

ELEANOR: So your mother and Waxy had some kind of relationship?

BOBBY: Yes. Theirs is like the plot of that film.

TONY/DYLAN: Moonstruck!

ELEANOR: They were lovers once, so she's not exactly been kidnapped as you said, Dylan?

DYLAN: Look, she had duck tape round her mouth and a sack over her head!

ELEANOR: But she probably went there willingly?

DYLAN: I don't fucking know!

MO: Actually it's 'duct' tape. Not 'duck' tape.

BOBBY: Look pal, you're in Yorkshire now, it's 'duck' tape.

MO: You tape up your ducks up with it, do you?

BOBBY: Yes, 'cause in Yorkshire if our fucking ducks gerr out of hand, we go to B&Q and get some fucking duck tape, alright?

DYLAN: If I have to tank a game –

BOBBY: – You don't have to.

TONY: Deffo. This is a bluff, Dylz. She'll never kill your mum.

MO: She might. What you don't understand yet is that the fifteen million that went on the Wongsawat game was Filipino money. It might be that Waxy is also under threat.

ELEANOR: A lone Filipino flew into Heathrow and took a connection to Leeds and Bradford Airport on Friday.

BOBBY: *(To ELEANOR.)* Why have brought him here tonight? He's not a cop.

ELEANOR: I want Mo to approve Dylan playing to lose.

TONY: No, I don't want –

MO: – I'm giving him, via the PBSA, let's call it, a one-off licence.

ELEANOR: – it's a police operation now.

TONY: No! I want a written guarantee that he will not get struck off.

MO: You have that guarantee.

TONY: Where?

MO: I will get it in writing.

TONY: Not an email. It's got to be on paper.

MO: A scan?

TONY: No that's not on paper.

MO: It would be on paper if it was printed off.

TONY: Er … let me think about that.

BOBBY: What's going on?

TONY: Shhh!

DYLAN: He's thinking about whether a scan, printed out, is in writing.

TONY: A scan's cool!

MO opens his briefcase and takes out a laptop or tablet.

MO: Have you got Wi-Fi?

DYLAN: Yeah. The passcode's over there.

BOBBY: I thought you said they'd kept the room exactly the same.

DYLAN: They have. But they've added good stuff.

BOBBY: It's not the same, then, is it?

MO: *(Showing scan to TONY.)* How's that?

TONY: How are you going to sign it!?

MO: I'm going to print it off.

TONY: I know that.

MO: And me, and Norman Twig will sign it.

TONY: Who's Norman Twig?

BOBBY: WPBSA.

TONY: Women's –

BOBBY: – World Professional Billiards and Snooker Association.

TONY: I knew that. Good. Bang! Sorted! Read that, Dylz.

DYLAN reads it.

DYLAN: It doesn't say frame four. That's the only frame I'm tanking.

MO: Frame four. OK. Tuesday before the game.

TONY: Shake on it.

DYLAN and MO shake hands. TONY shakes ELEANOR's hand and BOBBY's hand.

Everyone shakes. Come on!

Everyone shakes.

Excellent. A question. Mister Mo. Can I put money on frame four?

BOBBY: Yeah, can we put money on?

ELEANOR: No.

MO: The industry won't pay out. They're working with us.

TONY: You're going to suspend betting on the frame?

MO: We can't do that. But there'll be no paying out. Thanks, Dylan. I know how hard it is. But this is our chance to nail the Filipinos. That's massive, massive. You'll be doing the sport a service.

ELEANOR: Everyone can go now. I need to talk to Dylan, about security. Alone.

TONY: Oooh, no, matron! Soz. My bad. I'm gone.

TONY leaves.

DYLAN: I'm alright, Dad. You can go.

BOBBY: You don't need me?

DYLAN: I'm cool.

BOBBY: My point is, if they've added stuff, they haven't kept the room exactly as it was. I'm going.

MO: *(To ELEANOR.)* You OK?

ELEANOR: Cool.

BOBBY and TONY exit. DYLAN closes the door on them, pushes his back against the door. DYLAN sits on the bed. ELEANOR comforts him.

End of scene.

SCENE THREE

The Crucible Theatre. Set up for a first round match. 'The Boys are Back in Town' plays loud. Out walks the MC with a swagger.

MC: Good morning, Sheffield! Welcome to the second morning here at the cathedral of snooker, Sheffield Crucible. *(Begs a cheer from the audience.)*

The cheer is a bit weedy.

OK, OK. We'll do all that again. It's alright, you don't have to like me, you're doing this for the cameras, and Sheffield. So let me hear a big cheer. *(Begs a cheer.)*

CROWD: *(Cheer.)*

MC: Welcome to the second morning of the World Snooker Championships here in The Crucible Theatre, Sheffield!

He begs a cheer and this time gets one.

MC: And in this cathedral of snooker, please welcome the font of all knowledge, the referee for this morning, Mister Benny 'I've got white gloves and I know the rules', he's had his supper, Mister Benny Tupper!

Enter REFEREE.

MC: Now, let's get the boys on the baize! And we start the day with the unfinished first round match between one of the brightest stars in snooker, if not the Milky Way! He's in the aisle, he's from Carlisle, a hundred and fifty mile, he's full of guile, he's swum the Nile, never bitten by a crocodile, he makes his mum smile, it's Duncan 'the Ferryman' Ferryman!

Enter DUNCAN FERRYMAN acknowledging the cheers and his audience.

And now put your hands together for the local lad, he's just got outta bed, learned his snooker in a shed, he's Sheffield born and bred, he's in his home town, not wearing a dressing gown, it's Dylan 'the son of his folks' Spokes!

Silence. There's no sign of DYLAN.

Come on Dylan! You're on telly!

After a couple of beats DYLAN enters but does not acknowledge the crowd. The MC exits.

REFEREE: Dylan Spokes leads three frames to nil. Frame four. Dylan Spokes to the table.

The game is played out. Only the referee speaks, to update the score. FERRYMAN wins.

DYLAN exits down the tunnel at pace. FERRYMAN follows.

End of scene.

SCENE FOUR

WAXY's place. WAXY is standing at the snooker table. Enter ELEANOR, real name ROSA. She is carrying a holdall full of cash. Which she empties on to the snooker table.

WAXY: Rosa! I knew you'd be first back. The great looking bird always catches the worm. What odds did you get?

ELEANOR: Even Stevens. I need to eat.

WAXY: There's no smoke without salmon. Glass of champers or a line of Charlie?

ELEANOR: Smoked salmon, champers and Charlie?

WAXY: It's what I promised you. You alright?

ELEANOR: Yeah, why wouldn't I be?

ELEANOR snorts a line of coke. WAXY starts counting the money. Enter STELLA. She starts emptying her pockets of cash.

STELLA: *(To ELEANOR.)* Coulda give me a lift. Rosa?! I'm fucking talking to you! Din't yer see me walking up road?

WAXY: What odds did you get Stell?

STELLA: Evens. Some two to one ons, but mainly evens.

WAXY: Fabulous.

STELLA: What were you expecting?

WAXY: Short odds. But your lad wiped the floor with him in the first three frames so the odds lengthened. This is beyond my wettest dreams!

STELLA: Got your stake back yet?

WAXY: *(Indicating the tidy pile.)* We're ahead already.

STELLA picks out a fifty pound note and WAXY slaps her wrist.

STELLA: Don't see many fifties.

WAXY: I've always said, look after the fifties and the pennies can go fuck themselves.

WAXY starts dividing the money six ways, going round, like dealing cards.

ELEANOR: Can we sort the expenses?

STELLA: What's up with her?

WAXY: Later.

ELEANOR: That's what you said on the last job, and I didn't get any.

(ROSA/ELEANOR starts producing receipts as she speaks.) Dry cleaning, Police badges, urine sample kit, parking, parking, stage blood, it's expensive stage blood.

STELLA: – condoms.

ELEANOR: *(A look.)*

STELLA: He's my lad. I got a right to know.

ELEANOR: It's my body.

STELLA: She did! I told you Waxy, she did!

ELEANOR: You ripped him off. Your own son

STELLA: You don't know what them two done to me. They owe me fucking big time.

ELEANOR: *(To WAXY.)* Radios, petrol.

WAXY: How much?

ELEANOR: Nearly two hundred.

WAXY he gives her four fifties. Enter DANNY. He is very well dressed, with tweeds and a tie or bow tie, brogues etc. He has a cardboard box full of cash. Which he puts on the baize.

WAXY: I hope you've had a bath.

DANNY: I didn't take the bath to remove the smell, I was trying, in vain, to wash away my shameful, overtly racist portrayal of an *Oirishman.*

STELLA: But Fizzy you are Irish.

DANNY: And proud of it the full length of me shillelagh.

WAXY: Expenses?

DANNY: I had to buy a lot of fucking awful casual wear.
A hundred please.

WAXY starts counting out a hundred but ELEANOR jumps in with –

ELEANOR: You could've worn your own gear.

DANNY: Dear girl, I do not own any clothing inexplicably, gratuitously, covered in writing.

WAXY gives him a hundred, then continues counting money.

WAXY: Stella, give out them photocopies will you love?

DANNY: What's this?

STELLA approaches with photocopies of a newspaper article.

STELLA: The next job. *(To WAXY.)* Rosa?

WAXY: Give her a copy.

She gives them a copy each.

ELEANOR: Rafael Ribeiro signs for Manchester City.

STELLA: Thirty-six million. Two hundred thousand a week.

DANNY: When I think what Johnny Giles was earning at Leeds United.

ELEANOR: What nationality?

WAXY: Brazilian. His wife is homesick. Hot pot, clog dancing, George Formby. She doesn't like Lancashire. So who speaks Brazilian?

DANNY: My dear Waxy, nobody speaks Brazilian.

ELEANOR: Even Brazilians.

WAXY: How do they talk to each other then?

DANNY: In Portuguese.

WAXY: Why would anyone in Brazil speak Portuguese?

DANNY: Did you ever go to school?

WAXY: I did, yeah, twice.

DANNY: We need to be clear, who is the mark? The footballer, or his wife?

WAXY: His wife. Consuela. I thought this job might suit you Rosa.

ELEANOR: I'm not a lesbian.

WAXY: To get off with him. Psychologically, tip her over the hedge.

ELEANOR: Maybe I don't do that any more.

STELLA: Woah. Fizz? D'yer hear that? She's retiring.

DANNY: What is it my dear? You and Dylan?

WAXY: You got too close did you?

DANNY: I've seen it before. The honey trap traps herself.

ELEANOR: What is this?

STELLA: They're questions.

WAXY: We need to know.

STELLA: I want answers. He's my lad, and I'm his mother.

ELEANOR: What kind of mother rips her own son off?

STELLA: There's a debt that's been paid.

ELEANOR: If they, like, boiled down everyone's brains on Jeremy Kyle and poured the soup into a skull – that's yours.

STELLA: Dylan's not been hurt, he's lost no money. Nothing.

ELEANOR: Money?! Is that all you know?

DANNY: The damnable thing about money is that enough is never enough.

STELLA: I carried him, I had him. He's mine.

ELEANOR: You're unnatural.

STELLA lunges at ELEANOR and is held back by WAXY and DANNY.

STELLA: You weren't supposed to fuck him! My boy. Did you fuck him you bitch!?

ELEANOR: Wash your mouth out.

DANNY: Now this is daytime TV.

WAXY: What happened Rosa?

ELEANOR: That's my business innit.

DANNY: Love is the word. Do you love him? Rosa. If you've crossed that line and put the whole team in danger we need to know. Have you spoken to him?

WAXY: Everyone! Listen. Remember, we've done nothing legal.

DANNY: Illegal.

WAXY: Which one is it when you've done something wrong?

DANNY: Illegal.

WAXY: We've done nothing illegal.

Enter IQBAL, previously MO. He now speaks with a rough northern accent. He is carrying some plastic Sainsbury's shopping bags full of cash. He's badly dressed.

MO: Am I the last!?

WAXY: What odds d'yer get Ikky?

MO: Four to five on, evens, yeah, 'bout that.

MO empties his cash from the shopping bags.

ELEANOR: You're so pikey.

MO: Pikey? What's that's then. Pikey?

DANNY: The aesthetic.

MO: Wednesday is "wear what you like day" in Rochdale.

WAXY: Expenses?

MO: Er ... yeah. Radios, badges.

WAXY: Fuck off. Rosa got the badges

MO: OK. What's this?

STELLA: The next job.

MO reads the photocopies.

MO: Phwoargh, is that Ribeiro's missus?

WAXY: Fizzy is suggesting a long con.

DANNY: An old school long con I've worked before. Donkey sanctuary.

STELLA: Is that her weakness?

DANNY: Sick animals aye, according to this.

DANNY waves the newspaper article.

STELLA: I like animals, I could befriend her.

MO: Whilst Rosa hooks up with Ribeiro, and fucks her head up.

DANNY: Crude.

MO: That's how it works.

WAXY: She will turn to Stella for comfort, friendship.

DANNY: Then we offer her the position of Honorary President.

WAXY: Before explaining that we are desperate for funding.

DANNY: Medicines, vet's bills.

STELLA: Carrots.

WAXY: The objective is a monthly direct debit of five thousand.

STELLA: I like this. I need a steady income.

MO: But we'll need a farm or summat to do a mock up.

DANNY: My brother is a strong farmer in County Offaly. He'd give us a couple of fields for a week.

WAXY: Ireland would be good.

STELLA: Yeah, otherwise she'd want to pop in all the time, and see the donkeys.

MO: Which don't exist.

WAXY: We'll have to fly her out once.

MO: And we'll have to have proper donkeys for that.

WAXY: OK. Where do we get donkeys?

STELLA: I had a one-night stand with a track side marshall at Owlerton Speedway once.

DANNY: True love has many iterations.

WAXY: How does that help Stella?

STELLA: During the summer he helped his uncle's brother-in-law with the donkey rides at Cleethorpes.

WAXY: We have donkeys!

DANNY: We rent them, legitimately, for a week.

MO: We're a film company making a film or summat.

WAXY: Are you in Rosa?

ELEANOR: Let me think about it.

STELLA: No. I'm not working with her again. She went too far.

MO: You're supposed to tease, not please.

DANNY: Did you sleep with Dylan, we need to know?

STELLA's mobile phone rings.

STELLA: This is Dylan! Shhh!

(On the phone.) Hello love … I'm alright, yeah, straight away, she didn't hurt me … yeah she's sick … he was a vagrant and Waxy's killed before … you're not gonna go to the police? … you'd have to tell 'em you threw a game … where are you love? The hotel. I'll come and see you tomorrow … do you want some steaks? Tarra.

(Phone off.)

WAXY: Is he gonna fall over?

STELLA: Hard to tell innit.

DANNY: In my long, and I have to say, distinguished experience in the con game, I would say we are dependent on Rosa disappearing.

ELEANOR's mobile rings.

DANNY: If that's Dylan. Don't answer it.

WAXY: Go to London.

STELLA: Leave my lad alone.

ELEANOR: Coming from you that's –

DANNY: – Forget him.

ELEANOR: I don't have to.

MO: Wooo! She got it bad man!

DANNY: You will go to London my dear. Because I brought you into this team and I told Waxy you're a professional, and a good team player.

WAXY: I want you out of Sheffield now girl.

DANNY: You and I could do the glass eye shortcon for a couple of weeks, like we used to, around round the hotels. I got a new glass eye.

Produces it.

ELEANOR: You can't stop me seeing him.

WAXY: Yes I can. Seth! Get out of this town and don't come back.

Enter SETH.

Take this girl down to the station, make sure she gets on a train.

ELEANOR: I'm driving.

WAXY: Then drive.

DANNY: I'll be staying at the Savoy.

ELEANOR leaves.

She's a helluva fine woman. There'll be another man on his knees sobbing with lust within a week with that much beauty.

WAXY: Beauty is only skin.

DANNY: Skin deep?

WAXY: No. Skin.

STELLA: She's a whore!

DANNY: If she's a whore you're a pimp Stella. Your own son.

STELLA: She weren't supposed to sleep with him.

DANNY: I think it's called a vocational hazard.

MO: *(Studying the new job.)* One problem. I'm scared of donkeys.

End of scene.

SCENE FIVE

The British Legion snooker room, late at night. The snooker table is set for the start of a game, the lights are on, but there's no cue ball on the table. DYLAN is using a stanley knife to cut a cue tip and fix it to his cue. Enter BOBBY with shopping bag.

BOBBY: You alright Dyl? Do you want a sarnie? Cheese and tomato. No animals were injured during the making of these sandwiches.

DYLAN declines.

DYLAN: Is Mum alright?

BOBBY: Yeah. I phoned her. She's pissed. Which is normal.

DYLAN: Have you spoken to Waxy?

BOBBY: I don't speak to Waxy. If it's any consolation, son, I thought you threw the frame brilliantly.

DYLAN: Don't. Please, Dad. Don't.

BOBBY: No, I mean, I couldn't tell. You had that red, and I thought, he's gonna miss it, but you potted it. Brilliant. Stop prowling! Why are you prowling?

DYLAN: This is fucking killing me, Dad.

BOBBY: You beat him! You won the match!

DYLAN: What is the matter with you?!

BOBBY: What's the matter with you?! What happened there?

DYLAN: I can't believe you have to ask!

BOBBY: That gives the lie to all that psychology crap, dunnit? You tanked a frame which, by your theory has to fuck your mind, and fuck your game, but you went on and beat him ten six.

DYLAN kicks a chair. Then picks it up and smashes it. Damaging it slightly.

DYLAN: Fuck!

BOBBY: Oh, come on, son! The chair's done nothing.

DYLAN attacks the chair again, this time violently, and deliberately, and pedantically.

BOBBY: The chair's me, innit?

DYLAN: How could you tell?

BOBBY: I did Alcoholics Anonymous once for a week and we did a lot of stuff like that. Punching the shit out of pillows. Sorry. I'm a dick. But you beat him!

DYLAN picks up another chair.

Stop it. You're not bent! You got clearance from the cops, from the WPBSA. No one noticed. What you done is helping to clean up the game.

DYLAN: You got any beer?

BOBBY: Does Dolly Parton sleep on her back?

BOBBY gives him a beer.

If it'll make you feel any better.

Then two separate wads of cash on to the baize.

DYLAN: What's that?

BOBBY: Legal tender.

DYLAN: The horses?

BOBBY: Na! You.

DYLAN: Me?

BOBBY: Fucking you!

DYLAN: Me? Winning the first three frames?

BOBBY: No! You dick! Frame four. Losing it.

DYLAN: I don't understand. Dad? Who the fuck paid out?

BOBBY: I'm clever. Corbetts in Netherthorpe Place give me evens. And Causeway in Castle Street give me 5 to 4 on.

DYLAN: But they said none of them would be paying out on frame four.

BOBBY: I think they meant the big boys. Hills, BetFreds, KellyBet.

DYLAN: They didn't say that.

BOBBY: Whatever, I reckoned Causeway and Corbetts wouldn't be in the loop.

DYLAN: They're all in the loop! All betting shops are Gambling Commission licensed!

BOBBY: It in't Monopoly money!

DYLAN: How much did you win?

BOBBY: Dunno. I had a hundred quid in Causeway at 5 to 4 on. What's 5 to 4 on?

DYLAN: 80%.

BOBBY: So what's 80% of a hundred? It's about 65 quid innit?

DYLAN: And you were a drug dealer?

BOBBY: I wasn't a very good drug dealer.

DYLAN: 80% of a hundred is 80 quid.

BOBBY: 80% is 80? That's a bit of a coincidence, innit?

DYLAN is on his mobile.

Who are you ringing?

DYLAN: Hills.

(On phone.) Hi, er … I had a bet on Duncan Ferryman to beat Dylan Spokes in the fourth frame at the Crucible today but my mate said that you're not paying out … frame four … really?… ta man. Laters.

BOBBY: You had a bet on yourself?

DYLAN: No! I was trying to find out if Hills are paying out.

BOBBY: Are they?

DYLAN: Yes.

BOBBY: What?! They're paying out on frame four? Hills?! Fuck! And I schlepped all the way to Nether Edge.

DYLAN: What's the number for KellyBet?

BOBBY: Here. Speed dial.

He dials.

DYLAN: Dodgy this is Dad!

BOBBY: Have you phoned that copper bird?

DYLAN: Yes. She's coming here.

BOBBY: What did she say, on the phone?

DYLAN: She said, well done. I'll see you later. 'I'm sorry'.

BOBBY: What's she sorry for?

DYLAN: Dunno.

BOBBY: *(On the phone.)* Now then … are you paying out on frame four, first round … the snooker! Ferryman Spokes … frame four … why wouldn't you be indeed? Someone said you weren't. Ta. Have a nice day.

(Phone down.)

DYLAN: They're paying out?

BOBBY: Yeah.

DYLAN: They took bets and they're paying out.

BOBBY: So they didn't do what they said they would do.

DYLAN: Summat's fucking wrong Dad!

BOBBY: No, no, no.

DYLAN: Two officials from the WPBSA came round, half an hour ago.

BOBBY: Yeah.

DYLAN: They wanted a urine sample.

BOBBY: Another one?! What are they doing, drinking it!?

DYLAN: One of them was Norman Twig. I know him, I've met him before, Integrity Officer. I showed him Mo's business card.

DYLAN shows MO's card.

The International Centre for Sport Security.

BOBBY: What, and he'd never heard of it?

DYLAN: It exists, he'd heard of it. But they've got nothing to do with the snooker. Nothing.

BOBBY: That's a bottle of piss he owes you then.

DYLAN: We've been conned. Big time. By Waxy. By Mo. By Eleanor. Shit man, we've been done.

BOBBY: Wait, wait, wait! You saw the wino executed.

DYLAN: He had a sack over his head. Stage blood. Acting. Eleanor told me she went to drama school, trained as an actress.

BOBBY: No. Can't be a con. I'll tell you why.

DYLAN: Go on.

BOBBY: The copper, Eleanor, she's coming here.

DYLAN: She's not a copper. She's an actress. I shoulda … ah fuck!

BOBBY: What? You shoulda what?

DYLAN: I shoulda seen it. She knew Waxy was a woman.

BOBBY: Eh?

DYLAN: That is the one mistake she made. When I first told her who had asked me to tank a game, I said 'Waxy Chuff', and she said, 'who is she?' She! Who would presume that a gangster was a woman? But she knew because she's working for Waxy. Fuck!

BOBBY: But if it's a con, she wouldn't return to the scene of the crime.

DYLAN: She's not here, is she?! And, I'm not sure it is a crime. Or at least not a crime that is ever going to see the light of day. I mean, I'm not gonna go to the WPBSA and say hello I tanked frame four 'cause someone asked me to, am I? I'd get banned. For life.

BOBBY: 'Kinnell! It's brilliant! Ha! I take my hat off to you Waxy! At the end of the day, you gotta give it to him, her, ain't yer? It's the perfect crime. Genius!

DYLAN: Dad?

BOBBY: Sorry. So why's the girl coming here then? I'd be off if I was her.

DYLAN: She's not coming.

BOBBY: Have you had her?

DYLAN doesn't reply.

Bloody hell. You lucky bugger. Kaw! I tell you, I know you been ripped off, and totally fucked over, but fucking hell, it's been worth it.

DYLAN: I can't believe you.

BOBBY: Is it more? Than sex. With her?

DYLAN: I don't know.

BOBBY: That's a yes. Oh, fuck. Are you in deep? Is it love?

DYLAN: How do you know if it's love?

BOBBY: Have you stopped watching porn? If you've lost interest in porn, it's love.

DYLAN: It's love.

BOBBY: But man, you can't have. She's a grifter. Like in that film. Whatsitcalled?

DYLAN: Can we not do fucking films please!

Enter TONY.

TONY: Dylz! Hello Dadz. Dylz, good news. You've drawn Ronnie O'Sullivan in the next round.

DYLAN: Buggery.

TONY: No, it's not buggery, it's good news 'cause if you win I can nail down the sponsorship deal with Pret a Manger.

BOBBY: And if he loses?

TONY: Greggs.

BOBBY: And you've already beaten him at darts.

DYLAN: Everything's changed.

BOBBY: We been conned.

TONY: Eh? What do you mean?

DYLAN: A con team.

TONY: What's a con team?

BOBBY: A team of grifters. Like in that film.

TONY: What film?

DYLAN: No, Dad! Please!

ELEANOR enters unseen.

BOBBY: Had that gorgeous bird in it who's married to that bloke –

DYLAN: – Dad?!

BOBBY: No, famous actor, womaniser, something to do with where rabbits live.

TONY: Watership Down?

DYLAN: Warren Beatty.

BOBBY: Him. But he's not in the film, he's married to her, but he's not in the film, she's his – what do you call it –

DYLAN: – His wife.

BOBBY: That's it, his wife. But in the film, which Warren wasn't in –

TONY: But his wife was –

BOBBY: – was called …

TONY: Who else was in the film?

BOBBY: Big actress.

TONY: What's she look like?

BOBBY: A cross between Walter Mathau and a dinner lady. *(Beat.)* She was in The Milkman Always Rings Twice.

DYLAN: Postman! FUCKING POSTMAN!

ELEANOR: Anjelica Huston.

DYLAN turns, sees her. BOBBY turns.

DYLAN: Maybe you know. Maybe it's your specialist subject.

ELEANOR: What?

DYLAN: Trying to find the name of a film about con artists.

BOBBY: It's got Warren Beatty's wife in it.

ELEANOR: Annette Bening.

BOBBY: That's her, yeah!

ELEANOR: And John Cusack. They're both grifters.

BOBBY: Yeah, they're grifters, but what's the film called?

ELEANOR: Grifters.

BOBBY: That's it! Grifters!

DYLAN: Is this part of the con? You coming back? We worked it out.

ELEANOR: Yeah?

DYLAN: Yeah. Proud of yourself, are you?

ELEANOR: I'm sorry.

TONY: I shouldn't be here, should I? Dadz. We'd better go to the pub. Come on.

BOBBY: I was only saying a minute ago –

DYLAN: – Shut it Dad! Go. I can handle this.

BOBBY: But –

DYLAN: Really.

BOBBY: *(To ELEANOR.)* Impressed.

BOBBY heads for the door.

TONY: Dylzo! Practise! Ten thousand hours before Friday. Ronnie O!

BOBBY and TONY leave. TONY's phone goes off.

TONY: *(On phone.)* Yeah … I can't talk now mate, I'm in Paraguay. Just going into a tunnel. E … a … d … Crrr … crrr … crrr …

Door closes.

DYLAN: What about the Asian money? Have they gone home?

ELEANOR: The Filipinos?

DYLAN: Yeah, are they happy?

ELEANOR: There is no Filipino. No Asian syndicate. Never was.

DYLAN: Of course not. That's all part of the con.

ELEANOR: You never see the lies you believe.

DYLAN: I had to see a man shot in the head!

ELEANOR: A bit of theatre. He's fine.

DYLAN: He might be, but what about me?! I saw a man fucking murdered!

ELEANOR: You saw what you wanted to see.

DYLAN: You sound proud of what you've done.

ELEANOR: I'm a professional. Except for this.

DYLAN: 'Cept for what?

ELEANOR: Coming back here. Now.

DYLAN: What's your name, Eleanor?

ELEANOR: Rosa.

DYLAN: Rosa. What do you call mugs like me, Rosa?

ELEANOR: The mark.

DYLAN: The mark. I'm 'the mark', am I?

ELEANOR: Yeah. You were.

DYLAN: So, like, in an average year, how many 'marks' do you fuck?

ELEANOR: Like, none, actually.

DYLAN: I don't believe you! Why should I fucking believe you?! Why should I ever believe anything you ever fucking say ever again?

ELEANOR: I know. I can't expect anything from you.

DYLAN: You've already taken everything I ever had. Everything!

ELEANOR: My job –

DYLAN: – It's a job is it?! Fucking snooker players!?

ELEANOR: I want you to understand! My role in the team is to tempt, to keep the mark's interest, to stop him thinking rationally.

DYLAN: Bait.

ELEANOR: Dylan, please, it's usually older men, and it's like, look, I mean, older men are really gullible, yeah, and all I have to do is kinda suggest the possibility –

DYLAN: – you fuck their heads! You give them a dream.

ELEANOR: A fantasy.

DYLAN: No! A fucking sexual fantasy. Make them want to kiss you all over.

ELEANOR: Yeah.

DYLAN: Keep them on the boil. Tease, tease, tease.

ELEANOR: Yes! It's only ever a fantasy. Ours is reality. That's why we were different. Because we did sleep together.

DYLAN: How many of them fall in love with you?

ELEANOR: I remember what you said.

DYLAN: I hope it gives you some professional pride! Knowing how much you fucked me up.

ELEANOR: I'm fucked up too. I've never been like this. I'm no different.

DYLAN: Don't come near me! Don't turn to me! You're not real. You're a professional grifter. A honey trap whore!

He breaks his cue.

ELEANOR: No! I said, I have never ever slept with the mark. Never.

DYLAN: Why are you talking to me? Why aren't you in London spending your money? You're wasting your time here. I can't believe a fucking thing you say!

ELEANOR: I'm here, I –

DYLAN: – No! Listen to me! This is the only thing I've ever had! Snooker. And you've destroyed it. You've killed my game, my honour, my credit.

ELEANOR: Credit.

DYLAN: My edge is psychology.

ELEANOR: I'm sorry Dylan but that might be crap.

DYLAN: What do you know?

ELEANOR: You went on to beat him ten six! After you'd thrown the frame.

DYLAN: I don't know how.

ELEANOR: Maybe it's not psychology that is your advantage. Maybe you're just too good. Brilliant.

DYLAN: There is no silver lining in this!

ELEANOR: I wasn't trying to say –

DYLAN: I'm finished!

ELEANOR: Quite obviously not, since you're through to the next round. Dylan! No one need ever know. You can win. I believe in you. You could be world champion.

DYLAN tears his shirt off his back.

DYLAN: I know! I know! I can never not know! I have cheated! I'm a cheat! A fraud! Bent! I'm bent! I'm like this fucking cue, I'm broken! My whole game. You've killed me!

ELEANOR approaches.

Don't touch me!

ELEANOR: You loved me. No one's ever loved me.

DYLAN: Everyone's always fucking loved you.

ELEANOR: They've wanted me! Not loved me. Why can't you hear me, Dylan? I'm sorry. It was the same for me. I wasn't faking, I'm not faking. I'm here. I want to see you!

DYLAN takes the Stanley knife and puts it against his wrist.

DYLAN: Don't you fucking dare tell me that you love me, because I might want to believe you but I can't no more 'cause I know you're a liar. Get out of my fucking, fucked-up life you slapper!

He runs the knife over his wrist. We see blood.

That's not deep. That's the vein. But the artery is next. I know what I'm doing. Get out! Or I'll go for it.

End of scene.

SCENE SIX

The Crucible Theatre, two weeks later. In the scene change, 'The Boys are Back in Town' plays, and DYLAN leaves the set to change into his match suit. DANNY CARR and the referee enter. The KellyBet world championship cup is set on a table upstage. The REFEREE prowls. DYLAN sits and chalks his cue. The score board says Carr 60, Spokes 52. CARR pots an easy yellow, and sets himself up nicely for the easy green.

REFEREE: Sixty-two.

CARR moves to pot the green which is an easy pot. But he takes his time, powdering his cue, and chalking the tip, taking a breath.

COMMENTATOR: Danny Carr on the brink of greatness, chalks his cue, takes a breath, at the end of this extraordinary match, which must rival 1985, Dennis Taylor and Steve Davis, as the greatest final ever. Twenty frames to twenty frames. *(Whisper.)* There is nothing after this.

CARR goes to the table, lines up the green, and pots it.

REFEREE: Sixty-five.

COMMENTATOR: He's four pots away from becoming world champion and cashing a cheque for four hundred thousand pounds. Dylan Spokes, the outsider, the maverick, the local boy, can only watch. What an extraordinary two weeks he's had. His day will come whatever happens here tonight.

DANNY CARR pots the brown, and leaves himself nicely on the blue.

REFEREE: Sixty-nine.

COMMENTATOR: Can he hold his nerve? The occasion is either his friend or his enemy.

My goodness! Danny Carr has underhit the blue. This is extraordinary and reminds me of Steve Davis missing that relatively easy black – the 85 final. My goodness.

BOBBY: Come on, Dylan! Come on, son!

REFEREE: Quiet please!

COMMENTATOR: Dylan Spokes touched the green and handed five thousand pounds to Sean Murphy in Cardiff earlier this year. Well, goodness me, it's come back to him today. What do they call it? Karma.

DYLAN stands and lines up the blue. Which he pots.

BOBBY: Yes!

REFEREE: Quiet please! Fifty-seven.

COMMENTATOR: Dylan's father there, Bobby, bit of a character, can't contain himself, as usual. He built Dylan a snooker shed when he was eleven. It's paying off now. His lad has the pink and the black to become world champion. Incredible.

DYLAN pots the pink.

BOBBY: Yes! Sorry!

REFEREE: Sixty-three.

COMMENTATOR: Bobby's got his head in his hands now, he can't watch. Amazing scenes here in the championship final at the Crucible, Sheffield.

DYLAN lines up the black. ELEANOR shouts to him from the back of the auditorium.

ELEANOR: Dylan!

REFEREE: Quiet please!

ELEANOR: I'm here! I'm not going until you talk to me!

COMMENTATOR: Oh dear, we've got an idiot!

ELEANOR advances on to the stage.

REFEREE: Stewards please!

The REFEREE manhandles her.

DYLAN: Don't touch her! Please.

COMMENTATOR: Oh, my goodness, Dylan's getting involved.

ELEANOR: Dylan! I came back.

COMMENTATOR: Oh dear, I think Dylan knows her.

DYLAN: Eleanor –

ELEANOR: – Rosa.

COMMENTATOR: Maybe he doesn't know her.

REFEREE: Miss –

DYLAN: – It's OK.

ELEANOR: I just want to talk.

DYLAN: This is not a good time. *(Beat.)* And you're on telly.

ELEANOR: Oh no.

DYLAN: Oh yeah. This is the final.

ELEANOR: You made the final?! I knew you could! Sorry.

DYLAN: I'm on the black. To win.

ELEANOR: Like Dennis Taylor did with Steve Davis?

DYLAN: You remember?

ELEANOR: I remember everything. Do you?

DYLAN: I do, yeah. This is really embarrassing with everyone –

ELEANOR: – I don't care, I have to prove to you somehow that I believe in you. I believe in us. I love you and I don't care who's listening.

COMMENTATOR: An estimated eight million viewers.

A STEWARD approaches to throw her out.

DYLAN: *(To STEWARD.)* No! Please. She's my girlfriend. I love her.

COMMENTATOR: That's cleared that one up.

DYLAN: Let me play this shot. Rosa. Sit down.

ELEANOR sits. DYLAN chalks his cue. Lines up the black and pots it.

COMMENTATOR: Unprecedented scenes here at the home of snooker. Has Dylan Spokes, the local lad, got the steel, the composure, to recover from that extraordinary incident?

DYLAN pots the black.

COMMENTATOR: He's done it!

DYLAN goes to her. She runs to him. They kiss and hug. He lifts the trophy. Twenty pound notes fall like snow from the ceiling. Many flash lights. Music.

TO BLACK.

KISS ME

Characters

STEPHANIE, 32

PETER, 28

N.B. "Stephanie" and "Peter" are not their real names, but in the text these names are used as their cues throughout, even after they begin to use their real names.

Set

A rented room in a terraced house in Notting Hill. There is a double bed which dominates the room. It has an eiderdown, blankets and pillows. A bedside chair, a bath chair, a wardrobe, and chest of drawers. For Scene 1 the framed photograph is face down on the chest of drawers.

Kiss Me was first performed on 27 October 2016 at the Hampstead Theatre, London, with the following cast:

STEPHANIE	Claire Lams
PETER	Ben Lloyd-Hughes
Director	Anna Ledwich
Designer	Georgia Lowe
Lighting	Matthew Haskins
Sound	Sarah Weltman

SCENE 1

1929. STEPHANIE, a woman of about thirty, stands looking at two pairs of shoes. One pair has quite high heels and the other a low heel. She tries them both on, considers. She chooses the high heels. She looks at necklaces, one suggestive, one muted. She chooses the suggestive, and arranges on her cleavage. She takes off her wedding ring. She checks her lipstick. A bell sounds from the hall. She exits and returns, letting in PETER. He is a man slightly younger. He is wearing an outdoor coat, a brown bowler hat showing flecks of snow, and an umbrella walking stick. Under this he is smartly dressed with a neat shirt and tie. He uses a tie pin to secure the collar of his shirt. He is clean, and presentable. His presentation should feel like a costume.

STEPHANIE: Still snowing then?

PETER: Stopped now. But I walked over.

STEPHANIE: From?

PETER doesn't reply but raises his eyebrows questioningly.

STEPHANIE: Sorry. What do I call you? What would you like me to call you? I mean…what does Doctor Trollope want me to call you? I guess there are some parameters.

PETER: There are many parameters, yes. I start each visit by explaining them. That's the first thing I must do.

STEPHANIE: The first thing before the second thing.

PETER: Firstly, we're not to talk too much, not to get to know one another.

STEPHANIE: I can't…I need a name, at least.

PETER: Peter.

STEPHANIE: Is that your real name?

PETER: No.

STEPHANIE: Peter what? What's your surname?

PETER: It doesn't matter does it, because I'm not Peter anyway.

STEPHANIE: Make one up. For me. One you like.

Pause.

PETER: Boleyn.

STEPHANIE: Boleyn?

PETER: Yes.

STEPHANIE: Like Anne Boleyn?

PETER: I guess.

STEPHANIE: Peter Boleyn?

PETER: Yeah.

STEPHANIE: You can do better than that.

PETER: You don't like it?

STEPHANIE: She lost her head.

PETER: He didn't.

STEPHANIE: There was a Peter Boleyn was there?

PETER: I can't tell you my real name.

STEPHANIE: The parameters?

PETER: Yes. Doctor Trollope is fierce about that.

STEPHANIE: Doctor Trollope is pretty fierce all round.

PETER: She has to be. Or none of this could work for anyone.

STEPHANIE: What's she scared of?

PETER: Talk. Doctor Trollope has said to me that she would prefer to use a turkey baster. They don't talk.

STEPHANIE: And turkey basters, after they've done it, they don't want to do it again.

PETER: Turkey basters don't threaten established relationships, or raise any kind of moral dilemmas.

STEPHANIE: Unless you're using a turkey baster regularly for fun.

PETER: The real problem with turkey basters is they don't work.

STEPHANIE: Can I be Nancy?

PETER: I'd rather you didn't. That was my mother's name.

STEPHANIE: Oh dear. It's not fair to ask you to…you know… your mother. *(Beat.)* Stephanie?

PETER: It suits you.

She plays with her necklace.

STEPHANIE: So we can't talk. That's a disappointment because I like to talk. And listen. I'd like to travel, but I've not had the chance, obviously what with the war, and everything. I've got a sister in America. You look a bit foreign. Sorry. There's nothing wrong with being foreign, a bit foreign looking. It's rather exotic.

PETER: It's a tan. I'm English. I grew up in Barbados and I, we, still have business in Barbados.

STEPHANIE: You're telling me things about you. You're breaking your own rules.

PETER: Doctor Trollope has agreed that I have to explain the tan. The women ask, none of them –

STEPHANIE: – want a brown baby.

PETER: Yes. I'm one hundred percent English.

STEPHANIE: The only thing Doctor Trollope told me about you is that you don't have syphilis.

PETER: I don't have syphilis.

STEPHANIE: Lovely! Neither do I. Pubic lice?

PETER: No. That's all you need to know.

STEPHANIE: What are the other parameters? I mean, I know what my parameters are, what Doctor Trollope told me were my parameters, but do you have the same parameters?

PETER: We're not to try and get in touch beforehand, or afterwards. We're not to use our real names.

STEPHANIE: How did you find me, how did you know where to come, today, at the right time?

PETER: She sends a messenger.

STEPHANIE: A messenger! Gosh how romantic! Like a go-between. Ha! But what about your work. Do you just not go to work?

PETER: It's my father's business.

STEPHANIE: You're telling me things about you.

PETER: I run the London end, so I don't have to answer to anyone.

STEPHANIE: Lovely. Sounds like heaven.

PETER: It isn't heaven. I don't do this for pleasure.

STEPHANIE: I wish I had a job where I can just drop everything and run off to Notting Hill and make love to a stranger. Ha!

Beat.

PETER: We're not to kiss.

STEPHANIE: Yes, she told me that.

Beat.

Do you ever break that one?

PETER: No. Never. She means don't kiss on the lips.

STEPHANIE: I see. But you might sometimes kiss a woman somewhere else?

PETER: A lot of the widows find this very difficult.

STEPHANIE: They're nervous.

PETER: Yes. And…

STEPHANIE: – and women are slower anyway.

PETER: Yes.

STEPHANIE: Of course! Vive la différence! As they say in Ashby de la Zouch.

PETER: I find that a kiss on the neck can help.

STEPHANIE: Or the inner thigh.

PETER: Yes. The inner thigh. But initially the neck or the ears.

STEPHANIE: Yes! The ears! You're right. Good lord! Yes please! The ears. Both of them. At the same time! Ha!

PETER: Doctor Trollope considers kissing on the lips to be dangerous.

STEPHANIE: Spanish flu?

PETER: She believes that kissing on the lips is a gateway, her phrase, a gateway to love. And that for her is the final parameter. Our final parameter.

STEPHANIE: Love?

PETER: We're not to fall in love.

STEPHANIE: Of course. That would be terrible. Have you ever been in love?

PETER: If I answered that, you would know something about me.

STEPHANIE: Of course, silly me. I'm sorry I asked. I loved my husband. I shouldn't have told you that as we're not to know anything about each other, and now you know I once had a husband.

PETER: Doctor Trollope told me you were a widow, which presumes a husband.

STEPHANIE: And you could maybe presume that I loved him, once, and then you would know more about me than I know about you.

(STEPHANIE stands and takes the photo frame from the chest of drawers top and shows it to PETER. PETER averts his gaze.)

PETER: I'd rather not.

STEPHANIE: Anthony. Tony. My husband. That's not his real name. I made it up. Tony Boleyn. Sorry. Being silly now. He wouldn't approve of this.

(STEPHANIE puts the photo frame back face down on the chest of drawers.)

I was young, we were both young, and looking back, it was all very silly, but beautiful, and romantic… I was sixteen. I don't know what it was to be honest, but it took me over, and it was all mine.

PETER: Stop! Please. I don't want to know.

STEPHANIE: Don't listen then, because I'm not going to stop. I was working as a hairdresser, apprenticeship, I hated it, and he used to let the tyres down on my bike and at six o'clock, when I knocked off, he'd always be there ready to offer to pump them up. He even punctured them once and fixed the puncture. I asked him if he always walked around with a puncture repair kit in his pocket. He blushed. Sweet. Perhaps it wasn't love, maybe it was youth. Looking back. The war makes one so hard. And bitter. I'm thirty-two.

PETER: It is really important –

STEPHANIE: – that you don't know anything about me.

PETER: Yes.

STEPHANIE: You know I want a baby.

PETER: Of course.

STEPHANIE: I'm thirty-two and want a baby. That's old. For wanting a baby.

PETER: You're very attractive. I can see the girl in you.

STEPHANIE: That's the loveliest thing anyone's said to me so far today. I'll have to presume that you've never been in love, since you won't tell me.

PETER: You can presume that, if it helps.

STEPHANIE: You haven't then. You'd know. Even a man, couldn't help but know.

PETER: And isn't that a little tragic.

STEPHANIE: How old are you?

(Silence.)

Younger than me. Twenty-seven, twenty-eight? That's young for a man. Old for a cat, or a dog, or a woman who wants a child, but young for a man.

PETER: Doctor Trollope told me a woman of hers had a child at thirty-eight last week.

STEPHANIE: Thirty-eight!? Gosh, really. Gosh. One of yours?

PETER: No. No.

STEPHANIE: Why do you do it?

PETER: I do know why I do it –

STEPHANIE: – but you can't tell me. It's a shame we can't talk because you look interesting as if you've got interesting stories or surprising attitudes. The war. Travel. Women's position.

PETER: Women's position?

STEPHANIE: In society. I meant.

PETER: Oh.

STEPHANIE: What did you think I meant?

PETER: I didn't.

STEPHANIE: Oh I see. Ha. That's terrible! You're terrible!

PETER: I didn't!

STEPHANIE: It's funny.

PETER: Stephanie. I didn't.

STEPHANIE: Who's Stephanie?

PETER: You're Stephanie.

STEPHANIE: Oh Lord yes, I forgot! And you're Peter. Boleyn. Ha! I hope you keep your head. Barbados? My goodness, I bet it's beautiful. Everyone around here is so pale. Pale and dull. No-one's recovered from the war. It's like everyone's ill. And tired. And smelly. Do you smoke?

PETER: No.

STEPHANIE: I know something about you!

PETER: You can smoke.

STEPHANIE: It doesn't bother you? The smell? On clothes? On breath?

PETER: I quite like a woman to smoke.

STEPHANIE: Why? If you don't smoke, I mean.

PETER: The movies, I guess. Those beautiful women all smoke.

STEPHANIE: I read somewhere that smoking, in the movies, for a woman, when a woman does it, smokes, in the movies, she's really, what it means, is that she's saying that she's…you know.

PETER: Available?

STEPHANIE: Yes. Available and not averse to putting things in her mouth. After I read that. I stopped smoking in public. Sorry, a bit racy of me. Custard cream?

PETER: No thank you. You're incredibly modern.

STEPHANIE: I drive a lorry.

PETER: I can't know that.

STEPHANIE: You asked.

PETER: I didn't.

STEPHANIE: Our first argument. I've not had a cigarette today. I smoke at work, at the depot, in the yard, though even that's not allowed. Ha! I don't smoke when I'm driving. But I took the day off today. For this. Because, Doctor Trollope worked out that everything's right today. The timings. My cycles.

PETER: We're talking too much.

STEPHANIE: I have to talk! I'm sorry I can't not talk. You don't have to listen. I work in Munitions. I was working in the stores, and we used to keep the sulphur off-site. So someone had to drive and there were no men. It's easy, driving, I like it. I like the way people, men, look at you. Ha! There's a woman driving a big munitions lorry! Aaargh! We're all gonna die! Ha! Sorry!

PETER: If God had wanted women to drive lorries he'd have given them size 12 feet.

STEPHANIE: You're allowed to tell jokes are you?

PETER: Maybe.

STEPHANIE: Peter. I hope that was you being dry and funny, and not being truthful about what you think about women driving. Because if you really mean that about God and women, I won't sleep with you. Only kidding.

PETER: I can be dry.

STEPHANIE: That's two things I know about you then. So can I. *(Beat.)* Yeah. Would you like some more tea?

PETER: I brought some rum.

STEPHANIE: Rum and sex at eleven o'clock in the morning! This isn't the navy!

PETER: Most of the women are nervous.

STEPHANIE: Peter. Believe me, I'm nervous.

STEPHANIE looks at the bottle. It's a bottle of Cockspur Rum.

Cockspur?

PETER: Very popular in Barbados.

She stands, looks for glasses. There are only tumblers. These she puts on the table and PETER pours the rum into them.

My landlady Mrs Mitchell, that's her real name, is that alright knowing Mrs Mitchell's real name, I mean you're not going to have sex with her are you, not unless she's on Doctor Trollope's list, so it doesn't matter does it. She doesn't allow drinking in the house, but she's not here is she. Do the other women talk? As much as this?

PETER: No. I explain the rules and then they treat me a little like a doctor. Kind of let me run the show. For want of a better expression.

STEPHANIE: But don't any of them chat away beforehand, you know like me, like a mad chicken?

PETER: No.

STEPHANIE: Are they all girls, I mean, young?

PETER: I'm not to tell you.

STEPHANIE: I bet they are. War widows. Lucky you, eh. Can you…I mean, did, does Doctor Trollope let you, I don't know, what's the word, what do horses do? At fences. Fences they don't like the look of. Fences they think they can't jump.

PETER: Refuse.

STEPHANIE: Yes. Have you ever refused?

PETER: We are now talking too much.

He drinks his rum and puts the glass down purposefully. She picks her glass up, but doesn't drink, and puts it down again.

STEPHANIE: I've tried to be professional, today. I put some lippy on.

PETER: You look very beautiful.

STEPHANIE: I wouldn't normally wear this much make-up at eleven in the morning. Or these shoes.

PETER: They look good, on you.

STEPHANIE: You should try walking in them. Or driving. Stockings?

PETER: You really have tried.

STEPHANIE: Tony, my husband, not his real name, liked me in stockings. I'm sorry. How do we start?

PETER stands and takes off his overcoat, and then his jacket, and his tie pin which he puts in his hat.

STEPHANIE: I like a tie pin.

PETER: Thank you.

She watches, and stands. He puts his hands on her waist, and kisses her neck and ears, which she enjoys.

STEPHANIE: That's nice. But you never kiss a woman on the lips?

PETER: Not my women, no.

STEPHANIE freezes.

STEPHANIE: Your women? In what sense are they your women Peter?

PETER: "The women", then.

STEPHANIE: Because they're not your women are they? Even though you've had them. I'm sorry. I think what you do is possibly very noble. No. I hope what you do is very noble. I'd like to think what you do is very noble.

PETER: You don't know why I do this.

STEPHANIE: Maybe one day you can tell me.

PETER: There will only be today.

STEPHANIE: You think I'm very modern because I drive a lorry and drink rum, and talk about sex at eleven in the morning, but really, I'm not. I am finding this very difficult, and I'm talking a lot because I'm nervous. And I'm doing this because I'm thirty-two and I want a baby, and there are no men. My husband's buried in Belgium and all the other men are buried in France, or dead from Spanish flu, and if there were any men out there still alive there are younger, prettier women to make wives of. You're very pleasant looking, and you look respectable but that may be a show, I'm not to know, and maybe I don't want to know, but if this goes well, for me, I will not be respectable. I will be a single woman, pregnant. And the world and his gossiping wife will ask who the hell got her pregnant? I will definitely lose these lodgings. Where will I go? I do not know. I will lose my job. And I will be a whatsaname… it's like a fish, a South American fish, Brazil, river fish, very violent –

PETER: – piranha.

STEPHANIE: I'll be a piranha.

PETER: Pariah.

STEPHANIE: I know it's the wrong word Peter. I chose to say piranha. Comedy.

PETER: I'm sorry.

STEPHANIE: How come you survived?

PETER: I beg your pardon?

STEPHANIE: The war. Did you fight? In France. Belgium.

PETER: I wanted to.

STEPHANIE: But you didn't. Were you white feathered?

PETER: No. I was in Barbados. My work was essential to the war effort. Sugar.

STEPHANIE: Sugar?

PETER: Yes, with sugar you can win a war.

PETER touches her arm, to encourage her to continue.

STEPHANIE: No.

She turns away from him.

You didn't die then?

PETER: I didn't die. No.

STEPHANIE: I'm sorry, it's been very good of you to, you know, spare the time to come round, I'm sure you're busy, but I can't go ahead with this. I must ask you to leave. And I'm sincerely sorry, apologetic, for having wasted your time.

PETER: I understand.

STEPHANIE: I wouldn't expect you to understand. Thank you. It's been nice meeting you. Peter Boleyn. You're a very decent man. But I can't. I can't.

PETER: Because I didn't die?

STEPHANIE: You're asking questions. We're not supposed to know anything about each other, are we?

PETER: This is my war. This.

STEPHANIE: I don't want you to explain that. I'd like you to leave.

PETER collects his things. He picks up his hat but drops the tie pin from it which lands on the floor, unnoticed by PETER. He leaves. STEPHANIE closes the door behind him, and goes to the chest of drawers and turns the photo of Anthony upright. She then notices the tie pin and picks it up. She sits.

To black.

End of scene.

SCENE 2

Three weeks later. Evening, and it is dark outside. STEPHANIE is dressed differently but the intent is the same, to attract. She paces. She looks at the clock which shows eight thirty. PETER enters. He is still dressed for winter, but is not wearing the bowler hat.

STEPHANIE: Thank you for coming.

PETER: Slush.

STEPHANIE: Thank God it's melted. I was getting sick of it. None of us have the right clothes for snow. We're not Russians are we? No brown bowler hat. I liked the bowler.

PETER: Costume. For my visits. Thank you for finding me, and looking after the tie pin.

Silence.

I usually put it in my hat.

STEPHANIE: Sit down. You will stay a while won't you?

PETER: I can but –

STEPHANIE: – you weren't expecting to stay?

PETER: I –

STEPHANIE: – You thought you'd be picking up the tie pin and away?

PETER: I didn't know what to expect. What happened last month –

STEPHANIE: – is it a month ago? Have you been counting the days?

PETER: I don't understand your tone. Stephanie. It sounds sarcastic.

STEPHANIE: No. Playful. Something liberating about this, you know, conventions, the rules, the world, turned on its head.

PETER: What I do can only work within the parameters set by Doctor Trollope.

STEPHANIE: You've broken your own rule. You've come back. Returned to the scene of the crime. The non crime.

PETER: The tie pin was my uncle's. My favourite uncle's. He died in 1917.

STEPHANIE: In Palestine, with the West Indians?

PETER: No, Western Front. He was with the Ulsters. Battle of the Messines Ridge.

STEPHANIE: Not far from Tony. Passchendaele.

PETER: Ypres.

STEPHANIE: Or Wipers if you're not an officer. Which he wasn't. I've got the tie pin. It's safe.

PETER: So –

STEPHANIE: – no-one will know you came back. Unless you believe that God is watching.

PETER: I don't believe that God is watching.

STEPHANIE: So it'll be a secret. Do you like secrets?

PETER: I do, quite, yes. I went to boarding school. Spent my life hiding things.

STEPHANIE: You're telling me things about yourself. Is that because we are now outside of the parameters?

Beat.

PETER: How did you find my offices? Your letter was delivered by hand.

STEPHANIE: Sugar. There are not that many sugar refineries. Two in fact. I went to the wrong one first. Silvertown.

PETER: They refine sucrose from beet. We use sugar cane. We import raw sugar, but I'm trying to get my father to import syrup. The raw sugar's brown because it still contains molasses – are you interested in sugar refining?

STEPHANIE: No.

PETER: I'm sorry. A passion. So you just wandered into Silvertown and asked for Peter?

STEPHANIE: Why would I do that? That would be stupid. Do you think I'm stupid?

PETER: No. I don't think you're stupid. I don't know why I said that.

STEPHANIE: I asked for the son of the owner. A guess.

PETER: So in Silvertown that would be Cecil? We know each other as you can imagine.

STEPHANIE: Cecil was very pleasant. Though I was disappointed he wasn't you, as you can imagine. And then he was a little indiscreet.

PETER: In what way?

STEPHANIE: He told me where to find you.

PETER: Ha! He'll have thought he was doing me a favour putting an attractive woman my way.

STEPHANIE: Do other people…I mean…well, for example Cecil, does he know –

PETER: – no. Of course not.

STEPHANIE: You say of course not Peter, but I can imagine a situation where you and Cecil and maybe a whole battalion of young sugar men go up West and drink too much and you stand on a table and impress them all with your conquest stories.

PETER: No one knows what I do. No-one outside of Doctor Trollope's compass.

STEPHANIE: Your father? No, he's in Barbados.

PETER: No one. So you know my real name now?

STEPHANIE: Yes. It's a lovely name. William, though everyone calls you Billy. Suits you.

PETER: I don't know your name. You have an advantage now. Why didn't you leave the tie pin at my offices?

STEPHANIE: Because I want a baby.

Beat.

PETER: But we are now beyond –

STEPHANIE: – Yes! That's got to be good hasn't it? To be beyond something. For the sake of the child.

PETER: What do you mean?

STEPHANIE: What brought you back? A tie pin? Actually, I don't believe it is your uncle's, it's very modern. Sit. Or do you have to go home to someone? It is evening. Or perhaps you're going out with that special girl? You don't wear a ring. Maybe you take it off. I asked you what brought you back here. You haven't answered.

PETER: You found me, you trailed the streets of London to find me, and you asked me to come here.

STEPHANIE: It felt like the decent thing to do then? To turn up?

PETER: No. You. I wanted to see you again.

STEPHANIE takes his tie pin from a drawer and gives it to him.

STEPHANIE: Your tie pin.

PETER: Thank you.

STEPHANIE moves a book from a bookshelf revealing a bottle of Cockspur Rum.

STEPHANIE: Rum? Cockspur. Not easy to find. Had to go up West. It does feel like a mission doesn't it. As if she's saving the world. Doctor Trollope. I suppose she is. I hid the booze from Mrs Mitchell. I suppose that's a secret too. Suddenly we have so many secrets, Peter! Isn't it exciting! Isn't it?

PETER: Mrs Mitchell's out then?

STEPHANIE gets two brandies in glasses.

STEPHANIE: The pictures. "Orphans of the Storm". Lillian Gish. Have you seen it?

PETER: No, I don't think so.

STEPHANIE: Lillian Gish and her sister, I mean her sister in real life – whatshername, it's gone, something Gish obviously.

PETER: Dorothy.

STEPHANIE: Yes! They're sisters, kind of in the film too, which is the only reason Dorothy got the job if you ask me.

PETER: I like Dorothy Gish.

STEPHANIE: But you prefer Lillian.

PETER: Obviously.

STEPHANIE: I rest my case. Dorothy, is the illegitimate child of a wealthy – this is all set in the French Revolution –

PETER: – right.

STEPHANIE: Dorothy is born to an aristocrat –

PETER: – but illegitimate?

STEPHANIE: – I know it's a whatsaname –

PETER: – cliché.

STEPHANIE: Isn't it? And she's abandoned at birth –

PETER: – because she's illegitimate?

STEPHANIE: Yes! That's what the French aristocracy do you see Peter. In France, they're at it all day long making babies with any unfortunate peasant woman they trip over and then nine months later they throw the unwanted little bastard into a ditch. Excuse my French.

PETER: I like the French.

STEPHANIE: Then you can leave right now!

PETER: *(He laughs.)*

STEPHANIE: So the Gish sisters grow up as sisters, in the film, just like they did in real life, because Lillian's mother, in the film that is, not in real life because they've got the same mother in real life, one presumes, and she's not in the film, but in the film Lillian's mother, her film mother, finds Dorothy in the ditch and raises her as her own, even though she's also tragically blind, Dorothy not her mother, she's blind from the plague and then –

PETER: – is it a silent movie?

STEPHANIE: Yes, thank God!

PETER: It's a miracle you get all this information.

STEPHANIE: They've got a very good piano player at the Criterion.

PETER: Have you ever seen a talking movie?

STEPHANIE: You're not interested in "Orphans of the Storm" are you Peter?

PETER: If you hated it why did you recommend it to Mrs Mitchell?

STEPHANIE: Because it's three hours ten minutes long.

PETER: I've seen two talkies. I don't think I'll ever be inclined to see another silent movie.

STEPHANIE: Aren't you modern!

PETER: It is incumbent on us to move with the times. It's a new age, an age of machines, and what was only imagined ten years ago will be taken for granted very soon.

STEPHANIE: Peter, I drive a lorry, you're trying to convert the Pope.

PETER: I was looking at motor cars only yesterday. For myself.

STEPHANIE: Gosh. Your own car. Do you drive?

PETER: I don't.

STEPHANIE: But you're a man, who went to boarding school, you're entitled, you think you can do anything.

PETER: It can't be that difficult can it.

STEPHANIE: Because a woman can do it?

PETER: Are you a suffragette?

STEPHANIE: They were all posh weren't they? I'm lots of things but I'm not posh. You're posh, I can tell.

PETER: What does that mean? Posh.

STEPHANIE: Port out, starboard home.

PETER: We have a successful sugar business. We don't have slaves. I don't think the posh work.

STEPHANIE: Which of the posh schools did you go to? Not that I could tell one from another even it fell on me.

PETER: Charterhouse.

STEPHANIE: The playing fields of England.

PETER: Officers died too you know. Over seven hundred Old Carthusians.

STEPHANIE: Why are you talking about the war? I've forgiven you.

PETER: I've done nothing for which I could be forgiven.

STEPHANIE: And I've forgiven you your nothing!

PETER: Don't be cruel. It doesn't sound like you have forgiven me, for, for my nothing, for living, for not dying.

STEPHANIE: I have. That is my failing, not yours. To judge you, when I don't know you. I wanted the baby, my baby, to have something of Tony, something that acknowledged him, some connection. I wanted you to have been in the trenches, to have seen him, I don't know, to have carried his stretcher, to have gently, lovingly lied to him, to have said "everything's going to be alright". And when he'd gone, to have read a prayer, and cleaned him up and made him look nice for the Chaplain, and read a eulogy at his funeral. Lied.

PETER: Lied?

STEPHANIE: Said how he never had a wicked thought about anyone.

PETER: I was in Barbados when war broke out –

STEPHANIE: – yes, I –

PETER: – let me have my say! And if you accept that, I'll…stay.

STEPHANIE: I'm sorry.

PETER: I was running the plantation, my father was in London. I tried to enlist in the British West Indies Regiment in Barbados but they wouldn't have me.

STEPHANIE: Why not?

PETER: I'm white. The recruiting officer referred me to the British Ambassador who told me that I'd be more use "keeping the sugar coming" – as he put it.

STEPHANIE: The West Indians fought against the Turks didn't they?

PETER: In Palestine, yes. You knew that? I didn't think anyone knew that.

STEPHANIE: I asked my father-in-law. He's an expert on military campaigns, and has no other conversation.

PETER: Sixteen thousand West Indian troops on all fronts, two thousand dead.

STEPHANIE: You and he would get on like a house on fire.

PETER: Who?

STEPHANIE: My father-in-law, Tony's father. How many…do you know how many children you've fathered, in this…scheme.

PETER: Yes.

STEPHANIE: Doctor Trollope is not here. We are outside of her parameters.

PETER: You must speak to no one. No one.

STEPHANIE: No one will know.

PETER: Two hundred and two.

STEPHANIE: No.

PETER: Yes. Two hundred and two.

STEPHANIE: My goodness me. Gosh. Heavens. Good God! Blimey O'Reilly! I thought it'd be six or seven. It seems so extraordinary, that one man can –

PETER: – have brought so much life into the world.

STEPHANIE: Yes. But I can't get beyond thinking of all the women. Two hundred?

PETER: Two hundred and two. And they're only the ones that got pregnant.

STEPHANIE: Oh! Of course! Oh my God. Oh no. Thousands?!

PETER: Seven hundred and eleven.

STEPHANIE: No! Aargh. Oh my God. I'm shaking.

PETER: Yes.

STEPHANIE: You counted?

PETER: I don't count. Doctor Trollope keeps records.

STEPHANIE: Why did you tell me that? You really really broke the rules there.

PETER: I'm not here for Doctor Trollope. We're outside that now. And you, your situation is for me, your situation is quintessential.

STEPHANIE: Quintessentially what?

PETER: It fits. Why I do this. And I believe I'm happy to break the rules, for you, for me, actually.

STEPHANIE stands, turns her back on PETER and puts her glass on the side.

STEPHANIE: I'm sorry, I don't know how to look at you, now. I don't know… Crikey. We started by not knowing anything about each other, but now I know that you've slept with seven hundred and eleven women. And I'd be number seven hundred and twelve?

PETER: Only if we were to have sex under Doctor Trollope's umbrella.

STEPHANIE: I've never had sex under an umbrella. But I'm sure you have. What's the strangest place you've ever had sex?

PETER: Stoke Newington.

STEPHANIE: You're funny. Oh my God. So many women.

PETER: So many children. So much life.

STEPHANIE: What happens…no.

PETER: What?

STEPHANIE: I mean, I was thinking. When they're older, the children, not the women, one of them, might meet another, you know, unknowing, not knowing that they share the same father. Brother and sister.

PETER: Yes.

STEPHANIE: And they might fall in love. Incest.

PETER: Doctor Trollope keeps records. And when they're older, they're told.

STEPHANIE: About you?

PETER: No one gets to know my name.

STEPHANIE: Because of that I think maybe we should go back to Doctor Trollope.

PETER: No.

STEPHANIE: No? You said "no"?

PETER: We couldn't kiss then.

STEPHANIE: You? You'd like to kiss? You only kiss necks, and ears.

PETER: And I only do that to help the women be ready. And you're not one of them. You and I would be outside of all that.

STEPHANIE: I'm sorry but I don't believe you, anyway, about not kissing. How can anyone make love and not kiss?

PETER: Prostitutes don't kiss on the lips.

STEPHANIE: Good God, you don't go to prostitutes as well do you?!

PETER: Stop it! Of course not. But I can't make love without constraints. Discipline.

STEPHANIE: Make love? It's not love though, is it?

PETER: It is love! For Christ's sake it is love. It's all we've got. It's the opposite of death. And we need to mass our army.

STEPHANIE: You've got an army, of women. Why do you do this Billy?

PETER: It's complicated.

STEPHANIE: If you're going to make love to me because of something, something other than me, I'd like to know what it is.

PETER: Have you heard of Sigmund Freud?

STEPHANIE: Does he live round here?

PETER: You're kidding, you've heard of him.

STEPHANIE: Of course I have. I read the papers. I took his dreams book out of the library. Let's just say, I could put it down.

PETER: It's a little far-fetched, I agree but he has this idea of a life force, which he calls eros, after the Greek god Eros, and a death energy, which he calls thanatos, after the Greek god –

STEPHANIE: – let me guess, Thanatos!

PETER: Yes. Thanatos is the son of Nyx, goddess of the night, and Erebos, god of the dark. And during the war, it seemed to me, he, Thanatos, gained strength.

STEPHANIE: Do you believe in gods, and ghosts, and heaven and hell?

PETER: These are not ghosts, or gods even, really, they're myths. They're ideas, which although they're abstract are real.

STEPHANIE: But Tony is not dead in Belgium because the Greek god of –

PETER: – yes he is! These ideas are forces, you know, movements, spiritual movements, infections. And Europe now, and during the war was taken over by Thanatos, the god of death. He was at home in Flanders, and he ruled. One million dead in France and Belgium, and a living hell for many, and he had the upper hand.

STEPHANIE: And then, after the war, Spanish flu.

PETER: Another twenty million dead. Thanatos is still predominant. So although I could not fight, they wouldn't let me go to fight, this is now my fight. This is how I fight.

STEPHANIE: Billy, you're not the god of love.

PETER: I work for Eros.

STEPHANIE: No. You import rubber.

PETER: I'm on the side of the idea of love, of life.

STEPHANIE: You're certainly doing your bit.

PETER: And so are you. We need to be strong in the face of death.

STEPHANIE: So that's why you don't, can't refuse.

PETER: I have wanted to refuse. On occasion. Two occasions.

STEPHANIE: But you didn't?

PETER: Of course not.

STEPHANIE: You don't do this for pleasure. Were they, the ones you wanted to refuse, but didn't, were they, I don't know, were they awfully…oh, I don't know…

PETER: One was quite attractive actually, but you know how it is, the way that a man is attracted to a woman, and a woman –

STEPHANIE: – chemistry?

PETER: – yes, the chemistry, was sulphurous.

STEPHANIE: Sulphurous?! I work with sulphur. It's awful.

PETER: I suspect that particular woman –

STEPHANIE: – the attractive, but sulphurous one –

PETER: – yes, I think she felt…I think she was devout, and thought I was –

STEPHANIE: – the devil!?

PETER: Not the devil, but certainly, godless and, she certainly thought that what she, what we were doing, was wrong.

STEPHANIE: Did you manage it?

PETER: I got through it. Like a trip to the dentist.

STEPHANIE: And what about the second almost refusal?

PETER: Her husband was there.

STEPHANIE: No?! He was alive?

PETER: That's not uncommon. I have several times, on my visits, passed the husband in the hall.

STEPHANIE: But I thought –

PETER: – not all the women's husbands have been killed.

PETER: Some of them –

STEPHANIE: – some of who?

PETER: Some of the husbands, of Doctor Trollope's women –

STEPHANIE: – is that who we are? Doctor Trollope's women?

PETER: I –

STEPHANIE: – no. That's what we are. So some of the other women, their husbands are still alive?

PETER: Yes. Shell shock mostly. And some are physically injured. They don't have the equipment.

STEPHANIE: *(Sings.)*
I don't want a bayonet up my jacksie
I don't want my bollocks shot away
I'd rather be in England
Merry merry England

And fuck my bleeding life away
I blame the rum!

PETER: I guess you munitions girls know all the songs.

STEPHANIE: Yup. We're dead common!

PETER: Some of the men just go to the pub and they're not there when I arrive.

STEPHANIE: Of course.

PETER: But sometimes they want to meet me.

STEPHANIE: Oh my God, no?!

PETER: Yes. They wait in the parlour, and look me up and down.

STEPHANIE: Is that why you dress nicely?

PETER: Yes. And I try and look clean.

STEPHANIE: And you bathe. I guess you always bathe?

PETER: I have to bathe every day, in case the messenger comes.

STEPHANIE: Have any of the husbands ever been, you know, unpleasant about it?

PETER: Not unpleasant but occasionally, sullen.

STEPHANIE: Sullen? Mmm. What an awful thing for them. Awful.

PETER: So, that time –

STEPHANIE: The second non-refusal?

PETER: He wouldn't leave, and came into the bedroom –

STEPHANIE: – no!?

PETER: Yes, and held her hand.

STEPHANIE: What?!

PETER: Yes, he held her hand.

STEPHANIE: Whilst you –

PETER: – yes.

STEPHANIE: Oh my god! How sweet!

PETER: Touching, yes.

STEPHANIE: Do you enjoy the sex?

PETER: Not that time, no.

STEPHANIE: Ha! But usually you do?

PETER: I believe that it is important that I do. That's part of it.

STEPHANIE: That the child is conceived in one of Eros's moments?

PETER: Yes.

STEPHANIE: I thought men could enjoy it with anyone, or anything, you know, sheep, a hollowed out marrow. No-one eats marrows.

PETER: There was a third.

STEPHANIE: Refusal.

PETER: Non-refusal. Only last week. She was rather unfortunate looking.

STEPHANIE: A minger!?

PETER: Minger?

STEPHANIE: As my Scottish grandfather would say.

PETER: I don't know the expression. But I get the sense.

STEPHANIE: But you didn't refuse either?

PETER: No.

STEPHANIE: How –

PETER: – I closed my eyes.

STEPHANIE: All cats are grey when the lights are out.

PETER: I imagined she was someone else.

STEPHANIE: A fantasy woman.

PETER: You.

STEPHANIE: So that's why you came back. I'm glad.

PETER: I don't think of it as a series of individual widows or women with war-damaged husbands, who are impotent, I never think about the pleasure or, let's call it, difficulty, of any one of my women, the women, sorry, my pleasure, my satisfaction is more from the greater task, and –

STEPHANIE: – kiss me. I want you to kiss me. Will you kiss me, can you kiss me?

PETER: I can kiss you.

STEPHANIE: Not from over there you can't.

PETER kisses her. She sighs. He moves up and kisses her ears on the upstage side. She takes his head in her hands and pulls him to her so she can kiss him on the mouth which she does. It is a long and passionate kiss and she moves her hands inside his jacket to hold him. He presses her close to him, as they kiss, and she lets herself fall back on to the bed, and he moves himself on to her.

To black.

End of scene.

SCENE THREE

Summer. STEPHANIE is alone, wearing a summer dress. There is an opened letter on the side. A candle is lit, seemingly unnecessarily. Enter PETER, in shirt sleeves. STEPHANIE is still and quiet. He notices the candle. They kiss.

PETER: *(Re: the candle.)* What is it Jean?

STEPHANIE: It's a candle.

PETER: I know it's a candle. What or who –

STEPHANIE: – 31st July.

PETER: 31st of July? A date from the war?

STEPHANIE: For Tony.

PETER: Passchendaele.

STEPHANIE: He died on the first day. I always light a candle. These, I get them from the Co-op, they last about four hours, which is how long he lived. I don't mean he was four hours old when he died.

PETER: I know that.

STEPHANIE: He lived for four hours after the shrapnel got him. They keep going out so you have to watch it and keep lighting the bloody thing but if you do it'll last about four hours.

PETER: So you have to nurse the candle.

STEPHANIE: No, Billy, no. I know it looks like a neat whatsaname –

PETER: – analogy, metaphor –

STEPHANIE: – but to be honest I wish they weren't such rubbish candles.

PETER: But it helps you to –

STEPHANIE: – no! You're not listening, I wish they didn't go out, and I don't find it soothing to have to light the bugger over and over again.

PETER: But –

STEPHANIE: – no one ever told me that in those last four hours Tony looked like he'd died five or six times and had to be relit! A lump of iron sliced through his liver and he died four hours later. The nurses didn't sit there with a dry box of matches keeping him going.

PETER: No but –

STEPHANIE: – for Christ's sake! They're just rubbish candles! I don't know why I do it any more. He died ten years ago, and now there's you. I'll have my clothes off in half an hour and –

PETER: – don't.

He puts an arm around her.

I'm sorry. I wish I'd known him. All I know about him, which is not much, all I know makes me think I'd like him. I know I respect him.

STEPHANIE: Because he died.

PETER: He died so –

STEPHANIE: – we could have extramarital sex?

She starts giggling.

PETER: Don't do that.

STEPHANIE: I don't like that you wished you'd died.

PETER: Maybe that's just something I say.

STEPHANIE: You told me that you tried to enlist, that you wished you'd gone to war. And if you had gone to war the chances are that you would have died. Bit of Latin? Therefore –

PETER: – ergo.

STEPHANIE: Ergo, you wished you'd died.

PETER: There's certainly a bit of me that hates this intact, able-bodied, limbed man.

STEPHANIE: Limbed?

PETER: All my limbs.

STEPHANIE: I see.

PETER: There is a hole in my head filled with guilt. Hatred. Self-hatred.

STEPHANIE: Most men would feel guilty about sleeping with all the dead men's wives.

PETER: Not for pleasure. And only once. We're different. You're an aberration.

STEPHANIE: I've always wanted to be an aberration.

PETER: It's all we have to fight death. We all have the god within us.

STEPHANIE: Eros.

PETER: Death versus life.

STEPHANIE: Who's winning?

PETER: It's a long game.

STEPHANIE: A test match?

PETER: It's more than five days.

STEPHANIE: We've met fifteen times.

PETER: This is the sixteenth.

STEPHANIE: You're the numbers man.

PETER: It'll take twenty, thirty years, to push death back into its cave.

STEPHANIE: I'm glad you didn't die. But things have changed for me.

PETER: What's changed?

STEPHANIE: I joined this, your army of love, for a baby. But now I'm doing this because I can't imagine life without it. Without you.

PETER: If I'd died I would never have known you. I would never have made love to you. And if I had never made love to you, I would never have fallen in love with you.

STEPHANIE: Billy, stop it. You're telling me you love me again. You did this last time. You can't say that, you can't feel it. It's not allowed.

PETER: You say you love me.

STEPHANIE: I don't work for Doctor Trollope. She has no hold on me.

PETER: Nor on me, now. I love you Jean. I do.

STEPHANIE: You don't have to say "I do" we're not getting married, or are we?

PETER: No, we're not getting married.

STEPHANIE: Why not? What's wrong with me?

He moves to her and kisses her. He is avoiding the question.

You're also not supposed to do that. Kiss me on the lips.

PETER: I'll stop doing it then.

STEPHANIE: Good. You're only allowed to kiss me on the inner thigh.

PETER: *(Laughs.)* That was obviously a joke.

STEPHANIE: I didn't know it was a joke. It sounded plausible.

PETER: It wasn't my joke, I don't joke.

STEPHANIE: Are you saying you never said that Doctor Trollope allowed you to kiss her women on the neck, the ears and the inner thigh. To help them get ready.

PETER: It was your joke that you turned into my joke. Don't you remember?

STEPHANIE: No.

PETER: It's so implausible I thought it was obviously –

STEPHANIE: – so I'm stupid now?

PETER: No!

STEPHANIE: Looking back on it, I can see that it was an implausible instruction, and yes, of course I should've seen the joke, but when you started kissing me on the inner thigh, correctly, according to what I thought were Doctor Trollope's instructions, to be honest, at that moment, I wasn't thinking clearly, I was distracted. For God's sake someone was kissing me on the inner thigh!

They kiss.

Oh! I love what we have to do. Humans. I'm so glad I'm not a plant, and just split in two when I want to whatsaname.

PETER: Want to what?

STEPHANIE: Sounds like when you put things off.

PETER: Procrastinate?

STEPHANIE: That's it. Procreate.

PETER: Anyway, we are way way outside of her parameters now.

STEPHANIE: Sixteen meetings. Sixteen wonderful hours.

PETER: Two hours.

STEPHANIE: Whatever the average length of a Hollywood talkie is.

PETER: What if Mrs Mitchell walks out one day, doesn't like the film?

STEPHANIE: She'll never walk out. She's from a poor mining village. She'll stay to the end even if she hates it, to get her money's worth.

PETER: I don't care if she catches us –

STEPHANIE: I do. I don't want to be homeless.

PETER: We'd find somewhere else for you.

STEPHANIE: I like it here. I like your visits. It's what I live for.

PETER: It's all I look forward to.

STEPHANIE: You've got the others. How many this week?

PETER: Just one. Kilburn.

STEPHANIE: Sex in Kilburn? It shouldn't be allowed.

PETER: They do.

STEPHANIE: It's all going on behind the curtains isn't it? When is that?

PETER: Tomorrow. Morning. Half past eleven. Her husband's still alive.

STEPHANIE: Shell-shock?

PETER: I don't know

STEPHANIE: Won't you be, you know, not interested, after this? After me.

PETER: It doesn't matter whether I'm interested. It's war.

STEPHANIE: Eros v Thanatos. Be funny if you got to Kilburn tomorrow, and he's Greek. The husband. Opens the door in helmet, sandals, short sword, a toga.

PETER: Togas are Roman.

STEPHANIE: You know what I mean. Imagine if Tony had lived. Damaged, but alive, and you had to come round. To do this. It'd kill him.

PETER: Would he want to deny you a baby?

STEPHANIE: It's not about that. I was his. Property. He liked me being his. And, he wouldn't like the way you make love to me.

PETER: What wouldn't he like?

STEPHANIE: Your competence. Your skill. He was always sensitive to criticism, felt judged, he'd fly off the handle at little things. He never hit me, but he punched someone once, a cab driver, called him an effing idiot, he'd walked into the road, it was his fault, he was an idiot, you know, to walk into the road, but he couldn't take it, the, you know, judgement of his, anything. He wouldn't like your love-making, because, unlike his, I'm afraid, yours is wonderful.

PETER: I'm –

STEPHANIE: – I know, you're a kind of professional, and it's to be expected that you're brilliant, but he'd be hurt, he'd feel stupid. He'd be sitting downstairs and after five minutes he'd be wondering "what's taking so long".

PETER: I can be quick. I'm q –

STEPHANIE: – don't talk about it. He'd punch you. Punch you, and chop you up into little pieces and feed you to the ducks, which is a good thing, because I heard you're not supposed to feed them bread.

They kiss, and he touches her, and moves her to sigh with pleasure.

I feel as if there are parts of my body that, you know, will always technically belong to you.

PETER: Technically?

STEPHANIE: In the sense that they might as well have not existed before you came along. My clitoris, and the Cook Islands have a lot in common.

PETER: The Cook Islands?

STEPHANIE: Might have well not existed before being discovered, put on the map by Captain Cook. I should rename my clitoris, Peter.

PETER: Billy.

STEPHANIE: Peter. You were Peter when my Cook Islands were discovered.

PETER: Thank you. It's an honour.

STEPHANIE: Do you think Mrs Mitchell has ever had an orgasm?

PETER: In the cinema?

STEPHANIE: Stop it.

PETER: Of course she has. She'll be having orgasms all the time. She's Welsh.

STEPHANIE: And what, the Welsh have a lot of orgasms?

PETER: They're natural, passionate.

STEPHANIE: But not physically different.

PETER: Sex is an attitude of mind. The Welsh are interested in sex.

STEPHANIE: Is it more important than mining, rugby, sheep?

PETER: They're not English, not hung up, they don't have rules to follow, they're not affronted, frightened by passion.

STEPHANIE: I had a holiday in Llandudno once. It was the bleakest, least sensuous two weeks of my life.

PETER: You weren't with a Welshman then.

STEPHANIE: Tony. My honeymoon.

PETER: Oh dear.

STEPHANIE: Yes. It was oh dear.

PETER: Were you a virgin when you married?

STEPHANIE: All three of us were virgins.

PETER: All three?

STEPHANIE: Me, Tony and Father Michael.

PETER: But Father Michael didn't go on honeymoon with you?

STEPHANIE: He wasn't there, but his ignorance was. In me, in Tony. His Catholic, virgin, stupidity; his reserve, his shame. I do think it's unreasonable to expect two individuals to promise in a religious ceremony to undertake with one another, to the exclusion of all others, for a lifetime, something neither of them has ever done.

PETER: Where is Doctor Trollope's book?

STEPHANIE hands him the book from a hidden place.

Hidden?

STEPHANIE: Mrs Mitchell.

PETER: *(Opening the book.)* A foreword by the Archbishop of York.

STEPHANIE: He's Church of England! They're at it all the time! Jumping into bed with the Women's Institute. To us Catholics the Archbishop of York is the devil.

PETER: Did you ever have an orgasm with him?

STEPHANIE: The Archbishop of York?

PETER: Tony!

STEPHANIE: He'd tear my clothes off and mount me as if it was a life-threatening medical emergency. He was urgent, and I was, what's the word….

PETER: – slow.

STEPHANIE: Slow.

PETER: You're not slow. Even when I first met you. I knew you'd be, as you are, you know, modern.

STEPHANIE: That's the war. When you drive a lorry, you learn that you can do anything. But our honeymoon was before the war. I was a girl. He was not much more than a boy and, you know, we didn't know what we were supposed to do. It was as if someone had given us all the bits of the, I don't know, the Taj Mahal in a box, but no instructions, no drawings, and told us to get on with it.

PETER: *(Reading.)* "A woman is a delicate musical instrument".

STEPHANIE: Or if you're Tony, a drum kit.

They laugh. She looks to the candle.

Sorry Tony. It wasn't all your fault my love. I was a God-fearing, hell-inspired, little supplicant! I didn't know my own body. Masturbation is a sin. Touching yourself? You might as well hammer nails into Christ's hands. The pleasure of sex has to be paid for by some penalty, some suffering, shame, preferably pregnancy.

PETER: *(Reading.)* "The clitoris should lead the way to the vagina, and say wake up! Wake up, and do what we do!"

STEPHANIE: So, how much of your skill, is really hers?

PETER: She talked to me a lot. I read this, kind of learned it.

(Quoting.) "Touch her skin, kiss her lips, touch her face, kiss her neck, her ears, hold her breasts, kiss and touch the nipples". See, no mention of inner thigh.

STEPHANIE: Have you slept with Doctor Trollope?

PETER: I haven't, no.

STEPHANIE: But? I heard a "but" that you didn't say.

PETER: She wanted me to.

STEPHANIE: Oh my God.

PETER: She's like an artist, very free, communal.

STEPHANIE: She's twice your age, and you know –

PETER: – a bit of a minger?

STEPHANIE: I'm trying to imagine the situation, 'cause you're working for her aren't you, you're subservient and then she says she wants to have sex with you.

PETER: She made it clear that I could say "no".

STEPHANIE: Which you did?

PETER: I didn't use the word "no".

STEPHANIE: You used the word "yes"?

PETER: I put it off.

STEPHANIE: A refusal!

PETER: I postponed, the event.

STEPHANIE: It would be an event. I'd buy a ticket. Indefinitely postponed, I hope, since you love me.

PETER: Yes.

STEPHANIE: You love me. Fancy that. From a man whose job it is not to love.

PETER: Not to fall in love.

STEPHANIE: Why did she give you the job?

PETER: She knew my father. Knew our family. She knows and understands my desire to compensate, to make reparations for not having fought in the war. I'm not saying she didn't teach me nothing. That's a double negative. She has taught me other things. I knew nothing about the Bartholin's glands. They're the –

STEPHANIE: – urgh! I don't like the name.

PETER: Bartholin's gland?

STEPHANIE: Yes! How come a bit of my… my fanny is named after an 18th century Dutch bloke.

PETER: 17th century. Danish.

STEPHANIE: That's worse. He's Danish and a hundred years older than the Dutch fellah. How would you like it if a bit of your, I don't know, penis was called "Gertrude's bits".

PETER: Gertrude?

STEPHANIE: Back to Captain Cook and the Cook Islands. If, in Denmark, four hundred years ago, I don't know, Nurse Gertrude Mikelson-son found some incredibly important bits of the penis that everyone else had overlooked and she called them hers, Gertrude's bits, then every man, forever more, would have some Gertrude's bits, whether they liked it or not.

(Impression of cockney bloke.) Kaw! mi Gertrude's are giving me jip this morning china.

PETER: But she didn't did she.

STEPHANIE: I'm only saying, couldn't my glands, a woman's glands be at least Mrs Bartholin's glands.

PETER: She didn't discover them! He did!

STEPHANIE: Yes, but whose fanny was he looking at!?

PETER: His wife's presumably.

STEPHANIE: I rest my case. Should be Mrs Bartholin's glands!

PETER: We owe a debt to Bartholin and his like. They risked a lot, those pioneers. It's important to catalogue, to record, to understand how the body works, and God's intent. If those churchmen, those fierce killjoys, if they understood, if they had knowledge, they would see God's design, and understand that sex was given by Him as a, I don't know, creative and formative thing, perhaps even holy.

STEPHANIE: But not for us Billy. We're not married. This is sin.

PETER: A sin has to feel like a sin.

STEPHANIE: If we were caught, and Doctor Trollope was exposed would she go to prison?

PETER: What's the crime?

STEPHANIE: Isn't she a pimp, of sorts?

PETER: She'd get struck off.

STEPHANIE: And lose the clinic?

PETER: Yes.

STEPHANIE: So she's risking everything then – for us, for this.

PETER: If you'd got pregnant that first time she'd have taken you at the Camden Clinic, for the birth. But not now.

STEPHANIE: All this and then they'll take the baby off me.

PETER: What?

STEPHANIE: I'm pregnant.

He moves to her, puts his head against hers.

PETER: How long?

STEPHANIE: Two months.

PETER: Two months, but –

STEPHANIE: – yes, I'm sorry I deceived you. I'm not doing this for a baby, not now, not since last month. I'm doing this because I can't stop doing it.

PETER: Have you seen a doctor?

STEPHANIE: I'm not ill.

PETER: *(Turning away.)* This is fabulous news.

STEPHANIE: Number two hundred and eighteen.

PETER: Nineteen.

He has his back to her.

STEPHANIE: There was another last week?

PETER: Yesterday.

STEPHANIE: Congratulations.

PETER: Thank you.

STEPHANIE: But they probably won't let me keep the baby.

PETER: I don't think –

STEPHANIE: – If you're single, and there's no father, no husband, and you don't have the means.

PETER: Do you have the means?

STEPHANIE: I couldn't go back to my parents.

PETER: Why not?

STEPHANIE: They didn't approve of Tony, his class, they thought we were better than him, and they tried everything they could to break us up, and I ran away, with him, in the end. And I have no desire to see them again. And they would not approve. Of this. This method.

PETER: What will Mrs Mitchell do?

STEPHANIE: Kick me out. She might have a clitoris but she doesn't have a heart. *(Beat.)* You didn't laugh. At that. Not like you. When I say something funny, you laugh. Normally.

PETER: I'm sorry. I was thinking.

STEPHANIE: They might call me mad. They do that too. In this country. To women. Only mad women get pregnant outside of marriage.

PETER: This is, this is terrific news.

STEPHANIE: I'm worried that it's not good news. That it will change us. This. End this.

PETER: Yes.

STEPHANIE: Because, obviously trying, trying, and trying to have a baby, unsuccessfully was wonderful and has changed me. Without this much love, loving, without you, I don't know that life would be…anything.

PETER: No. Me too.

STEPHANIE: What will this do to us Billy? Do you know?

PETER: No.

STEPHANIE: We can't keep trying for a baby because I've got one.

PETER: No.

STEPHANIE: You've gone all mono-whatsit.

PETER: Monosyllabic.

STEPHANIE: That an'all.

PETER: It's good that you've got what you wanted.

STEPHANIE: But I don't know anymore, that I want a baby! I only want this. Us! What do we do Billy?

PETER: I don't know.

STEPHANIE: It's never happened before has it?

PETER: No.

STEPHANIE: That you have fallen in love with someone who has fallen in love with you, and they get pregnant.

PETER: Never.

STEPHANIE: I don't believe you.

PETER: You're my first.

STEPHANIE: Numbers again.

PETER: I've never fallen in love with any of them, it's only ever one visit.

STEPHANIE: We could marry.

PETER: No, no.

STEPHANIE: I'm asking. You know, as a solution, it just popped up into my head. Bit conventional. I could go to the church in a lorry.

PETER: No. We can't.

STEPHANIE: No?

PETER: No.

STEPHANIE: You love me.

PETER: I do. I do love you. Yes. That's –

STEPHANIE: – you can carry on loving me.

PETER: In an ideal world. Yes. It's not an ideal world. It's the real world.

STEPHANIE: I know that.

PETER: I want nothing more than to marry you, and raise our son, our daughter, together, married.

STEPHANIE: Our own house.

PETER: Yes.

STEPHANIE: In the country.

PETER: No.

STEPHANIE: Not necessarily in the country.

PETER: Anywhere with you, would be an ideal world. Heaven. It would make me happy, fulfilled, whole. And I would love you, exclusively. There'd be no others. No war.

STEPHANIE: We could carry on our own little war. Or at least exercises.

PETER: These sixteen days, they're the sixteen most precious days of my life.

STEPHANIE: We feel the same then, but I don't do the numbers thing. Numbers, they're yours.

PETER: Jean.

STEPHANIE: Yes.

PETER: I'm already married.

She says nothing, but during the next pulls her head down and begins to rock gently. Then crawls on to the bed and begins to cry, pulling the covers over her. PETER sits and watches. There is a considerable silence, broken only by her muted sobbing. Then he reaches out an arm to comfort her. She flinches.

STEPHANIE: Don't touch me!

She rolls over, away from the touch.

PETER: I can speak to Doctor Trollope. To see if she will take you back at the clinic. To have the baby. I think she will. She's not –

STEPHANIE: – heartless?

PETER: I love you. I've never known love like this. I have never felt so close, so accepted, so loved –

STEPHANIE: – but!?

PETER: I'm married.

STEPHANIE: Do you love your wife?

PETER: No. We had to marry.

STEPHANIE: She was pregnant?

PETER: Yes.

STEPHANIE: Did you have a second child?

PETER: We became a family, and so we lived…we did the family thing.

STEPHANIE: Does she know about your work with Doctor Trollope?

PETER: Yes. Because she doesn't love me she –

STEPHANIE: – doesn't give a damn?

PETER: She doesn't object, but she doesn't understand, like you do.

STEPHANIE: I don't want you to talk to Doctor Trollope. I don't want anything to do with her.

PETER: I'm sorry. You have the baby.

STEPHANIE: I don't want the baby! I want you! I want our love!

PETER: And so do I. But we can't. The world –

STEPHANIE: – no, no, no.

PETER: You will want the baby.

STEPHANIE: No.

PETER: You must.

STEPHANIE: It's your war, it's your baby.

PETER: What will you do?

STEPHANIE: Go to America. My sister's.

PETER: Yes.

STEPHANIE: I can lie then. Can say my husband died. In a bizarre accident with a, I don't know, a threshing machine.

PETER: They are very –

STEPHANIE: – free, accepting, modern?

PETER: More so than here. You will love again.

STEPHANIE: You don't love me do you? You never did.

PETER: I do.

STEPHANIE: I'm trying not to hate you now. You lied to me.

PETER: I never lied. You never asked if I was married.

STEPHANIE: Not allowed to know anything about you. Convenient rules.

PETER: After we were outside her parameters, you still didn't ask.

STEPHANIE: I knew all I wanted to know about you. *(Beat.)* You should've told me.

PETER: You didn't tell me you were pregnant.

STEPHANIE: Hardly the same, whatsaname.

PETER: Magnitude.

STEPHANIE: Magnitude.

PETER: I'd better go.

(He stands, and collects his clothes.)

STEPHANIE: I'll be alright. I drive a lorry. I can go to America. There are a lot of lorries in America that need me. They don't think they need a woman lorry driver but they do. Yes, I'm needed by a lot of factories, and businesses in America, if not by you. You can dispose of me but that's not the end of me. And if I drive well, and if I'm conscientious, and cheerful, and smoke, and give cigarettes away, and swear, and call everyone Mac, I might be loved, though no one will ever use that word. Maybe my sister can look after the baby, so I can drive.

PETER: America then?

STEPHANIE: America or a back-street abortion. It's a difficult choice.

PETER: You might meet someone.

STEPHANIE: Yes! I might run someone over. A handsome Lithuanian immigrant. And if he didn't die, and if I said I was sorry, and smiled, and gave him the kind of mouth-to-mouth resuscitation he'd never had in Lithuania, and if I explained that I was a single thirty-two-year-old with a baby and nowhere to live they might find me attractive and take me home.

PETER: I must go.

STEPHANIE: That's what you do best isn't it?

PETER: What?

STEPHANIE: Going. Loving is one of your skills, but you're more of a genius at leaving. Go then, Peter. Go. You must leave. The war goes on.

He goes. She sits, thinks. Then opens a drawer and takes out an envelope, an airmail letter. She then takes a fresh, new airmail envelope and copies the address on to the front of it.

The End.